THE RHETORIC OF AMERICAN POLI____
A STUDY OF DOCUM___
by William R. Smith

In this volume Willian _____ lyzes thirteen carefull_ _____ documents, including m_____ ___ a personal, governmental, and institutional nature. These primary sources are accompanied by Professor Smith's commentaries, which collectively present his theory that the study of original documents reveals the philosophical and political assumptions of their authors and of the times in which they were written. The first two chapters introduce the author's theory and pattern for studying rhetoric, a sophisticated method deriving from a unique combination of the techniques of rhetorical analysis and an understanding of recent work in the philosophy of history. Professor Smith's model is sufficiently broad and flexible to allow for adaptation to the peculiarities of each case under study.

The subsequent documents and their analyses reveal such important historical points as: the colonialist spirit inherent in the Northwest Ordinance of 1787; the appeal to Calvinist doctrine in Abraham Lincoln's Second Inaugural Address; the 1890 Populist Party platform's challenge to the American notion that politics is simply defined as a scramble for power; Woodrow Wilson's view of himself as world savior; the New Deal's error in choosing to subsidize the farmer rather than the worker in the Agricultural Adjustment Act of 1933; Harry S. Truman's structuring of cold war policy and rhetoric; and Earl Warren's failure to take the action demanded by his argument in *Brown* v. *Board of Education*.

The Rhetoric of American Politics

In this important work, Professor Smith does contemporary historiography a dual service by demonstrating the validity and usefulness of his unusual analytical method, and by illuminating the contents and implications of significant historical documents.

William Raymond Smith is currently Fulbright Professor of American Studies at the University of Utrecht. He attended the University of Chicago, receiving his Ph.D. in History of Culture from that institution in 1961. Since then he has taught literature, history, and philosophy at Pennsylvania State University, and at Haverford, Scripps, and Shimer Colleges. He has published numerous articles and reviews in both popular and scholarly journals, and is the author of *History as Argument: Three Patriot Historians of the American Revolution* (1966).

The Rhetoric of
AMERICAN
POLITICS

A Study of Documents

WILLIAM RAYMOND SMITH

GREENWOOD PUBLISHING CORPORATION
WESTPORT, CONNECTICUT

IN MEMORY OF

Otto Jolle Matthijs Jolles.

Contents

Preface

Our knowledge of the past raises philosophical questions analogous to the questions raised by our knowledge of nature. Basically, what is the relationship between the known and the grounds of knowing? This question is not easy to answer in either case. In science, our grounds of knowledge consist of experiments and the reasoning based upon their results that lead us to construct hypotheses. It is then these hypotheses which, when combined with new experimental results, allow us to understand natural phenomena. The feeling is that we understand an event when it relates to an hypothesis in such a way as to allow us to anticipate its consequences. However, it is not only legitimate but necessary for us to question this feeling. Does it result simply from the observation that hypotheses in the past have allowed us to explain events? Can there be grounds more relevant than this?

The historian attempts to understand events through procedures analogous to those used by the physical scientist. It is sometimes facilely assumed that physical scientists are in a better position than historians to construct hypotheses because they deal with phenomena that can be experimentally repeated. To repeat an event experimentally, however, is not the same thing as to actually repeat it. No stone ever falls precisely the same way twice, even under exacting laboratory conditions. What the scientist does is to abstract from the total circumstances factors he hypothetically considers constant. If we substitute "documents" for experiments and "theories of history" for natural laws, we see that statements of scientific method and descriptions of historical procedure are analogous. It is from his documents that a historian reconstructs events. The way in which he narrates events depends for support upon the documents he has investigated. We feel that we understand an event when we can explain why it happened as it did, why it followed preceding events, and why it led into subsequent events. It is the historian's theory of history, or the pattern he sees in events, that allows these questions to be answered, just as the natural laws, or hypotheses, in science allow anticipation of the consequences of an event.

The questions that concern the relationship between the known and the grounds of knowing require continuous philosophical investigation and debate because our capacity for experience shifts with new discoveries in natural and human phenomena. With the questions of these relationships, this book does not deal directly. Rather, I concentrate upon the primary material of historical inquiry—documents—and attempt to develop a way to understand them—a method which is then applied to a number of specific examples.

Anything left from the refuse of life can become a document for historical inquiry. Anthropologists have developed sophisticated techniques for reconstructing the life style of a primitive people from bits and pieces of broken pots at the sites of long burned out campfires. Historians of literate people usually find written records more to their purpose than antique furniture. Whatever it may be, a document represents an event frozen in time. Actually we cannot stop time to study an event any more than a natural scientist can really repeat an event. But we consider documents as frozen events in order to discover the original form of the life they represent. The attempt is like the reconstruction of, say, a seventeenth-century house encased in three centuries of modification. We can hypothesize its initial structure from what we know about seventeenth-century building techniques in general. We must then trace through the modifications until we reach the original structure. If our hypothesis was incorrect, we may remove a structural member that will bring the house crashing down. But should we succeed in removing the accretions, we can begin to construct an hypothesis about what it felt like to live in the house by collecting seventeenth-century objects of everyday life. History, then, is a subjunctive inquiry based upon documents. Unlike physical science, which sets up future experiments that can confirm or deny hypotheses, experiments in history consist of the application of hypothesis to documents. Contradiction means denial in both sciences, just as noncontradiction means confirmation. While the physical scientist may predict the future of natural phenomena, the historian can only prophesy about past events and circumstances.

Basing inquiry upon documents, how is the historian who deals with written remains to reconstruct them so as to bring back the form of life they represent? Just as historians typically attempt to explain an event by relating it to its antecedents and consequents, its temporal causes and effects, too frequently they seem to relate documents to each other without explicit analysis of individual documents. We, of course, need to know how documents relate to each other just as we wish to know the temporal relationship of events; but unless we understand the particular document, the sequences we construct will be ropes of sand. We need, then, explicit procedures for analyzing particular documents.

The science of diplomatics, the branch of paleography that deals with methods for establishing the authenticity of documents, was established systematically by Jean Mabillon (1632–1707), in connection with the collections of documents of French history that the Benedictine monks of the congregation of Saint-Maur were making. Before the work of these monks, editors had altered texts at their own discretion, had been slipshod about citations, and had had no model for judging the genuineness of a text. Sloppy procedure did not of course stop after Mabillon's publication of *De re diplomatica* (1681), but his model turned interest in the direction of exactness. A standard had been set for the nineteenth-century outpouring of documents to support national aspirations.

As more and more documents have been found and edited during the last two centuries, the standards have become increasingly more exacting. To take only the American example, the work of Peter Force and Jared Sparks during the earlier part of the nineteenth century is naive compared to the standards of editing done by John Franklin Jameson, Worthington C. Ford, and Paul Leicester Ford early in the twentieth century; and this work in turn does not stand up to the exactness of the editing done since World War II by such men as Julian P. Boyd on the *Jefferson Papers,* W. T. Hutchinson on the *Madison Papers,* and Lyman H. Butterfield on the *Adams Papers.*

The editing of documents found a use in the teaching of American history as early as 1883 with the beginning of the *Old South Leaflets*. These were followed by Albert Bushnell Hart's four-volume *American History Told by Contemporaries* (1897–1901) and William MacDonald's selected documents illustrating the colonial, Revolution-to-Civil-War, and Civil-War-and-after periods of American history (1898, 1899, and 1903). The most long-lasting and popular collection has been Henry Steele Commager's *Documents of American History*, first published in 1934 and issued in a seventh edition in 1963. The collections of selected documents moved from library to coffee table with Daniel Boorstin's edition of *An American Primer* (1966), which, despite its high cost, is the most useful of the selected collections because professional historians introduce each document with its antecedents and follow it with its consequents, or "afterlife," as each of these short essays is called. With increased availability of documents, the standard structure of history courses has increasingly revolved around their discussion.

In the main, the editions of these documents are trustworthy. The old diplomatics has done its job. What now seems needed is a new diplomatics that will serve as a model for understanding particular documents as they exist in themselves, as frozen events in time. My aim in this book is to provide such a model.

A model includes a method for analysis and its application to test cases. The method developed in Chapter I is based upon techniques of rhetorical analysis as these have developed since Aristotle. The test cases range from a speech by an Englishman on his way to America in 1630 to a Supreme Court decision given in 1954. Of the thirteen test cases, five are speeches, three are manifestoes, three are laws, and two are court decisions. They are intended to be indicative of the range of American political rhetoric, but they do not exhaust the possibilities. With the exception of the Agricultural Adjustment Act, the documents presented are complete. The analysis following each document adapts the method presented in Chapter I to the material peculiar to the document. A model for analysis must always be considered suggestive. It can never be applied exactly to the material for analysis. The material is always unique, while the model is always general. The problem is to adapt the general to the particular. When the procedure is the other way round, plausibility is squeezed out like the last dab of toothpaste in the tube.

I have written this book for the general audience of all those interested in the study of history, broadly conceived. With such an audience in mind, I have made no attempt to restrict my personal judgment of the ethical merit of the documents as I might have done had I restricted myself to writing for either students or teachers of history. Especially in dealing with the twentieth-century documents, I have expressed severe reservations concerning their ethical status. One's view of his own time is, of course, shaped by the tendencies he sees. Whether or not my bleak view of the tendencies expressed by these documents follows logically from the analysis and argument is for the reader to decide. I, of course, feel that it does.

My hope for this book is that it will provide a model, or a suggestion for a model, that will allow a fuller understanding of the inner workings of documents. This task, I would argue is the first job in the historian's attempt to construct a causal chain linking events in time. Why do events happen as they do and not another way? This is the question for all those interested in history. It cannot be answered convincingly until we are able to understand the isolated event.

This study was planned at the suggestion and with the help of Herbert Charles Cohen. His suggestion was that I apply the method I had used in *History as Argument* (The Hague: Mouton & Co., 1966) to a broader context. In the early stages Professors W. T. Hutchinson and Ari Hoogenboom made valuable suggestions. Professor Wayne Booth was kind enough to read the manuscript before it was edited, and he made valuable comments. Doubtless, where I have gone wrong, I have ignored the advice of these four friends.

I wish to thank the National Council of Teachers of English for permission to use a revised version of my essay, "The Rhetoric of the Declaration of Independence," which appeared in *College English* (January, 1965).

In the bibliographical essay at the end of the book I have cited the sources for the reprinted texts and short quotations, and given suggestions for those interested in pursuing topics raised throughout the book.

W. R. SMITH

Mount Carroll, Illinois
October, 1968

I

The Analysis of Documents

Uniqueness and Our
Knowledge of the Past

SITTING before my typewriter, staring from the window at the trucks speeding along the highway, I begin to wonder who I am and how I am to know myself. The trucks pass in an instant, not long enough for me to be certain of their makes, colors, or shapes. I notice leaves falling from the trees on a cold and wet day in late fall. Turning my gaze inside my office, I see differently colored and shaped books and papers in the fluorescent indoor light. Looking at my watch, I see that half an hour has passed since I last noticed it. My gaze falls on the paper in my typewriter and I see words written there. As I read them, I wonder what exactly was meant? Why do the sentences follow as they do? As I wonder about them, the words on the page become a document to be analyzed in my attempt to discover myself of half an hour ago. I become an historian of myself.

From the time we develop memory as very young children, we all become self-historians. The things that we save—toys, drawings, love-letters, ribbons won in summer-camp athletics, papers given A's by teachers, commendations from the boss, hats bought on summer vacations, gold watches inscribed with fifty-years' service—are the documents one collects during a long life. By fixing our thought on one of them, we recreate our past by using this frozen moment in time to unlock our memory, which in turn breathes life back into the document of our past that we hold in our hands. Only in this way can we know what we have been and sense the direction in which we are going. What we are at this moment is largely unknowable. The continuum rushes forward as the trucks speed by my view from the window. To know the trucks I must stop them, which I cannot do from here. To know myself fully, I must find some documents that my self has left behind.

But with the documents in hand, they are no more completely knowable in themselves than I am able to know myself completely at the present moment. To be known, an object must be related to another object that is already understood. Typically, an historian relates the document to be known to the effects it produced and then infers the probable causes of the document. The *Magna Carta* was long considered the foundation of English liberties. But the document is full of words, such as "free man," whose meaning in the thirteenth century was quite the reverse of twentieth-century usage. Upon close observation, the language is seen to apply to a particular situation at a particular time. The power of the king was displacing the powers of the barons and churchmen, and the nobles used general discontent with John's reign in 1215 to force the central government to restrict its operations. In narrative, the analytic process is turned around and we are given the synthetic temporal order of causes to effects. Yet, although the document has been related to its past and its future, we have not seen the thing in itself.

In order to see the thing properly, we need to relate it to

something other than itself. The unknown must be related to the known in order to be understood. Having failed to get at the uniqueness of the unknown through its causes and effects in time, the alternative is to construct a model for analysis that will allow us to relate the unknown to the model.

RHETORICAL ANALYSIS

One possible model is rhetorical analysis. Obviously, such a model can only deal with documents whose medium of expression is language. Rhetoric is the art of convincing others that we have something valuable to say. Any linguistic utterance necessarily attempts this. There is a metaphorical sense in which the plastic arts, music, and architecture also must convince us that they are worthwhile. But it is only by analogy that we speak of the Greek revival style as expressing certain emotional states.

Restricting our inquiry to the rhetorical analysis of linguistic documents, then, how are we to proceed? First of all, what is involved in an utterance? A speaker implies an audience, even if it is only he listening to himself. The utterance is produced because of a certain purpose on the part of the speaker. He wishes to make the kind of statement that will affect his audience in some way. In order to make an effect, he must use language appropriate to the subject at hand, and his words must be put into an appropriate form. The success or failure of the utterance depends upon the result the intended effect actually has upon the audience.

Confronted with a document, there are four kinds of questions we may ask. What is the document's purpose? What materials does the document use? Into what form are these materials shaped? And, what impact upon its audience does the document attempt to achieve?

QUESTIONS OF PURPOSE

Study of the means of persuasion, like most other studies in Western civilization, began with the Greeks, who, being fortunate enough to be first—or at least to leave the earliest well-formed observations—could speculate on everything without the handicap of feeling that if they looked it up in a book there would be no further need for discussion. Rhetoric, apparently, was one of their first studies, for Greek literature is full of formal speeches and debates long before the sophists began teaching rhetorical tricks to the Athenians around the end of the Persian wars in 448 B.C. During the fourth century, through the philosophical analyses of Plato and Aristotle, the study of rhetoric was given a form that has controlled all investigations of the art of persuasion since.

Categories of Rhetoric

Persuasive discourse was categorized during this period into political or deliberative, forensic or legal, and epideictic or ceremonial rhetoric. A speaker trying to persuade a group to take a certain course of action uses *deliberative rhetoric.* When judging actions already committed, *forensic rhetoric* is used. *Epideictic rhetoric* concerns itself with praising or blaming the moral worth of a man at the present time, that is, his capacity for performing certain kinds of actions. Thus, these categories are partly based on future, past, and present time, and partly on modes of action. More importantly, the categories of rhetoric represent the kinds of purposes men have for persuasive discourse.

What good are these ancient categories today? Don't they simply turn into pigeonholes for sorting and forgetting? Of course, categories may become pigeonholes for those who think that naming is all there is to knowing. But if it is understood that classification of things into categories helps us to understand the specific things better, categorization can be a useful device for learning. We should never expect that the characteristics of a category would be identical with the characteristics of any object within that category, but we can expect that an understanding of a category will help us begin our investigation of the things within it.

The traditional categories for characterizing the purpose of speeches can help us understand how specific examples of persuasive discourse work on us. Advertising is probably the most pervasive form of persuasive discourse today, and television commercials are one of the more effective forms of advertising. Through a TV commercial, it is obvious that copywriters are trying to persuade us to adopt a course of action; they want us to buy the product whose manufacturer pays them to write the ads so that they can continue to make money by writing ads. So far, anyone who understands the meaning of the term can tell us that they are using deliberative rhetoric. But that alone would be mere pigeonholing, not analysis; in order to really know how such deliberative discourse works on its audience, we must develop this answer to the question of advertising's purpose and complement it with questions about the materials, form, and effect of commercials.

One cannot look at TV commercials very often without

realizing that the anecdotes are a form of debate between competing products (why they are written in anecdotal form will be examined further on). The action in the anecdote for one product, often blatantly, sometimes subtly, refutes the claims made for a similar product. In order to understand the characters and action in the anecdote, the audience, frequently, must be familiar with other anecdotes. Looked at closely, we see that the copywriters employ all of the traditional categories that characterize rhetorical purpose, and frequently their real deliberative purpose is submerged beneath forensic and epideictic purposes for effect.

The debate over the value of competing hair tonics provides a convenient, and perhaps an amusing, example, at least for a balding writer. The early TV anecdotes showed an athlete, fresh from the shower, being advised by a well-groomed friend to use a white cream containing lanolin. This hair cream, the suave friend tells the bushy-haired neophyte, will replace the natural oils baked out by the sun and washed out by the shower. The neophyte accepts a handful of his friend's hair cream, gives his scalp a brisk rubdown, runs a comb through his hair, and emerges from the gym with suavity. The rhetoric here is simply deliberative. As audience, the anecdote urges us to go and do likewise. Frequently, such commercials end with a salesman making an explicit pitch.

The reply to this kind of commercial complicates the rhetorical purpose. A suave young man fixes up his bashful friend with a blind date. We see the friends picking up their dates; the suave one's hair is lying naturally in place, but his bashful buddy has that plastered-down look. At the movies, the suave friend's date laughs and cuddles, but the bashful friend's date is deliberately cool. On their way home, the friends talk it over, and our bashful boy learns that the whole trouble is that he is still using that greasy kid-stuff instead of a natural hair dressing. In the next scene, we see that the friend's bashfulness has indeed disappeared with the acquisition of the natural hair dressing, while the girl who was cool before is now provocative. In addition to the sexual complications, the persuasion has been complicated and made more effective by the addition of a forensic purpose. The anecdote intends to convince us in deliberative fashion to use one hair cream by attacking in forensic fashion another. A past mistake is used as the means to convince us to take the right course of action in the future.

The hair-tonic debate becomes complicated even further with the introduction of a number of competing clear jellies. In an early commercial for one of the jellies, we find the standard characters, noticeably younger than in the other ads, landing a plane or a boat. The boy playing the bushy-haired bit pulls out a tube of white hair cream when his well-groomed friend tells him that the girls are coming. The well-groomed friend nearly panics at the sight of the hair cream, and through squeezing tubes into his bushy-haired friend's hands, he convinces him that it is better to have the clear jelly on his hair than a head full of greasy-looking stuff. This scene is cut, without showing us rubdown and combing (presumably, we all know how it is done by this time), and we are shown the couple up in a plane or speeding through the water in a motor boat. The girl is admiring the boy's hair with a look that tells him he has a good chance to score with her later on. The rhetorical appeal in this anecdote is more subtle than in earlier commercials. The audience the copywriter is trying to reach is specified through the age and activities of the characters (the problem of audience will be taken up in detail later). The forensic purpose of the anecdote is low-keyed, since we do not actually see one of the characters commit the wrong action by using the greasy-looking stuff. An epideictic aspect enters the commercial through the tone the characters use in voicing the product's name. Thus, this anecdote uses all of the traditional categories of rhetorical purpose to make its deliberative point.

In the anecdote answering that one, the product is not only clear, but invisible as well. The opening scene shows a young man of college age walking through a group of young children shouting "jelly-head" at him. When he gets back to his room, his roommate tells him that he needs something that won't stick to his hair. The roommate puts two paper towels on the table, squeezes the clear jelly into the palm of one hand and the invisible jelly into the other. When he slaps the towels, the hand with the clear jelly picks up the towel, but the hand with the invisible jelly comes up clean. This demonstration shows the potential worth of the invisible jelly and the potential danger of the clear jelly. In this anecdote, the sexual connotations are suppressed because the debate between the competing hair creams has made them too obvious to need repeating. The forensic purpose is brought out through the ridicule of the young children, and the epideictic aspect of the anecdote is shown in the demonstration. The real purpose of the anecdote, its deliberative rhetorical appeal, is brought out through a combination of forensic and epideictic aspects.

In the commercial that completes this debate so far, the rhetoric is predominately epideictic. A mermaid addresses the audience directly about a product that not only grooms the hair but substitutes for a shampoo as well. Its superior worth is demonstrated not directly by showing us how it controls a bushy head of hair, but indirectly through its capacity to react with water. Both the deliberative rhetoric of this commercial —that we should buy the product—and the forensic rhetoric

—that it will not produce oily-looking hair—are suppressed in favor of the commercial's epideictic appeal. The product is worthy of our praise because of its capacity to control hair and keep it clean. This potentiality obviously makes the product something that we should use, and so the real deliberative purpose of the commercial is fulfilled by an epideictic discourse.

A review of the great hair-tonic debate shows the usefulness of the traditional categories of rhetorical purpose. Direct persuasion through the deliberative rhetorical means that urge the audience to action tends to lose its effectiveness through repetition. The effectiveness can be retained by covering a direct appeal to action with judgments about past actions that did not produce the desired effect. This allows us as the audience to deduce the desired action for ourselves and, because inferences that we ourselves draw tend to stick in our memories, the deliberative persuasion regains its effectiveness. When we grow tired of attacks on past actions, epideictic means of directly praising the capacity of a product for producing the desired effect again forces us to make the deduction that we ought to buy it. Thus the skillful copywriter changes his rhetorical devices for achieving his deliberative purpose. Aware of these possibilities, we should be better able to control our own reactions to persuasion.

The Speaker's Character

Variation of the categories of rhetorical purpose is only one among the many ways the skillful rhetorician seeks to persuade. Given any of the three categories of purpose, there are three traditional means used in persuasion. A speaker may appeal to the audience's *reason* through logical arguments, to its *emotions* through ordering descriptions, or use of language, and he may exhibit his own character through his speech as an *ethical appeal.* The rational and emotional appeals to the audience will be discussed when we come to questions about the form and effects of persuasive discourse. Because a man's character must in some sense determine the range of purposes he may have in speaking, the ethical appeal is best discussed here with other questions of purpose.

The ethical appeal consists of all the things in a particular discourse that lead the audience to accept the speaker as a man who has a right to say what he says in the way he says it at the time he speaks. We may, for example, agree that what a man says makes sense, but we may reject his conclusions because we feel that he is speaking out of turn. This is frequently the attitude that many people take toward those who criticize policies of the national government in time of national emergency. The tone that a man uses is another factor that may lead an audience to reject his conclusions even though they accept his premises. If he uses a sarcastic tone about matters that people consider sacred, they will mark him as a man without common human feeling, and so reject his arguments. Men considered specialists in the subject are frequently more acceptable than those who can have no claim to special knowledge, although occasionally an audience may react against the specialist in favor of men of common sense. For example, we generally think that men of long experience have a better right to make statements about education, foreign policy, or economics than those who have never worked in these areas. But when the specialists debate issues using an incomprehensible jargon, we may turn to men who use common language. All these things are aspects of what is today called a man's "image." Concern for the image that we present, as a nation, organization, or individual, represents preoccupation with ethical appeal.

To return to our example of the hair-tonic debate, we can

see that the character representing the product's virtues in each of the anecdotes possesses the characteristics Aristotle, in his *Rhetoric,* claimed that a speaker should exhibit in order to make an ethical appeal to his audience. He is "sensible" because he knows the relative worth of the different hair creams. He is "moral" because he is concerned with the welfare of others, and his "benevolence" is shown when he instructs his friend in the arts of good grooming. His own obviously well-groomed hair shows us that he speaks with practical knowledge. Thus, he is the sort of person that we tend to identify with: a good person, concerned with others, knowing what to do and doing it. The copywriter's desire for an effective ethical appeal is one of the main reasons for presenting the commercials in anecdotal form.

The ethical appeal in the mermaid commercial is more complex than in the anecdotes. It is easy for one to identify with the character and situation of the actors in the anecdotes, but how can we be expected to accept the word of a mermaid when it comes to hair tonic? Stretched out seductively on her side at the edge of the ocean, the mermaid speaks directly to her male audience about a "fantastic new experience." We know that it's a bit silly, but the very fact that we smile softens our feelings into imagining what it would be like to make love to a mermaid. Once we have done this, the mermaid's opinions about hair grooming tend to stand for the opinions of all desirable women. Since the desire for sexual attractiveness is a major reason for paying attention to the way our hair looks, the character of the mermaid in the commercial exercises the most powerful ethical appeal in any of the hair-tonic commercials.

An effective ethical position is one of the strongest devices available in persuasive discourse. Whether a speaker's purpose is to persuade his audience to take some course of action through the use of deliberative rhetoric, to direct, by forensic means, its judgment concerning an action already committed, or to convince it through the use of epideictic means of the nobility or ignobility of some person, institution, or thing, he must present himself as a man capable of making such judgments. The image of him that we as an audience will see depends largely upon how he shapes the materials of his arguments to achieve his effects. Even though we may have a clear picture of what a man is like before any particular speech, this picture will be redefined by what he does on the occasion. The kind of materials—both the sorts of arguments and the language in which they are presented—that a speaker chooses strongly affect the moral character that he presents.

QUESTIONS OF MATERIALS

Like the categories of rhetorical purpose and the possible appeals that a speaker may make to his audience, the kinds of arguments a speaker may produce about his subject were categorized by the Greek and Roman students of rhetoric as "topics." These topics are ways in which the relationship between things can be seen. It is standard practice to use the phrase, "an argument from . . . ," when identifying a speaker's use of particular topics. Thus, in analyzing persuasive discourse, we speak of arguments from definition, comparison, relationship, circumstance, and testimony. Men tend to use a small number of these topics habitually, and when we discover their favorites, we are beginning to have a good grasp of their individual style of persuasion.

Kinds of Arguments
Arguments from *definition* tend toward more formal devel-

opment than arguments from the other topics. In his *Topica,* Cicero gave this example of an argument based upon genus and species:

> The civil law is a system of equity established between members of the same state for the purpose of securing to each his property rights.
> The knowledge of this system of equity is useful.
> Therefore, the science of civil law is useful.

In this form the argument is not a syllogism, but by some rearrangement and elimination of the explanatory material, it can be reduced to a syllogism:

> The civil law is a species of all systems of equity; knowledge of systems of equity is useful; therefore, knowing the civil law is useful.

There is no need to get into the technical details of logic here, although it should be clear that there is an intimate connection between logic and rhetoric, in that rational argumentation is one of the most persuasive aspects of polemical writing. The syllogism, once the premises are accepted as true, gives us undeniable proof of its conclusion.

A syllogism is rarely explicitly stated in persuasive discourse. For example, the opening sentence of the Declaration of Independence is a definition by genus and species that contains an implicit syllogism:

> When in the Course of human events, it becomes necessary for one people to dissolve the political bands which have connected them with another, and to assume among the powers of the earth, the separate and equal station to which the Laws of Nature and

of Nature's God entitle them, a decent respect to the opinions of mankind requires that they should declare the causes which impel them to the separation.

Reduced to a definition, this sentence asserts that the species "American people" is a part of the genus "people." The syllogism underlying this definition is: Each separate people is entitled by God to its own government; the Americans are a separate people; therefore they are entitled to their own government. The form this definition and syllogism take in the sentence makes for more effective persuasion than would an explicit statement, because the reader is forced to engage his mind actively in discovery.

The second pattern of argument from definition Cicero listed was the enumeration of parts:

So-and-So is not a free man unless he has been set free by entry in the census roll, or by touching with the rod, or by will.
None of these conditions has been fulfilled.
Therefore, he is not free.

Here again, we would have to do some rearranging to present this argument in correct syllogistic form. Enumeration frequently forms the second statement in an argument that is implicitly syllogistic. To look at the Declaration again, we see that its implicit syllogism (an attempt to establish despotism necessitates revolution; George III attempts to establish despotism; therefore revolution is necessary) uses as a minor premise an enumeration of the acts George III has committed against the colonies. This constitutes a definition of him as a tyrant: "A Prince, whose character is thus marked by every act which may define a Tyrant, is unfit to be the ruler of a free people." After such an exhaustive enumeration, the colonies' statement, "that they are Absolved from all Allegiance to the British Crown," carries greater persuasive weight because of their successful definition of their former sovereign as a tyrant.

The argument from definition, whether by genus and species, or by enumeration of parts, has long been thought the most persuasive of arguments. Plato, in his dialogue concerning rhetoric, *Phaedrus*, asserts that there are two principles of good rhetoric: "First, the comprehension of scattered particulars in one idea; . . . the speaker should define his several notions and so make his meaning clear"; second, the "division into species according to the natural formation, where the joint is, not breaking any part as a bad carver might." And Aristotle, in his stress on the enthymeme (an abbreviated syllogism requiring the reader to supply one of the premises or the conclusion), and in his insistence that rhetoric was the counterpart of dialectic (the art of persuasion, that is, cannot be carried on without logical discourse), recognized that we cannot persuade without defining.

Although there are several other methods of defining, none is so persuasive as definition by genus and species and enumeration of parts. Definitions constructed from the nature of language, either by synonyms or etymologies, appear artificial. If a man argues that an aristocratic form of government would be a good thing because the term itself is a combination of two Greek words, one meaning "best" and the other meaning "to rule," or if he asserts that "president" is just another word for "master," we are not likely to continue listening to him. When descriptions and examples are used as definitions, we tend to become impatient to get at the real thing. The speaker who begins by telling us, "I cannot define happiness, I can only describe a happy man," or who tells us a long story which concludes, "that's happiness," only gives us examples that may not apply in all circumstances. Happiness may be a blanket for Linus in *Peanuts,* but a blanket is only one of the things that will make me happy on a cold night.

We are more satisfied, and therefore more easily persuaded, by definitions from genus and species and enumeration of parts because the man who can construct them asserts hypotheses concerning the nature of things. When Edmund Burke asserted, in "On Conciliation with the Colonies," that "abstract liberty, like other mere abstractions, is not to be found," he was defining liberty as an actual property of a people. "Liberty," he continued, "inheres in some sensible object; and every nation has formed to itself some favorite point, which by way of eminence becomes the criterion of their happiness." This line of argument becomes very persuasive when we see him go on to specify the characteristics of the colonists that make them see questions of taxation as issues of liberty.

Equally persuasive was the line of argument Thomas Paine took when he sought in *The Rights of Man* to refute Burke's application of this definition of liberty in his *Reflections on the Revolution in France.* To Burke's argument that the French had destroyed their liberties when they overthrew their constitution of government, Paine replied that man "acquires a knowledge of his rights by attending justly to his interest, and discovers in the event that the strength and powers of despotism consist wholly in the fear of resisting it, and that in order 'to be free it is sufficient that he wills it.'" Burke's definition that liberty could only have meaning in terms of actual circumstances was nonsense to Paine, who saw despotism as the circumstances of the French people. If liberty is defined as a man's right to life and happiness, then his present circumstances can have no direct bearing on the nature of his liberty. But if, as Burke believed, liberty can only be the result of a fortuitous combination of circumstances regulated to achieve what each particular people believes is its happiness, these circumstances are the very essence of each people's liberty.

Contradictory definitions can be equally persuasive in the context of the arguments developed from them. But in order to be ultimately persuaded by an argument from definition, we must accept the implications a definition has for the nature of things. Paine's definition of liberty implies some kind of eternal order governing the affairs of men. This order expresses itself in the mind and heart of each individual, because we have only to look into ourselves to know what our liberty ought to be. Whatever eternal order there may be governing human affairs is unknowable for Burke. His definition of liberty implies that we are prisoners of our immediate situations. The most we can do is attempt to regulate our affairs in our own interest, whatever we may consider it to be.

The implications of these two contradictory definitions of liberty help account for the different styles of the two men. Paine's optimism grows out of a metaphysical presupposition concerning the order of the universe and the ability of men to know and then act upon their knowledge. Burke's epistemological skepticism prevents him from developing a position relating the order of the universe to the affairs of men, and this makes absolute definitions impossible. In turn, the impossibility of definitive judgment accounts for Burke's pessimism. Whether we are persuaded by the argument of Burke or by the argument of Paine depends upon our acceptance of the implications in their definitions.

Their definitions, in either case, are the most persuasive parts of their arguments. A definition, because it has implications for the nature of things, is necessarily an hypothesis for prediction, and it is such hypotheses that constitute the fruits of knowledge for most men. A man whose argument implies the future is a man to be believed.

Men like Paine, whose definitions imply an ordered universe, tend to rely heavily upon these definitions in their arguments. But men like Burke, whose definitions imply either the impossibility of knowing order in the universe, or a chaotic universe, attempt to support their definitions with arguments from comparison, relationships, circumstances, and testimony.

Those who draw *comparisons* in their arguments, whether they show similarity or difference between the materials, or whether they judge their values, depend upon probability for persuasion. These topics are frequently used in debates about political action, an area about which, unlike the nature of government itself, men feel incapable of making real definitions. Early in the *Federalist Papers,* Hamilton and Madison used a series of essays (numbers 15–20) to argue that the Articles of Confederation could not maintain the kind of government that the American states needed. After characterizing the situation under the Confederation as failing to meet the needs for which government is established in the first place, Hamilton and Madison used historical examples of confederations as arguments from comparison to show that the American confederation would suffer the fate of those in the past. Their examples range over the whole of European history, from ancient Greece, to medieval Germany, to modern Holland, all attempting to show that because anarchy between the members, not tyranny in the ruling body, has been the result in the past, Americans would be unreasonable to expect anything different from their confederacy. The validity of arguments from comparison is stressed again and again in this series, and Madison concluded with a paragraph asserting their value:

> I make no apology for having dwelt so long on the contemplation of these federal precedents. Experience is the oracle of truth; and where its responses are unequivocal, they ought to be conclusive and sacred. The important truth, which it unequivocally pronounces in the present case, is that a sovereignty over sovereigns, a government over governments, a legislation for communities, as contradistinguished from individuals, as it is a solecism in theory, so in practice it is subversive of the order and ends of civil polity, by substituting *violence* in place of *law,* or the destructive *coercion* of the *sword* in place of the mild and salutary *coercion* of the *magistracy.*

Although the explicit conclusion—that America will be reduced to the militaristic tyranny which follows anarchy—is not stated here, its effectiveness as persuasion is the greater because no reader could fail to draw the conclusion.

Such arguments depend for their persuasive power on the opinion most of us have that, if two things are alike in most aspects, they will probably be alike in all aspects. If A, let us say, has the aspects u, v, w, x, y, and z, and if B has the aspects u, v, w, x, and y, it is reasonable to assume that B will also have the aspect z. At the very least, when we find this much similarity, we should expect z to appear and should prepare for it. This argument can be reversed by finding differences between A and B. If we discover that B has an aspect t that A does not have, we can construct an argument from difference that asserts z is not likely for B because z only appears when the series begins with u, as it does in A. The argument from comparison can be further complicated if differences of degree are discovered. If we find that in the case of

A, the aspects are really u^1, v^1, . . . z^1, whereas in B the aspects are u^2, v^2, . . . , it can be argued that the different values assignable to the aspects make us believe that A and B are only superficially similar.

Arguments concerning war and peace frequently turn upon comparisons. To take the example of the debate over the proper policy to take in Vietnam, we find one position maintaining that the history of the twentieth century shows that aggression must be stopped as soon as it appears or the result will be a major war. The United States and its allies stand in a position to China analogous to the position occupied by England and France toward Germany during the late thirties. We now know that if England and France had taken a stronger position at the Munich conference, Germany would have backed down on its demands concerning Czechoslovakia and World War II could possibly have been averted. The United States should, therefore, take a very strong position toward the Communists in Vietnam, for if it does not, Communism will spread, and we will find ourselves fighting on many fronts at once.

The opponents of this line of argument, using an argument from difference, assert that the analogy does not hold. There is no similarity between the expansionist policy of Germany in the late thirties and the civil war going on in Vietnam. Of course, the Communist governments in other countries are supporting the rebels in South Vietnam, but outside aid to revolutionaries is as old as the French assistance to the Americans in the American Revolution. The policy of the United States in fact encourages world Communism because opponents of corrupt governments are led to believe that they can be helped only by Communist countries, and outside aid is always necessary for successful revolution. If the United States, therefore, is to serve its own best interest in not alienating the underdeveloped nations, its best policy would be to withdraw from South Vietnam.

Arguments from degree can strengthen these two positions. To those who argue from the comparison between Nazi Germany in the thirties and the Communist nations in the sixties, Communism is really a greater threat to world peace than was Germany. Germany wanted to control the European continent, but the Communists want to control the world. To this, those who argue from the difference between Nazi Germany and the Communists can reply that the threat posed by Germany was a military one, whereas the Communists pose rather a political threat. Furthermore, the whole tenor of German policy threatened the very existence of civilization. The willingness to put racial theories into practice with the killing of millions of Jews and Gypsies destroyed the very basis of the morality that supports civilization. Communists, on the other hand, at least assert the brotherhood of man, and although their means toward achieving this are potentially tyrannical, the end, at least, is in keeping with the goals of civilization. But those arguing from the similarity between Nazi Germany and Communism can retort that a military threat can be overcome by military means, whereas a political threat is much more difficult to combat, especially in the case of Communism, which uses a bogus goal of brotherhood to turn men into machines.

Such arguments rarely find a conclusion. To each point raised by the advocates of a strong policy in Vietnam, the opponents of the policy can produce a counterargument. What appears as a similarity to one group can become a difference to the other, and the difference of degree of value assigned to different facts and positions by the two groups further complicates the debate. The resolution of such arguments is only found in clear definitions. In this example, clear definitions of the terms in which both sides argue would be necessary before the audience could be finally persuaded of the right course of action. The two sides would have to agree on what is meant by "Communism" and "democracy," "aggression" and "revolution," and "civilization" and "government" before these central terms in their arguments could become premises with which to construct conclusive arguments. Their inability to define such terms conclusively leads men to adopt arguments from *relationships*.

When we argue from comparison, we are asserting the probable truth or falsity of something. When we find similarities or differences of aspects or degrees between two things, we are wise if we consider the likelihood that they are similar or different in all their aspects or degrees. But, as we have seen, comparisons cannot produce arguments that are conclusively persuasive. The discovery of relationships between the two things we compare, however, can produce conclusive arguments because when we show that A cannot happen unless acted upon by B, or that D never occurs unless preceded by C, or that if Q is the case, R cannot be the case, or if Z is false, Y must be true, we have established a necessary connection between the two things. Something necessary is something we cannot doubt. The only retort to a conclusion established through relationships is to bring the definitions of the objects related into question.

Looking back at our example of the great hair-tonic debate, we can see that each of the anecdotes tries to convince us that there is a cause and effect relationship between the way a man's hair looks and the hair tonic he uses. Unless he uses a particular hair tonic, his hair will not be well-groomed. Competing products, the anecdotes suggest, produce effects that are the reverse of those intended. There is little attempt in the anecdotes to clearly define the central terms of the argument, "well-groomed," "greasy look," etc., because we all know what they mean even if their implications were not presented by the anecdote's action. We all know, even if we are not completely familiar with the rules of logic that govern cause and effect relationships, that the anecdote's claim for a causal relationship between hair tonic and good looks is specious. A hair tonic can at best be only a contributing factor in good grooming for which many other things, at the least a good head of hair, are necessary.

When men cannot establish a causal connection between the terms of their argument, they frequently rely upon an antecedent-consequence relationship. This relationship maintains that among the many factors in a situation, X is crucial because it leads to Y, which may be a good or a bad thing. The hair tonic, for example, is presented in the anecdotes as being an antecedent for the consequence of good grooming. This kind of argument frequently occurs in this form: "if one is old enough to fight, he is old enough to vote." There is no necessary causal relationship between fighting and voting, but it is felt that voting gives one a voice in the policies of the government, and that one should certainly be able to give an official opinion on matters, such as going to war, that affect him directly. In this form, the argument from antecedent to consequence implies definitions that, made explicit, would allow the argument to be reduced to syllogistic reasoning. The implied argument from definition accounts for the persuasive power of the argument from antecedent to consequence, but this power can be undermined by exposing the implicit definitions.

In order to refute competing positions, we frequently rely upon arguments from contraries and contradictions. The argument from contraries shows that although two things belong to the same general kind (for example, both are hair tonics), this relationship is not as essential as the results they produce (for example, one hair tonic produces a greasy look, while the other produces well-groomed hair). When arguing from contraries, we must remember that, although if one proposition is true, the contrary proposition must be false, it is not the case that if one proposition is false, its contrary must be true, because both may be equally false. Neither hair tonic may produce the desired well-groomed effect.

The argument from contradiction is more persuasive than the argument from contraries, because if two propositions contradict each other, one of them must necessarily be false. Two contradictory propositions do not, however, establish the necessary truth of one because both may be false. If it is the case that the clear jelly will produce well-groomed hair, then the hair cream containing lanolin cannot. Such argument depends upon the adequacy of the implied definition of "well groomed." If the definition is inadequate, the relationship drawn between the contradictory propositions is beside the point and implies neither truth nor falsity of either proposition. In order to establish adequate definitions about the things we ordinarily debate, men often turn to an examination of circumstances.

Men arguing from *circumstances*—what is the case at present—are, like those arguing from comparison, concerned with probabilities; but through the form that this kind of argument takes, because the statement of circumstances occupies the position of a definition in a set of propositions resembling a syllogism, it develops enormous persuasive power. When arguing from comparison, we set up two things that are known to resemble each other in many respects and predict that they will resemble each other in even more ways. The argument from circumstance, on the other hand, begins with a statement of present conditions in the position of a major premise. The action necessitated by these conditions occupies the place of a minor premise. Expediency then dictates the action that stands as a conclusion. This quasi-syllogism persuades more effectively than the argument from comparison, because, although logically it only tells us what may be probable, its form seems to show us what is necessary. It is, therefore, frequently used in debates concerned with political action in conjunction with arguments from comparison that help to establish the nature of the present circumstances.

If we have, for example, developed an argument from comparison that shows the probability that z, which terminated case A, will be the conclusion of case B, because both cases have developed analogously through $u, v, w, x,$ and y, we can use this probability as a definition of the circumstances of case B. The action that seems best in case B to encourage or prevent the development of z will then be our minor premise, and we will conclude this quasi-syllogism with an appeal for the expediency of this action.

Chief Justice John Marshall, for example, developed a sustained argument from circumstances in his *Life of George Washington,* which was actually a history of the United States from the discovery of America to the death of Washington. Writing during the administration of Thomas Jefferson, Marshall wished to counter the states' rights position on the Constitution with the nationalistic position that he was beginning to assert in his Supreme Court decisions. He used colonial history to assert that the American states were a unity in which the necessity of the part implied the necessity of the whole, whose needs in turn dictated the proper action for each state. By showing that lack of effective centralized power had produced colonial wars and economic difficulties, and that weak national government under the Articles of Confederation had prolonged the Revolutionary War and had produced the economic chaos following it, he argued that strong central government was the necessity of the American union. This point was reinforced by stressing the effectiveness of the national government under the administration of Washington. In his argument, Marshall deliberately avoided justifications for the American Revolution that were common at the time, such as the argument that the Revolution was the effect of the will of God. Because he brought no metaphysical position of that kind into his argument, Marshall could not use the ultimate definitions of world order that were common to other advocates of the Revolution and the American system of government. Instead, he had to derive his definitions from the circumstances of the United States as these were made clear through analogy with its past history.

Arguments from circumstance do not always use analogy with the past to make clear their initial premise defining the actual conditions. If we look again at the debate concerning the proper policy for the United States in Vietnam, we will see that one group of opponents of the official policy argue that the circumstances of Asian politics, the topography of Vietnam, and the attitudes of the Vietnamese make it inexpedient to conduct a major war there. This group refutes the assessment of world circumstances, which claims through analogy with Germany of the thirties that the expansion of world Communism must be contained at any and all places it appears. The inability of reconciling such a debate leads the participants to an appeal to "facts," by which they mean testimony from authorities, personal experience, statistics, maxims, laws, and precedents.

The argument from *testimony* is quite often the final appeal in debate. As such, it is familiar to us through its use in advertising and in politics. Recalling our example of the great hair-tonic debate, we can easily pick out such arguments. When products give their chemical formula, they are appealing to our respect for authority. If a hair tonic has been analyzed by a chemist, it must be a sound product. The anecdotes themselves give us a view of the personal experience of using the different hair tonics, for if we see something work for one person, we believe it will work for us. The use of statistics as an argument in advertising convinces us that if such a high percentage of our fellowmen find the product useful, we should also be able to use it. Slogans for products frequently gain the currency of maxims that persuade because of their very repetition. Laws and precedents also find a use in advertising when the product is of the kind that protects us against accidents. For example, a tire commercial may cite the driving laws and show us that the advertised tires make it easy to stop even when traveling at high speed. These are the kinds of evidence we evoke in our arguments when we say that there is no disputing the facts.

In politics, testimony is also a powerful persuader. The authority of the President in foreign affairs, it is argued, is not to be doubted because he possesses more information than any ordinary citizen could. This authority can be brought into question, as it is in the debate over Vietnam policy, by those who have had personal experience with the issue in question. Journalists and anthropologists who have worked in Vietnam, for instance, may argue that the Vietnamese themselves want the American army out of their country. The statistics produced in the State Department's 1965 White Paper on Vietnam gave figures on the movement between North and South Vietnam that were designed to convince us that North Vietnam was actually an aggressor. But statistics can be brought into question by other statistics, as was the case with the replies to the White Paper. Maxims concerning the virtues of strength and the uses of negotiation frequently come into play when we argue about government policy. President Kennedy's Inaugural Address contained a number of maxims, such as "Let us never negotiate out of fear. But let us never fear to negotiate," a precept that has found constant use in foreign policy debates since. Laws and precedents based upon the law figure heavily in such debates. As we have seen, all sides of the Vietnamese question cite both the 1954 Geneva agreements that ended the war the French were fighting in Indochina and the treaties that the United States negotiated with some of the countries of Southeast Asia and with the government of South Vietnam following the close of that war.

But arguments from testimony, like the arguments from circumstance, relationship, and comparison, do not end debates. For each testimony one side brings forth, the other side has a contrasting testimony. With testimony, as with other arguments that lack ultimate definitions as a starting point, there is no really persuasive conclusion. Unless men agree on the ultimate definitions of the terms in which they argue, for every point that one side brings up, the opposing side can cite a counterargument. Ultimate definitions are, of course, difficult to arrive at. Because any definition contains implications of a metaphysical nature, we find that all arguments pushed far enough end in philosophical speculation.

Philosophical Implications

It is for this reason that examination of the topics a rhetorician habitually uses to present his materials is an important part of the explication of his style of persuasion. When men consistently argue from testimony, they reveal their assumption that there is something or someone not actually connected with the issue at hand whose statement will clarify everything. Fundamentalists, whether they argue for the literal application of the Bible, the United States Constitution, or some other sacred set of statements, exemplify this attitude. Those arguing from circumstance reverse the procedure of the fundamentalists, whose view of right action always depends upon past authority. For the circumstantialist, right action always depends upon personal benefit and the welfare of the group with which he associates himself. His kind of argument looks to the future for judgment and justification of the expedient actions he advocates for the present. Those arguing from relationships, on the other hand, are concerned mainly with the present. For them, controversy is settled by exposing the logical connection between the terms in the debate. The making of comparisons into arguments also shows concern with the present; but in this kind of argument, a man shows his concern for the probability that the world is composed of analogous units, rather than his feeling for the necessity expressed in logical connections. When a man argues from definition, his concern is beyond time, with what either is the case or what ought to be the case, eternally.

Arguments from definition, then, are favored by men who see the world as an eternal constant, a view we tend to identify with systematic philosophers and their followers. That the world is actually a unity, each part implying the whole, and the whole being a vast series of correspondences, is a view characteristic of religious thinkers and mystics, who tend to argue in terms of comparison. What we call the scientific attitude, which demands rigorous tests of logic in its investigations, favors arguments in terms of relationships. Politics, concerning itself with the manipulation of forces for personal or group interest, tends toward argument from circumstance. The ordinary, unreflective man, who feels that there must be a higher power than his own, finds arguments from testimony persuasive.

All these topics imply a view of the world. The argument from testimony implies that the world is controlled by some outside force. Circumstantial arguments imply that the flux of world forces must be controlled by groups or individuals for personal interest. If the world is a set of inexorable relationships, one can adapt to them by understanding them. An argument from comparison implies the individual's place in the all-encompassing unity. Systematic definitions imply the eternal nature of the world. Of course, anyone uses all these arguments in different situations, but the tendency to use certain of them marks the individuality of one's thought and style of persuasion. When we have discovered the leading argument, the way of organizing materials that seems most persuasive to an individual, we have found a sure indication of his style, and can so characterize him.

Language and Argument

An individual's style of persuasion is reflected in the language he uses. In the Declaration of Independence, for example, the measured, deliberative statements of what exists, rather than the use of imperative statements of what ought to exist, reveal use of an argument from definition. Were the Declaration arguing from circumstance, it would have appealed to the "best interests of men and nations," "expedience," "enlightened opinion," and "the strength of our determination and arms." Instead of expressing the wish that everything be regulated according to the desires of men, the Declaration manifests the feeling that men must order their affairs with nature. Men *are* created; they *are* endowed; governments *are* instituted. Whereas if custom identified through an argument from circumstance had conditioned the attitudes in the Declaration, the language would have been imperative: each national group *ought* to have a nation, instead of being *entitled to* a separate and equal station; the people *must* throw off tyranny, instead of *it is the right of the people* to alter or abolish arbitrary government.

Tone in polemical writing frequently reflects the leading argument in this way. We have all experienced the smug belligerence of those who feel that their arguments from testimony end all discussion. Strident insistence on "self-interest" frequently reflects the politician's argument from circumstance, as in Burke's *Reflections on the Revolution in France*. The dry explication of logical alternatives often characterizes the language of arguments from relationships, as in many of Einstein's popular essays. The tone of wonder and the frequent use of metaphor, as in the writings of Thoreau, point to the use of arguments from comparison. The calm deliberation of speeches, such as Lincoln's, is the natural expression of arguments from definition.

We have seen, then, that both the kinds of arguments and the tone of language (the materials used in polemical writing) are guides to the persuasive style of the writer. It would be a mistake, however, to isolate individual arguments and uses of language from the context of a complete discourse. A man whose purpose is deliberative normally argues from definition and uses a calm, measured tone, but he may adopt other means to make a point to a particular audience. A college professor who wants to enter a debate on public policy, for example, may realize that a popular audience has no patience with involved definitions. Should he begin his discourse, as he normally would to an audience of other professors, with a statement of principles that when applied to the situation will determine the proper action, the audience will put him down as an egghead and stop listening. Therefore, he might begin with an argument from circumstance that would allow him to show his audience that the principles he advocates actually define its own self-interest. Such an argument would actually be an argument from definition, masked by an argument from circumstance for persuasive effect.

QUESTIONS OF FORM

In order to investigate how the materials of polemical discourse are shaped into complete speeches and extended arguments, we must turn from questions of the materials of rhetoric to questions about the forms of rhetoric.

Anyone who does much writing has frequently experienced the frustration of being unable to start, develop, or conclude an essay. He may have the subject well in mind. What he wants to accomplish is clear. The materials, arguments, evidence, etc. may be clearly outlined, but somehow he cannot write the first sentence, or he cannot think of a way to continue what he has already written. The problem in such a situation is not that he has nothing to say. Frequently he feels that he has so much to say that he doesn't know where to begin and that he cannot get into the essay everything he has amassed on the subject. If only he knew a little less about the subject, his ignorance would allow him to say what he knows without getting into complications that confuse the reader and impair the unity of the essay.

When we experience this kind of writer's block, the problem is not that we know too much—for when we think about it, we always "know" too little—but that we have failed to develop a form for presenting our purpose and materials. In such a situation, we experience an inability to choose. The questions we keep asking ourselves, without getting an answer, are "What should I say now?" and "How should I put it?" Our problem is one of selection. From the vast number of things we might say, we have to find a way of rejecting the extraneous and selecting the essential material.

Frequently, instructors of writing tell us that making an outline before we begin to write will prevent this difficulty. Such a suggestion is based on the assumption that outlining will force us to select and reject material for the purpose of our essay. Sometimes this does help, but more frequently we find that we are unable to follow the outline, and the attempt to do so becomes another block to writing. Only when we throw away the outline do we frequently find that we are able to continue writing by a process that resembles something like an animal charging with his head down.

When a writer charges through the writing of an essay successfully, his habitual way of thinking makes the choices without his being conscious of it. In this happy situation, words follow words, sentences follow sentences, and paragraphs, paragraphs without straining. He feels that what he writes is automatically right. It reads well and the arguments follow each other naturally. "That essay wrote itself," he remarks afterward.

Such writing is rare for most. The experience of an essay writing itself is one that occurs one day but is not repeated the next. The more experienced a writer becomes, the less trouble he is likely to have in making choices. But until he develops an habitual way of thinking that automatically determines the choice of materials necessary in writing, he will continue to have days when the words just won't come, even though he "knows" what he wants to say.

This habitual way of making choices constitutes the form a writer gives to his writing. In any successfully unified essay, there will be a recognizable way of making choices that we can discover by imagining the range of material the writer had at his disposal. When we find the principle he used in selecting and rejecting material out of the possible amount he might have used, we have discovered the form his essay takes. Established writers tend to use the same sort of form again and again, and it is for this reason that we can recognize an author's "style" in an unsigned passage when we have had wide experience studying his writings.

In discussing questions of materials in polemical writing, we said that the arguments and language a writer uses are guides to his persuasive style. This is so because they are reflections of assumptions about the nature of the universe that characterize his thought. We now see that these assumptions, arguments, and language are all part of the way a writer makes choices in his writing, the form he gives his work.

Sometimes "form" is restricted to a characterization of the kind of language used or the sorts of arguments employed. This is a confusing restriction because both language and arguments depend upon the kind of choices one habitually makes in writing. Such choices can only be the product of a writer's most general assumptions. These assumptions themselves are not the form of his writing, but are the principles that govern the form. Form, itself, is a concept characterizing the way that the choices in writing are made.

Looking back at the great hair-tonic debate, we said that the copywriter's desire for an effective emotional appeal was one of the major reasons for the anecdotal form. In analyzing polemical writing, we call the choices the writer makes regarding his emotional appeal to his audience the rhetorical structure of his argument. The rational structure of his argument is made of the choices dictated by the logical appeal of his argument. Advertising is frequently formed exclusively by emotional appeal.

Rhetorical Structure

When a writer seeks to persuade an audience to take an action or make a judgment through an emotional appeal, he tries to get it to identify itself with the action or judgment under question. He wants to show the audience that it will make a difference to each person's day-to-day life, or that each is already living by the principles the writer advocates. To do this, he uses materials that appeal to the imagination. His words may be those that quicken the heart—honor, duty, love, country. The actions he describes may be those we instinctively wish to participate in—battle in the cause of justice, perseverance in the face of adversity, magnanimity. Or he may wish us to identify ourselves in the condemnation of cowardice, selfishness, or rashness. The copywriter on a mundane level appeals to us in his hair-tonic anecdote in the same way that the heroic orator does. When presented with characters with our problems—unmanageable hair, inadequacy in social situations—who overcome these difficulties by the simple expedient of a new hair tonic, we feel that what works for those like us will work for us. When the copywriter constantly keeps this emotional appeal in view, the choices of actions to be presented in the anecdote naturally follow from the form.

Winston Churchill, in his wartime speeches, was one of the great masters of the emotional appeal that gives rhetorical structure to persuasive discourse. In his speech to the House of Commons, on June 4, 1940, reporting the "colossal military disaster" at Dunkirk, he managed to turn the place of defeat into a rallying cry that did much to preserve British resistance and helped to build American sentiment for entering the war. After presenting the situation without mitigating qualifications, he concluded with an appeal for "duty" as the only recourse.

> I have, myself, full confidence that if all do their duty, if nothing is neglected, and if the best arrangements are made, as they are being made, we shall prove ourselves once again able to defend our Island home, to ride out the storm of war, and to outlive the menace of tyranny, if necessary for years, if necessary alone.

This picture of an heroic people alone he immediately qualified with the vision of "the British Empire and the French Republic, linked together in their cause and in their need," defending "to the death their native soil, aiding each other like good comrades to the utmost of their strength." This comradeship insured that "even though large tracts of Europe and many old and famous States have fallen or may fall into the grip of the Gestapo and all the odious apparatus of Nazi rule, we shall not flag or fail." He then concluded with a rolling sentence that specified a possible geographical progression that the war might take before eventual victory.

> We shall go on to the end, we shall fight in France, we shall fight on the seas and oceans, we shall fight with growing confidence and growing strength in the air, we shall defend our Island, whatever the cost may be, we shall fight on the beaches, we shall fight on the landing grounds, we shall fight in the fields and in the streets, we shall fight in the hills; we shall never surrender, and even if, which I do not for a moment believe, this

Island or a large part of it were subjugated and starving, then our Empire beyond the seas, armed and guarded by the British Fleet, would carry on the struggle, until, in God's good time, the New World, with all its power and might, steps forth to the rescue and the liberation of the old.

This concluding paragraph presents a paradigm of the entire speech. Churchill begins at a low pitch with the flat statement that the best arrangements "are being made." The pitch increases as he specifies the actual situation of Europe under the "apparatus of Nazi rule," implying by the word "apparatus" that Nazi rule is a mechanical imposition. As he specifies the progression the war might take, his tone heightens as the position of Great Britain worsens. The roll call of natural positions for fighting finally leads to the ultimate intervention of the United States. This will be, the pattern of his final sentence tells his audience, the natural result of the unnatural Nazi activities. The conception that men will meet the necessity of their circumstances through their feelings of duty, and that the natural will finally displace the unnatural, forms the emotional appeal of Churchill's speech.

Rational Structure

Making choices that present materials with which an audience can identify is only half the problem for the writer seeking to persuade. No one likes to be made a fool of, and unless the emotional appeal has a rational basis, the audience will be likely to reject it. To appeal to an audience's reason, a speaker must obviously be logical. In a sense, no one attempting to persuade anyone of anything will be deliberately illogical. It is, however, the case that in certain circumstances, speakers will appeal to a logic above the logic of the schools, as Hitler appealed to the logic of the blood, or back-country politicians in the United States sometimes appeal to what they call the logic of the heart. These appeals to other "logics" are effective for a time to the immediate audience under peculiar circumstances, but viewed dispassionately or in retrospect, they lose their force. Anyone with normal intelligence usually recognizes logical argument when he sees it, and though any of us may be fooled for a time by what logicians call informal fallacies—ambiguities in the language in which arguments are presented, or irrelevances that confuse the argument—we almost always, on second thought, feel that something has been wrong somewhere. The chain of logical proofs that appear in a piece of persuasive writing, then, is only part of what we call its rational structure.

In order to understand the rational form that accounts for the presentation of logical proofs in persuasion, we must imagine what choices the writer made in selecting and rejecting material for his finished product. To do this, it is useful to examine the pattern of topics—arguments from definition, comparison, etc.—actually used in the piece of writing under question. In our examination of these topics earlier in this chapter, we saw that each one of them has implications for a view of the nature of things. These implications, when we discover that certain of them form a pattern, tell us the writer's assumptions about the way things are or ought to be. Choice can only be made within the range of possibilities that our assumptions of the nature of things allows. The rational structure a writer gives to his persuasion is rational to him because it typifies the way he sees the world.

As an example, let us look at Lincoln's "Gettysburg Address."

Fourscore and seven years ago our fathers brought forth on this continent, a new nation, conceived in Liberty, and dedicated to the proposition that all men are created equal.

Now we are engaged in a great civil war, testing whether that nation, or any nation so conceived and so dedicated, can long endure. We are met on a great battlefield of that war. We have come to dedicate a portion of that field, as a final resting place for those who here gave their lives that that nation might live. It is altogether fitting and proper that we should do this.

But, in a larger sense, we can not dedicate—we can not consecrate—we can not hallow—this ground. The brave men living and dead, who struggled here, have consecrated it, far above our poor power to add or detract. The world will little note, nor long remember what we say here, but it can never forget what they did here. It is for us the living, rather, to be dedicated here to the unfinished work which they who fought here have thus far so nobly advanced. It is rather for us to be here dedicated to the great task remaining before us—that from these honored dead we take increased devotion to that cause for which they gave the last full measure of devotion—that we here highly resolve that these dead shall not have died in vain—that this nation, under God, shall have a new birth of freedom—and that government of the people, by the people, for the people, shall not perish from the earth.

Although we may now view the battle of Gettysburg as the turning point of the Civil War, events were not so clearly defined when Lincoln delivered his address at the dedication of the cemetery in November following the battle of early July. The battle of Chickamauga a month before had ended in qualified victory after the Union line had initially cracked and broken. During the following spring, the indecisive battles of The Wilderness, Spotsylvania, and Cold Harbor led up to the long and costly siege of Petersburg. Lincoln could feel that the outcome was sure, but he could not predict when or at what cost. He obviously needed to use the occasion of the dedication of the cemetery at Gettysburg to rally conviction in the justice of the Union cause.

Lincoln might have delivered his address in the "spread-eagle" style popular at the time, with its wide-ranging appeal to the American past and its vision of the glorious American future. He might have stressed the point that Gettysburg was the furthest the Confederate Army had yet penetrated north, and exhorted his audience to see to it that it never happened again. He might have detailed the causes of the war, heaped blame upon Confederate atrocities, or told the story of the battle at Gettysburg. He might have justified the war on Constitutional grounds, or justified his own actions within the Constitution. He might have spent two hours instead of the few minutes that he spoke. That he did none of these things, but chose to define the nature of the war for all time, made his speech an instant success, as is evident from the five times he was interrupted by applause in its delivery and by the "long-continued applause" at its conclusion, which was reported in the first newspaper accounts. Critical acclaim followed quickly with a congratulatory note the next day from Edward Everett, who delivered the major two-hour address at Gettysburg, and with several reprintings.

The "Gettysburg Address" begins with a definition of the nation's origin put in terms of the images of conception, birth, and christening. This definition gives world scope and biblical importance to the birth by specifying time in biblical language and place as "this continent." The rhetorical effectiveness of the first sentence was shown through the applause that interrupted Lincoln's delivery after his statement of the abstract proposition that dedicated the nation.

In the second paragraph, Lincoln begins to give concrete meaning to this abstract proposition. He defines the war as a test of the proposition. Such a test is almost a logical exercise to discover if the proposition conforms to the nature of things. By specifying their meeting place as a part of the battle-field reserved for a cemetery, he itemizes the human cost of this logical exercise. The concluding sentence of the second paragraph asserts the naturalness of the ceremony in which he and his audience are participating.

In the first three sentences of the third paragraph, Lincoln defines the nature of this ceremony. The rhetorical effectiveness of his definition of the ceremony as the battle itself, not the dedication of the cemetery, was shown through the applause that interrupted him after the second and third sentences. The last two sentences contain the exhortation to his audience and the concrete embodiment of the abstract proposition of dedication. Applause after the fourth sentence indicated that the audience had felt both the logical and emotional force of his appeal to its "unfinished work." In his concluding sentence, he makes of death the spur to action that will finally force life into the abstract proposition that dedicated the nation. Applause after the phrase "shall not have died in vain" indicated that the audience accepted the role of greater dedication and increased devotion to the abstract proposition for which the battle was fought. The long, continued applause after the conclusion of the speech indicated the success of Lincoln's restatement of the proposition—"that government of the people, by the people, for the people, shall not perish from the earth." It is the acceptance by his audience of renewed dedication that shall bring forth "a new birth of freedom."

The movement of Lincoln's speech through conception, birth, christening, and death to new birth indicates the argument from the nature of things that stands behind his remarks. The calm tone of heroic vision that he projects shows that he has no doubt that in the nature of things the Union will triumph. It is in the nature of life that new life has to be paid for by death, and this is a price that he wishes his audience to accept, not with resignation, but with devotion. Almost every statement in this short address defines something—the nation, the occasion, the battle, the task of the living, the new meaning of the nation. Lincoln's choice to make this address a series of cumulative definitions is reflected in the form of the speech. In this form there is no clear separation between emotional appeal and rational appeal, between rhetorical structure and rational structure. The abstract proposition that dedicated the nation to be tested by war and to emerge from it with that proposition made concrete is a rational argument that arouses appropriate emotions. It was his clear grasp of this form that allowed Lincoln to reject all the remarks that he might have made on the occasion and to select the few statements that forever defined not only the Civil War, but the purpose of the United States as well.

Throughout our discussion of polemical writing, we have found that considerations of the audience have to be brought in, whether we are discussing questions of purpose (the traditional categories of rhetoric and the ethical appeal of the speaker), materials (the kinds of arguments used, their implication, and their effect on the speaker's language), or form (the way that choices were made in selecting and rejecting material for the finished discourse). This is so because the audience that a speaker assumes he will be addressing determines to a large degree the kind of rhetoric—deliberative, forensic, or epideictic—and the ethical character he presents. The variety of language, the kinds of arguments, and the emotional and rational structure he chooses also depend upon his picture of his audience. Persuasion is not the mere assertion of the speaker's views, but the adaptation of means that will present these views to others in such a way that they will accept them for their own.

In the criticism of polemical writing, we are more concerned with the picture of his audience the writer had when drafting his speech than we are in the actual audience to which he delivered the speech, because it is this picture that led him to construct the speech in the way that he did. We may also touch on the historical response of the audience, as we did in mentioning the applause that interrupted the "Gettysburg Address," in order to show how well the speaker judged his immediate audience. But we should not confuse this kind of historical investigation with rhetorical criticism, which is concerned with the construction of the speech itself. The fact that Lincoln's audience at Gettysburg interrupted his concluding sentence with applause shows that he misjudged that audience slightly when he did not punctuate this sentence to allow for a full stop after the phrase "shall not have died in vain." But when we view the speech from the position of rhetorical criticism, we see that the gathering momentum of that long sentence is necessary for its full meaning. For the audience Lincoln had in mind, and he obviously had in mind an audience that would stretch out in time throughout the history of the republic, the concluding sentence is a unity whose final clause defining the nature of the republic is justified by the four preceding clauses.

QUESTIONS OF EFFECT

In turning to our fourth and last question about polemical writing, the question of effect, we need mainly to amplify what we have already discussed concerning audience, for it is consideration of audience that determines the effect the speaker designs. The audience a speaker pictures indicates his conception of the nature of man. When a speaker tries to persuade his audience to take some action, judge something or someone to be good or bad, or feel that some action or person is worthy of its praise, he is assuming that he addresses people capable of such things. He must present himself as an ethical being and his position in rational and emotional terms so that his audience can sympathize. The way that he chooses his arguments and the language in which he presents them shows the kind of argument and language he feels will be best received. When a speaker presents himself as an outraged moralist, for example, he reveals his belief that men are conscious moral agents. A deliberately rational presentation shows us a man who believes men are capable of reasoning. The speaker who plays exclusively upon his audience's emotions is a man who believes men are creatures of their feelings. Let us look once again at the Declaration of Independence to see how the intended effect upon its audience accounts for its means of persuasion.

By expressing their feeling, in the first sentence of the Declaration, that "a decent respect to the opinions of mankind requires" such a declaration, the members of the Continental Congress state their belief that most men are decent enough to listen to a forensic appeal. Rationality, then, was a human characteristic upon which the Declaration was predicated. In the next three sentences, which define the rights of mankind, the nature of government, and the circumstances under which government ought to be changed, the members of Congress present themselves, in an ethical appeal, as men who have thought about fundamental questions of human nature and government. This presentation is followed by two more sentences qualifying the circumstances necessary for a change of government, and in doing this the "prudence" of Congress is exhibited. The long and somewhat boring list of indictments against George III builds up this picture of the prudence of Congress. The appeal to their "British brethren" reveals their own "magnanimity" as it exhibits the meanness of the people of Great Britain. The qualification to the conclusion denouncing separation from Britain—"and hold them, as we hold the rest of mankind, Enemies in War, in Peace Friends"—reinforces this picture of prudent, magnanimous men acting only under extreme necessity. Even in their formal declaration of independence, which completes the Declaration, Congress continues to stress this picture of itself. By appealing to God to show the rectitude of its intentions, Congress adds piety to its image, and by supporting their declaration with reliance on God and a mutual pledge of their lives, fortunes, and sacred honor, each member stresses his belief in a moral universe controlled by God's will, not by the force of guns.

The audience addressed by the Declaration, then, was a mankind living in a moral order directly controlled by the will of God. God's will in such a universe was knowable through human reason. Congress was taking an awful risk in the Declaration, because if its intentions were not just, events would prove it so. That events did prove the members to be just men acting in moral fashion powerfully impressed their generation of Americans and Europeans, as shown by such events as the French Revolution. The choice they made in presenting their Declaration in syllogistic form shows their belief in human reason. It is their picture of man as a rational, moral creature, governed by a God whose will is analogous to human reason, that accounts for their appeal to their audience through definitions of human rights and government instead of assertions of its own best interests.

The emotions aroused by such an appeal contain feelings that such patient, rational, magnanimous men could not be wrong in their action. This is precisely the effect desired in such a situation. Revolution in the late eighteenth century was, although not unprecedented, thought to be a dangerous action. Government, most men believed, was an institution ordained by God, and to tamper with God's work was impious. By asserting that men had rights from God antecedent to the institution of government, and that their government had interfered with these rights, the Declaration showed that it was their former government, and not themselves, who had acted against God's will. In doing this, the Declaration attempts to change opinion by changing what men thought was the case.

There is a kind of persuasion, associated with demagogy, that attempts merely to direct the feelings an audience already possesses toward the speaker's own selfish ends. Hitler's anti-Semitic tirades, for example, played upon the feeling, latent in Germany between the two world wars, that the Jews had gained an international control over finance and were using it to impoverish the German people. By bringing this feeling into the open, Hitler gained the reputation of a man who knew the reality of the situation, and was thus able to secure a majority in a free election that gave him personal power.

We must admit that Hitler was a powerful rhetorician. But his immoral means of using the opinions his audience already possessed violates the nature of ethical rhetoric. Persuasion, as we have mainly considered it in this chapter, is a device whose use determines its moral worth. If the effect we wish our persuasive discourse to have is just, there is nothing immoral in adapting our means of persuasion to the character of our audience. But when men seek to corrupt the morality of their audiences, their skill in using the means of persuasion compounds the immorality of their speeches.

The model for analysis I suggest, therefore, concerns itself quite as much with ethical potentials as with motives, choices of data, and their arrangement. These four aspects of the concept "why" seem to exhaust the possible categories of questions that may be asked about a document. If so, the model of rhetorical analysis will serve as an adequate tool for the first stage in the historian's job of explaining the development of events. This first stage is the understanding of the unique event frozen in time as represented by a document. Uniqueness cannot be understood in itself. We can only grasp the particular through its relationship to something else. Attempting to understand a particular event through its antecedents and consequents restricts us to temporal aspects alone. By dealing only with the temporal aspects of an event represented by a document, we neglect its materials and form. The connection between antecedents, consequents, materials, and form can be arbitrarily broken for analysis. But for the synthesis that we mean by understanding, the connection must be reestablished.

In the chapters that follow, rhetorical analysis is taken as a hypothetical model. An hypothesis is to be used to understand something whose understanding does not necessarily establish the hypothesis. A model must be used as an aid, never as a dogma to be substantiated. We need a model to understand the particular, but we must remember that it is the particular that we wish to understand. In the studies of documents that follow, I have tried to use rhetorical analysis in this way.

II

Hope and Fear for the Band of Christian Brothers

A MODELL OF
CHRISTIAN CHARITY

Written
On Boarde the Arrabella,
On the Attlantick Ocean.
By the Honorable John Winthrop *Esquire*

In His passage, (with the great Company of Religious people, of which Christian Tribes he was the Brave Leader and famous Governor;) from the Island of Great Brittaine, to New-England in the North America.

ANNO 1630.

CHRISTIAN CHARITIE.

A MODELL HEREOF.

God Almightie in his most holy and wise providence hath soe disposed of the Condicion of mankinde, as in all times some must be rich some poore, some highe and eminent in power and dignitie; others mean and in subieccion.

THE REASON HEREOF.

1. REAS: *First,* to hold conformity with the rest of his workes, being delighted to shewe forthe the glory of his wisdome in the variety and differance of the Creatures and the glory of his power, in ordering all these differences for the preservacion and good of the whole, and the glory of his greatnes that as it is the glory of princes to haue many officers, soe this great King will haue many Stewards counting himselfe more honoured in dispenceing his guifts to man by man, then if hee did it by his owne immediate hand.

2. REAS: *Secondly,* That he might haue the more occasion to manifest the worke of his Spirit: first, vpon the wicked in moderateing and restraineing them: soe that the riche and mighty should not eate vpp the poore, nor the poore, and dispised rise vpp against theire superiours, and shake off theire yoake; 2ly in the regenerate in exerciseing his graces in them, as in the greate ones, theire loue mercy, gentlenes, temperance etc., in the poore and inferiour sorte, theire faithe patience, obedience etc:

3. REAS: *Thirdly,* That every man might haue need of other, and from hence they might be all knitt more nearly together in the Bond of brotherly affeccion: from hence it appeares plainely that noe man is made more honourable then another or more wealthy etc., out of any perticuler and singuler respect to himselfe but for the glory of his Creator and the Common good of the Creature, Man; Therefore God still reserues the propperty of these guifts to himselfe as Ezek: 16. 17. he there calls wealthe his gold and his silver etc. Prov: 3. 9. he claimes theire seruice as his due honour the Lord with thy riches etc. All men being thus (by divine providence) ranked

into two sortes, riche and poore; vnder the first, are compre-
hended all such as are able to liue comfortably by theire owne
meanes duely improued; and all others are poore according to
the former distribution. There are two rules whereby wee are
to walke one towards another: JUSTICE and MERCY. These are
allwayes distinguished in theire Act and in theire obiect, yet
may they both concurre in the same Subiect in eache respect; as
sometimes there may be an occasion of shewing mercy to a
rich man, in some sudden danger of distresse, and allsoe doe-
ing of meere Justice to a poore man in regard of some perticuler contract etc. There is likewise a double Lawe by which wee
are regulated in our conversacion one towardes another: in
both the former respects, the lawe of nature and the lawe of
grace, or the morrall lawe or the lawe of the gospell, to omitt
the rule of Justice as not propperly belonging to this purpose
otherwise then it may fall into consideracion in some perticuler Cases: By the first of these lawes man as he was enabled
soe withall [is] commaunded to loue his neighbour as himselfe
vpon this ground stands all the precepts of the morrall lawe,
which concernes our dealings with men. To apply this to the
works of mercy this lawe requires two things first that every
man afford his help to another in every want or distresse Sec-
condly, That hee performe this out of the same affeccion,
which makes him carefull of his owne good according to that
of our Saviour Math: [7.12] Whatsoever ye would that men
should doe to you. This was practised by Abraham and Lott
in entertaineing the Angells and the old man of Gibea.[1]

The Lawe of Grace or the Gospell hath some differance
from the former as in these respectes first the lawe of nature
was giuen to man in the estate of innocency; this of the gospell
in the estate of regeneracy: 2ly, the former propounds one man
to another, as the same fleshe and Image of god, this as a

brother in Christ allsoe, and in the Communion of the same
spirit and soe teacheth vs to put a difference betweene Christians and others. Doe good to all especially to the household
of faith;[2] vpon this ground the Israelites were to putt a difference betweene the brethren of such as were strangers though
not of the Canaanites. 3ly. The Lawe of nature could giue noe
rules for dealeing with enemies for all are to be considered as
freinds in the state of innocency, but the Gospell commaunds
loue to an enemy. proofe. If thine Enemie hunger feede him;
Loue your Enemies doe good to them that hate you Math:
5. 44.

This Lawe of the Gospell propoundes likewise a difference
of seasons and occasions there is a time when a christian must
sell all and giue to the poore as they did in the Apostles times.
There is a tyme allsoe when a christian (though they giue not
all yet) must giue beyond theire abillity, as they of Macedonia.
Cor: 2. 6. likewise community of perills calls for extraordinary
liberallity and soe doth Community in some speciall seruice
for the Churche. Lastly, when there is noe other meanes
whereby our Christian brother may be releiued in this distresse, wee must help him beyond our ability, rather then
tempt God, in putting him vpon help by miraculous or extraordinary meanes.

This duty of mercy is exercised in the kindes, Giueing,
lending, and forgiueing.

QUEST. What rule shall a man observe in giueing in respect
of the measure?

ANS. If the time and occasion be ordinary he is to giue out
of his aboundance—let him lay aside, as god hath blessed him.
If the time and occasion be extraordinary he must be ruled
by them; takeing this withall, that then a man cannot likely
doe too much especially, if he may leaue himselfe and his
family vnder probable meanes of comfortable subsistance.

OBIECTION. A man must lay vpp for posterity, the fathers lay vpp for posterity and children and he is worse then an Infidell that prouideth not for his owne.[3]

ANS: For the first, it is plaine, that it being spoken by way of Comparison it must be meant of the ordinary and vsuall course of fathers and cannot extend to times and occasions extraordinary; for the other place the Apostle speakes against such as walked inordinately, and it is without question, that he is worse then an Infidell whoe throughe his owne Sloathe and voluptuousnes shall neglect to prouide for his family.

OBIECTION. The wise mans Eies are in his head (saith Salomon)[4] and foreseeth the plague, therefore wee must forecast and lay vpp against euill times when hee or his may stand in need of all he can gather.

ANS: This very Argument Salomon vseth to perswade to liberallity. Eccle: [11.1.] cast thy bread vpon the waters etc.: for thou knowest not what euill may come vpon the land Luke 16. make you freinds of the riches of Iniquity; you will aske how this shall be? very well. for first he that giues to the poore lends to the lord, and he will repay him euen in this life an hundred fold to him or his. The righteous is ever mercifull and lendeth and his seed enioyeth the blessing; and besides wee know what advantage it will be to vs in the day of account, when many such Witnesses shall stand forthe for vs to witnesse the improuement of our Tallent. And I would knowe of those whoe pleade soe much for layeing vp for time to come, whether they hold that to be Gospell Math: 16. 19. Lay not vpp for yourselues Treasures vpon Earth etc. if they acknowledge it what extent will they allowe it; if onely to those primitiue times lett them consider the reason wherevpon our Saviour groundes it, the first is that they are subiect to the moathe, the rust the Theife. Secondly, They will steale away the hearte, where the treasure is there will the heart be allsoe.

The reasons are of like force at all times therefore the exhortacion must be generall and perpetuall which [applies] allwayes in respect of the loue and affeccion to riches and in regard of the things themselues when any speciall seruice for the churche or perticuler distresse of our brother doe call for the vse of them; otherwise it is not onely lawfull but necessary to lay vpp as Joseph did to haue ready vppon such occasions, as the Lord (whose stewards wee are of them) shall call for them from vs: Christ giues vs an Instance of the first, when hee sent his disciples for the Asse, and bidds them answer the owner thus, the Lord hath need of him;[5] soe when the Tabernacle was to be builte his [servant] [6] sends to his people to call for their silver and gold etc.; and yeildes them noe other reason but that it was for his worke, when Elisha comes to the widowe of Sareptah[7] and findes her prepareing to make ready her pittance for herselfe and family, he bids her first provide for him, he challengeth first gods parte which shee must first giue before shee must serue her owne family, all these teache vs that the lord lookes that when hee is pleased to call for his right in any thing wee haue, our owne Interest wee haue must stand aside, till his turne be serued, for the other wee need looke noe further then to that of John 1. he whoe hath this worlds goodes and seeth his brother to neede, and shutts vpp his Compassion from him, how dwelleth the loue of god in him, which comes punctually to this Conclusion: if thy brother be in want and thou canst help him, thou needst not make doubt, what thou shouldst doe, if thou louest god thou must help him.

QUEST: What rule must wee obserue in lending?

ANS: Thou must obserue whether thy brother hath present or probable, or possible meanes of repayeing thee, if ther be none of these, thou must giue him according to his necessity, rather then lend him as hee requires; if he hath present meanes of repayeing thee, thou art to looke at him, not as an Act of mercy, but by way of Commerce, wherein thou arte to walke by the rule of Justice, but, if his meanes of repayeing thee be onely probable or possible then is hee an obiect of thy mercy thou must lend him, though there be danger of looseing it Deut: 15. 7. If any of thy brethren be poore etc. thou shalt lend him sufficient that men might not shift off this duty by the apparant hazzard, he tells them that though the Yeare of Jubile were at hand (when he must remitt it, if hee were not able to repay it before) yet he must lend him and that chearefully:[8] it may not greiue thee to giue him (saith hee) and because some might obiect, why soe I should soone impoverishe my selfe and my family, he adds with all thy Worke etc. for our Saviour Math: 5. 42. From him that would borrow of thee turne not away.

QUEST: What rule must wee obserue in forgiueing?

ANS: Whether thou didst lend by way of Commerce or in mercy, if he haue noething to pay thee [thou] must forgiue him (except in cause where thou hast a surety or a lawfull pleadge) Deut. 15. 2. Every seaventh yeare the Creditor was to quitt that which hee lent to his brother if hee were poore as appeares ver: 8 [4]: saue when there shall be noe poore with thee. In all these and like Cases Christ was a generall rule Math: 7. 22. Whatsoever ye would that men should doe to you doe yee the same to them allsoe.

QUEST: What rule must wee obserue and walke by in cause of Community of perill?

ANS: The same as before, but with more enlargement towardes others and lesse respect towards our selues, and our owne right hence it was that in the primitiue Churche they sold all had all things in Common, neither did any man say that that which he possessed was his owne[9] likewise in theire re-

turne out of the Captiuity, because the worke was greate for
the restoreing of the church and the danger of enemies was
Common to all Nehemiah exhortes the Jewes to liberallity and
readines in remitting theire debtes to theire brethren, and
disposeth liberally of his owne to such as wanted and stands
not vpon his owne due, which hee might haue demaunded of
them,[10] thus did some of our forefathers in times of persecu-
cion here in England, and soe did many of the faithfull in
other Churches whereof wee keepe an honourable remem-
brance of them, and it is to be obserued that both in Scrip-
tures and latter stories of the Churches that such as haue
beene most bountifull to the poore Saintes especially in these
extraordinary times and occasions god hath left them highly
Commended to posterity, as Zacheus, Cornelius, Dorcas,[11]
Bishop Hooper, the Cuttler of Brussells and divers others obserue againe that the scripture giues noe causion to restraine
any from being over liberall this way; but all men to the liberall and cherefull practise hereof by the sweetest promises as
to instance one for many, Isaiah 58. 6: Is not this the fast that
I haue chosen to loose the bonds of wickednes, to take off the
heavy burdens to lett the oppressed goe free and to breake
every Yoake, to deale thy bread to the hungry and to bring
the poore that wander into thy house, when thou seest the
naked to cover them etc. then shall thy light breake forthe as
the morneing, and thy healthe shall growe speedily, thy right-
eousnes shall goe before thee, and the glory of the lord shall
embrace thee, then thou shalt call and the lord shall Answer
thee etc. 2. 10: If thou power out thy soule to the hungry, then
shall thy light spring out in darknes, and the lord shall guide
thee continually, and satisfie thy Soule in draught, and make
fatt thy bones, thou shalt be like a watered Garden, and they
shall be of thee that shall build the old wast places etc. on the

contrary most heavy cursses are layd vpon such as are straight-
ened towards the Lord and his people Judg: 5. [23] Cursse ye
Meroshe because the[y] came not to help the Lord etc. Pro:
[21. 13] Hee whoe shutteth his eares from hearing the cry of the
poore, he shall cry and shall not be heard: Math: 25. [41] Goe
ye curssed into everlasting fire etc. [42.] I was hungry and ye
fedd me not. Cor: 2. 9. 16. [6.] He that soweth spareingly shall
reape spareingly.

Haueing allready sett forth the practise of mercy according
to the rule of gods lawe, it will be vsefull to lay open the
groundes of it allsoe being the other parte of the Commaunde-
ment and that is the affeccion from which this exercise of
mercy must arise, the Apostle tells vs that this loue is the full-
filling of the lawe,[12] not that it is enough to loue our brother
and soe noe further but in regard of the excellency of his
partes giueing any motion to the other as the Soule to the body
and the power it hath to sett all the faculties on worke in the
outward exercise of this duty as when wee bid one make the
clocke strike he doth not lay hand on the hammer which is the
immediate instrument of the sound but setts on worke the first
mouer or maine wheele, knoweing that will certainely produce
the sound which hee intends; soe the way to drawe men to the
workes of mercy is not by force of Argument from the goodnes
or necessity of the worke, for though this course may enforce
a rationall minde to some present Act of mercy as is frequent
in experience, yet it cannot worke such a habit in a Soule as
shall make it prompt vpon all occasions to produce the same
effect but by frameing these affeccions of loue in the hearte
which will as natiuely bring forthe the other, as any cause doth
produce the effect.

The diffinition which the Scripture giues vs of loue is this
Loue is the bond of perfection.[13] First, it is a bond, or liga-

ment. 2ly, it makes the worke perfect. There is noe body but consistes of partes and that which knitts these partes together giues the body its perfeccion, because it makes eache parte soe contiguous to other as thereby they doe mutually participate with eache other, both in strengthe and infirmity in pleasure and paine, to instance in the most perfect of all bodies, Christ and his church make one body: the severall partes of this body considered aparte before they were vnited were as disproportionate and as much disordering as soe many contrary quallities or elements but when christ comes and by his spirit and loue knitts all these partes to himselfe and each to other, it is become the most perfect and best proportioned body in the world Eph: 4. 16. "Christ by whome all the body being knitt together by every ioynt for the furniture thereof according to the effectuall power which is in the measure of every perfeccion of partes a glorious body without spott or wrinckle the ligaments hereof being Christ or his loue for Christ is loue 1 John: 4. 8. Soe this definition is right Loue is the bond of perfeccion.

From hence wee may frame these Conclusions.

1 first all true Christians are of one body in Christ 1. Cor. 12. 12. 13. 17. [27.] Ye are the body of Christ and members of [your?] parte.

2ly. The ligamentes of this body which knitt together are loue.

3ly. Noe body can be perfect which wants its propper ligamentes.

4ly. All the partes of this body being thus vnited are made soe contiguous in a speciall relacion as they must needes partake of each others strength and infirmity, ioy, and sorrowe, weale and woe. 1 Cor: 12. 26. If one member suffers all suffer with it, if one be in honour, all reioyce with it.

5ly. This sensiblenes and Sympathy of each others Condicions will necessarily infuse into each parte a natiue desire and endeavour, to strengthen defend preserue and comfort the other.

To insist a little on this Conclusion being the product of all the former the truthe hereof will appeare both by precept and patterne i. John. 3. 10. yee ought to lay downe your liues for the brethren Gal: 6. 2. beare ye one anothers burthens and soe fulfill the lawe of Christ.

For patterns wee haue that first of our Saviour whoe out of his good will in obedience to his father, becomeing a parte of this body, and being knitt with it in the bond of loue, found such a natiue sensiblenes of our infirmities and sorrowes as hee willingly yeilded himselfe to deathe to ease the infirmities of the rest of his body and soe heale theire sorrowes: from the like Sympathy of partes did the Apostles and many thousands of the Saintes lay downe theire liues for Christ againe, the like wee may see in the members of this body among themselues. 1. Rom. 9. Paule could haue beene contented to haue beene separated from Christ that the Jewes might not be cutt off from the body: It is very obseruable which hee professeth of his affectionate part[ak]eing with every member: whoe is weake (saith hee) and I am not weake? whoe is offended and I burne not; and againe. 2 Cor: 7. 13. therefore wee are comforted because yee were comforted. of Epaphroditus he speaketh Phil: 2. 30. that he regarded not his owne life to [do] him seruice soe Phebe. and others are called the seruantes of the Churche[14] now it is apparant that they serued not for wages or by Constrainte but out of loue, the like wee shall finde in the histories of the churche in all ages the sweete Sympathie of affeccions which was in the members of this body one towardes another, theire chearfullnes in serueing and suffering together how liberall they were without repineing harbourers without grudgeing and helpfull without reproacheing and all from hence they had feruent loue amongst them which onely make[s] the practise of mercy constant and easie.

The next consideracion is how this loue comes to be wrought; Adam in his first estate was a perfect modell of man-kinde in all theire generacions, and in him this loue was per-fected in regard of the habit, but Adam Rent in himselfe from his Creator, rent all his posterity allsoe one from another, whence it comes that every man is borne with this principle in him, to loue and seeke himselfe onely and thus a man con-tinueth till Christ comes and takes possession of the soule, and infuseth another principle loue to God and our brother. And this latter haueing continuall supply from Christ, as the head and roote by which hee is vnited get the predominency in the soule, soe by little and little expells the former 1 John 4. 7. loue cometh of god and every one that loueth is borne of god, soe that this loue is the fruite of the new birthe, and none can haue it but the new Creature, now when this quallity is thus formed in the soules of men it workes like the Spirit vpon the drie bones Ezek. 37. [7] bone came to bone, it gathers to-gether the scattered bones or perfect old man Adam and knitts them into one body againe in Christ whereby a man is become againe a liueing soule.

The third Consideracion is concerning the exercise of this loue, which is twofold, inward or outward, the outward hath beene handled in the former preface of this discourse, for vn-folding the other wee must take in our way that maxime of philosophy, Simile simili gaudet or like will to like; for as it is things which are carued with disafeccion to eache other, the ground of it is from a dissimilitude or [*blank*] ariseing from the contrary or different nature of things themselues, soe the

ground of loue is an apprehension of some resemblance in the
things loued to that which affectes it, this is the cause why
the Lord loues the Creature, soe farre as it hath any of his
Image in it, he loues his elect because they are like himselfe,
he beholds them in his beloued sonne: soe a mother loues her
childe, because shee throughly conceiues a resemblance of
herselfe in it. Thus it is betweene the members of Christ, each
discernes by the worke of the spirit his owne Image and resemblance in another, and therefore cannot but loue him as
he loues himselfe: Now when the soule which is of a sociable
nature findes any thing like to it selfe, it is like Adam when
Eue was brought to him, shee must haue it one with herselfe
this is fleshe of my fleshe (saith shee) and bone of my bone
shee conceiues a greate delighte in it, therefore shee desires
nearenes and familiarity with it: shee hath a greate propensity
to doe it good and receiues such content in it, as feareing the
miscarriage of her beloued shee bestowes it in the inmost closett
of her heart, shee will not endure that it shall want any good
which shee can giue it, if by occasion shee be withdrawne
from the Company of it, shee is still lookeing towardes the
place where shee left her beloued, if shee heare it groane
shee is with it presently, if shee finde it sadd and disconsolate
shee sighes and mournes with it, shee hath noe such ioy, as to
see her beloued merry and thriueing, if shee see it wronged,
shee cannot beare it without passion, shee setts noe boundes of
her affeccions, nor hath any thought of reward, shee findes
recompence enoughe in the exercise of her loue towardes it,
wee may see this Acted to life in Jonathan and David. Jonathan a valiant man endued with the spirit of Christ, soe
soone as hee Discovers the same spirit in David had presently
his hearte knitt to him by this linement of loue, soe that it is
said he loued him as his owne soule, he takes soe great pleas-

ure in him that hee stripps himselfe to adorne his beloued,
his fathers kingdome was not soe precious to him as his beloued David, Dauid shall haue it with all his hearte, himselfe
desires noe more but that hee may be neare to him to reioyce
in his good hee chooseth to converse with him in the wilder-
nesse even to the hazzard of his owne life, rather then with
the greate Courtiers in his fathers Pallace; when hee sees
danger towards him, hee spares neither care paines, nor perill
to divert it, when Iniury was offered his beloued David, hee
could not beare it, though from his owne father, and when
they must parte for a Season onely, they thought theire heartes
would haue broake for sorrowe, had not theire affeccions
found vent by aboundance of Teares: other instances might
be brought to shewe the nature of this affeccion as of Ruthe
and Naomi and many others, but this truthe is cleared enough.
If any shall obiect that it is not possible that loue should be
bred or vpheld without hope of requitall, it is graunted but
that is not our cause, for this loue is allwayes vnder reward it
never giues, but it allwayes receiues with advantage: first, in
regard that among the members of the same body, loue and
affection are reciprocall in a most equall and sweete kinde of
Commence. 2ly [3ly], in regard of the pleasure and content
that the exercise of loue carries with it as wee may see in the
naturall body the mouth it at all the paines to receiue, and
mince the foode which serues for the nourishment of all the
other partes of the body, yet it hath noe cause to complaine;
for first, the other partes send backe by secret passages a due
proporcion of the same nourishment in a better forme for the
strengthening and comforteing the mouthe. 2ly the labour of
the mouthe is accompanied with such pleasure and content as
farre exceedes the paines it takes: soe is it in all the labour of
loue, among christians, the partie loueing, reapes loue againe

as was shewed before, which the soule covetts more then all the wealthe in the world. 2ly [4ly]. noething yeildes more pleasure and content to the soule then when it findes that which it may loue fervently, for to loue and liue beloued is the soules paradice, both heare and in heaven: In the State of Wedlock there be many comfortes to beare out the troubles of that Condicion; but let such as haue tryed the most, say if there be any sweetnes in that Condicion comparable to the exercise of mutuall loue.

From the former Consideracions ariseth these Conclusions.

1 First, This loue among Christians is a reall thing not Imaginarie.

2ly. This loue is as absolutely necessary to the being of the body of Christ, as the sinewes and other ligaments of a naturall body are to the being of that body.

3ly. This loue is a divine spirituall nature free, actiue strong Couragious permanent vnder valueing all things beneathe its propper obiect, and of all the graces this makes vs nearer to resemble the virtues of our heavenly father.

4ly, It restes in the loue and wellfare of its beloued, for the full and certaine knowledge of these truthes concerning the nature vse, [and] excellency of this grace, that which the holy ghost hath left recorded 1. Cor. 13. may giue full satisfaccion which is needfull for every true member of this louely body of the Lord Jesus, to worke vpon theire heartes, by prayer meditacion continuall exercise at least of the speciall [power] of this grace till Christ be formed in them and they in him all in eache other knitt together by this bond of loue.

It rests now to make some applicacion of this discourse by the present designe which gaue the occasion of writeing of it. Herein are 4 things to be propounded: first the **persons**, 2ly, the worke, 3ly, the end, 4ly the meanes.

1. For the persons, wee are a Company professing our selues
fellow members of Christ, In which respect onely though wee
were absent from eache other many miles, and had our im-
ploymentes as farre distant, yet wee ought to account our
selues knitt together by this bond of loue, and liue in the
exercise of it, if wee would haue comforte of our being in
Christ, this was notorious in the practise of the Christians in
former times, as is testified of the Waldenses from the mouth
of one of the adversaries Aeneas Syluius, mutuo [solent amare]
penè antequam norint, they vse to loue any of theire owne
religion even before they were acquainted with them.

2ly. for the worke wee haue in hand, it is by a mutuall
consent through a speciall overruleing providence, and a more
then an ordinary approbation of the Churches of Christ to
seeke out a place of Cohabitation and Consorteshipp vnder
a due forme of Goverment both ciuill and ecclesiasticall. In
such cases as this the care of the publique must oversway all
private respects, by which not onely conscience, but meare
Ciuill pollicy doth binde vs; for it is a true rule that perticuler
estates cannott subsist in the ruine of the publique.

3ly. The end is to improue our liues to doe more seruice to
the Lord the comforte and encrease of the body of christe
whereof wee are members that our selues and posterity may
be the better preserued from the Common corrupcions of this
euill world to serue the Lord and worke out our Salvacion
vnder the power and purity of his holy Ordinances.

4ly for the meanes whereby this must bee effected, they are
2fold, a Conformity with the worke and end wee aime at,
these wee see are extraordinary, therefore wee must not content our selues with vsuall ordinary meanes whatsoever wee
did or ought to haue done when wee liued in England, the
same must wee doe and more allsoe where wee goe: That
which the most in their Churches maineteine as a truthe in

profession onely, wee must bring into familiar and constant
practise, as in this duty of loue wee must loue brotherly without dissimulation,[15] wee must loue one another with a pure
hearte feruently[16] wee must beare one anothers burthens,[17]
wee must not looke onely on our owne things, but allsoe on
the things of our brethren, neither must wee think that the
lord will beare with such faileings at our hands as hee dothe
from those among whome wee haue liued, and that for 3
Reasons.

1. In regard of the more neare bond of mariage, betweene
him and vs, wherein he hath taken vs to be his after a most
strickt and peculiar manner which will make him the more
Jealous of our loue and obedience soe he tells the people of
Israell, you onely haue I knowne of all the families of the
Earthe therefore will I punishe you for your Transgressions.[18]

2ly, because the lord will be sanctified in them that come
neare him. Wee know that there were many that corrupted
the seruice of the Lord some setting vpp Alters before his
owne, others offering both strange fire and strange Sacrifices
allsoe; yet there came noe fire from heaven, or other sudden
Judgement vpon them as did vpon Nadab and Abihu[19] whoe
yet wee may thinke did not sinne presumptuously.

3ly When God giues a speciall Commission he lookes to
haue it strictly obserued in every Article, when hee gaue
Saule a Commission to destroy Amaleck hee indented with
him vpon certaine Articles and because hee failed in one of
the least, and that vpon a faire pretence, it lost him the kingdome, which should haue beene his reward, if hee had obserued his Commission:[20] Thus stands the cause betweene God
and vs, wee are entered into Covenant with him for this
worke, wee haue taken out a Commission, the Lord hath
giuen vs leaue to drawe our owne Articles wee haue professed
to enterprise these Accions vpon these and these ends, wee

haue herevpon besought him of favour and blessing: Now if the Lord shall please to heare vs, and bring vs in peace to the place wee desire, then hath hee ratified this Covenant and sealed our Commission, [and] will expect a strickt performance of the Articles contained in it, but if wee shall neglect the observacion of these Articles which are the ends wee haue propounded, and dissembling with our God, shall fall to embrace this present world and prosecute our carnall intencions, seekeing greate things for our selues and our posterity, the Lord will surely breake out in wrathe against vs be revenged of such a periured people and make vs knowe the price of the breache of such a Covenant.

Now the onely way to avoyde this shipwracke and to provide for our posterity is to followe the Counsell of Micah, to doe Justly, to loue mercy, to walke humbly with our God,[21] for this end, wee must be knitt together in this worke as one man, wee must entertaine each other in brotherly Affeccion, wee must be willing to abridge our selues of our superfluities, for the supply of others necessities, wee must vphold a familiar Commerce together in all meekenes, gentlenes, patience and liberallity, wee must delight in eache other, make others Condicions our owne reioyce together, mourne together, labour, and suffer together, allwayes haueing before our eyes our Commission and Community in the worke, our Community as members of the same body, soe shall wee keepe the vnitie of the spirit in the bond of peace,[22] the Lord will be our God and delight to dwell among vs, as his owne people and will commaund a blessing vpon vs in all our wayes, soe that wee shall see much more of his wisdome power goodnes and truthe then formerly wee haue beene acquainted with, wee shall finde that the God of Israell is among vs, when tenn of vs shall be able to resist a thousand of our enemies, when hee

shall make vs a prayse and glory, that men shall say of succeeding plantacions: the lord make it like that of New England: for wee must Consider that wee shall be as a Citty vpon
a Hill,[23] the eies of all people are vppon vs; soe that if wee
shall deale falsely with our god in this worke wee haue vndertaken and soe cause him to withdrawe his present help from
vs, wee shall be made a story and a by-word through the world,
wee shall open the mouthes of enemies to speake euill of the
wayes of god and all professours for Gods sake; wee shall
shame the faces of many of gods worthy seruants, and cause
theire prayers to be turned into Cursses vpon vs till wee be
consumed out of the good land whether wee are goeing: And
to shutt vpp this discourse with that exhortacion of Moses
that faithfull seruant of the Lord in his last farewell to Israell
Deut. 30. Beloued there is now sett before vs life, and good,
deathe and euill in that wee are Commaunded this day to loue
the Lord our God, and to loue one another to walke in his
wayes and to keepe his Commaundements and his Ordinance,
and his lawes, and the Articles of our Covenant with him
that wee may liue and be multiplyed, and that the Lord our
God may blesse vs in the land whether wee goe to possesse it:
But if our heartes shall turne away soe that wee will not obey,
but shall be seduced and worshipp [serue *cancelled*] other
Gods our pleasures, and proffitts, and serue them; it is propounded vnto vs this day, wee shall surely perishe out of the
good Land whether wee passe over this vast Sea to possesse it;

> Therefore lett vs choose life,
> that wee, and our Seede,
> may liue; by obeyeing his
> voyce, and cleaueing to him,
> for hee is our life, and
> our prosperity.

NOTES

[1] Genesis, xviii–xix.
[2] Galatians, vi. 10.
[3] I Timothy, v. 8.
[4] Ecclesiastes, ii. 14.
[5] Matthew, xxi. 2–3.
[6] Zerubbabel, Ezra, iii; Haggai, ii.
[7] I Kings, xvii. 8–24; Luke, v. 26.
[8] Deuteronomy, xv. 7–11; Leviticus, xxv. 35–42.
[9] Acts, ii. 44–45; iv. 32–35.
[10] Nehemiah, v.
[11] Luke, xix. 8–10; Acts, ix. 36–42 and x.
[12] Romans, xiii. 10.
[13] Colossians, iii. 14.
[14] Romans, xvi. 1.
[15] Romans, xii. 9–10.
[16] I Peter, i. 22.
[17] Galatians, vi. 2.
[18] Amos, iii. 2.
[19] Leviticus, x. 1–2.
[20] I Samuel, xv; xxviii. 16–18.
[21] Micah, vi. 8.
[22] Ephesians, iv. 3.
[23] Matthew, v. 14.

Hope and Fear for the
Band of Christian Brothers

COMMENTARY

We are often trapped by our categories into thinking that, because we have a name for something, it must exist. The study of national expression often seems such a trap. How can American literature—narrowly defined as belles lettres, or broadly conceived as everything written in a form with permanent value—be distinguished from everything else written in English? Certainly the job would be pretty hopeless for the seventeenth century; and for the twentieth, it is hard to tell whether certain major writers, T. S. Eliot or W. H. Auden, for example, are English or American. Perhaps the whole distinction makes no logical sense except as a matter of personal convenience.

In choosing John Winthrop's lay sermon, "A Modell of

Christian Charity," as the first example of American political rhetoric, I have picked something written before its author ever laid eyes on any piece of land that could be called America. This sermon was delivered somewhere in the middle of the Atlantic in the spring of 1630 to the future settlers of Massachusetts Bay. The form and language were standard for the time, but the warning Winthrop gave became one of the tests used throughout American history in attempts to distinguish the peculiarities of the American experience: "We shall be as a city on a hill, the eyes of all people are upon us; so that if we shall deal falsely with our God in this work we have undertaken and so cause him to withdraw his present help from us, we shall be made a story and a by-word through the world. . . ."

Such a dramatic pronouncement can be put to many uses. You may recall that John Kennedy used it in an address to the Massachusetts legislature shortly after he became President. To discover what Winthrop meant by it, I will make a rhetorical analysis of the sermon. This does not mean that I will attempt to discover the kind of rhetoric Winthrop thought he was using (Perry Miller has done that adequately in his various discussions of the logic and rhetoric of Peter Ramus); rather, I will run the sermon through a machine for rhetorical analysis in an attempt to reveal the presuppositions that determined what Winthrop said.

Winthrop developed the sermon in the standard Puritan way from doctrine through reasons to application. In its straightforward numbering of distinctions and inferences, it conforms to George Orwell's rules for writing in his essay "Politics and the English Language," which gives us a good illustration of what is meant when historians of the development of prose style stress the Puritan influence. Nothing diverts the reader's attention from the points being made. No striking phrase or metaphor prevents us from being carried from point to point. Everything is included for the end, nothing is there for itself.

To a philosopher, Winthrop's points may be questionable in themselves. The rhetorician, on the other hand, is interested not only in the sense the points make in themselves, but in the sense of Winthrop and his audience that can be inferred from the way in which he makes his points. The rhetorician examines not only the meaning of statements (such as, "wee are entered into Covenant with him"), but also the meaning given statements by the context of the sermon.

The machine for rhetorical analysis has four main components: questions of purpose, materials, form, and effect. Questions of purpose deal with the issues of aim, occasion, and ethical appeal of the speaker's character. Materials involve the kinds of arguments used, their implications for the speaker's view of the nature of things, and the effect of this view on his use of language. The form a speech takes depends upon the speaker's choice of an emotional and a logical appeal. The picture a speaker has of his audience determines the emotions he attempts to arouse in order to affect their opinions. These four components must obviously work together in any successful piece of rhetoric.

To begin, then, how did Winthrop use the occasion of his lay sermon to achieve his purpose in speaking? Nothing is known of the immediate circumstances in which the sermon was delivered. The partly corrupt scribe's copy used as the text for the *Winthrop Papers* was probably one of those used to "publish" the sermon in manuscript, as was common at the time. However, from general knowledge of the Massachusetts Bay Company's aims and situation and from Winthrop's remarks, we can make some inferences.

The men who formed the Massachusetts Bay Company felt

that they were living in evil times. Although God would save the souls of individuals living according to Christian principles, when the time came to punish communities in this world, his wrath would fall on the just and on the unjust alike. After a moderate adherence to Calvinist theology during the reign of Elizabeth—a theology Puritans interpreted as consistent with their own—the Anglican Church had been given over to Arminians by James I and Charles I. The Arminian belief that men could gain faith and win salvation through their own power was heresy to the Puritans, who saw that the grace of God was necessary for men to believe what appeared as absurdity to natural reason. Arminians appeared to the Puritans to be absorbed in the pleasures of the moment, whether the pleasures of good living or the pleasures of the church service, rather than keeping constantly attentive to salvation, which the Puritans considered to be life's end. The trend toward Arminianism seemed to be accelerating, and when Charles dissolved Parliament on March 10, 1629, many Puritans felt that God would soon strike England.

This fear led to the conviction that, as Edmund Morgan put it in his biography of Winthrop, "the only hope was to cross the water and establish a government of Christ in exile." The Puritans who formed the Massachusetts Bay Company reached this decision even though their social views condemned separation from a bad situation and enjoined men to live in their world and work for its improvement. The charge that they were running out on their friends and countrymen bothered them, and Morgan sees their many protestations that they were not separatists as evidence of "a half-recognized sense of guilt."

Given the fact that the Puritans aboard the "Arrabella" had reason to feel guilty about escaping from a bad situation,

Winthrop might have used his sermon to justify their actions, with either the forensic or the epideictic appeal of traditional rhetoric. Using a forensic appeal, he might have attacked the Arminians and defended the Puritans by reciting the history of the conflict, ending with the justice of the emigration. With an epideictic purpose, he could have praised his ship-mates for their courage in carrying out the word of God and concluded by asserting the honorable nature of their actions. Instead of either of these approaches, he restricts himself to a deliberative discourse on the bases of social organizations, especially Christian societies.

Winthrop's reasons for doing this may seem a bit clearer if we remember what it was that Marlow learned to fear in Conrad's *Heart of Darkness*. His experience in the Congo showed him that social behavior was a thin veneer over an essentially bestial human nature. When men left their inherited restrictions, the savagery within broke free. Winthrop's belief, that since the fall of Adam only strict government prevented natural selfishness from destroying the state, would have led him to experience fears analogous to Marlow's. Although most of those traveling to New England were visible saints, there were strangers among them who had been enrolled for special services and to fill out the passenger lists. Even among the saints, one could never be sure of an individual's salvation. Freed from the many social, economic, and political restrictions of old England, the hypocrites might throw off their masks. Thus Winthrop carefully explicated the economic and social bases of a Christian society and stressed the special responsibility that was involved in a self-conscious attempt to build a model for all Christian society.

In his position as governor of the Company, Winthrop appeared as the guardian of all. This position constituted an ethical appeal to his audience or, in more contemporary terms, it gave him a certain "image." Although he expressed knowledge of private interest in questions concerning giving, lending, and forgiving, he was concerned in each question to show the priority of community interest. Constant reiteration of this heightened his ethical appeal as the Christian governor. Clergy aboard ship would quite properly have given sermons on grace, regeneration, and salvation, while Winthrop's position limited his purpose in speaking to the salvation of the community.

What materials did Winthrop use to construct his sermon on conditions for success in this experiment of founding a Christian society? The sermon is developed by drawing inferences from definitions. Each inference in turn becomes a new definition for renewal of the process. In his "doctrine" and first two "reasons," he defines the nature of God's dealings with man. God is an all-powerful being who orders human relationships for his own glory. The ordering then becomes the basis for man's well-being, and from it Winthrop derives the rules of Justice and Mercy. Justice does not concern him here, so he goes on to show that Mercy implies both the natural law and the law of grace. The law of grace, embodied in the Gospel, implies obligations further than the natural obligation to do as much good for others as one does for oneself. The Christian must be willing to undertake total sacrifice. This obligation implies economic rules, which Winthrop develops in the four questions and answers. In answering objections to the economic inferences he draws, he refutes fundamentalist readings of the Bible with readings drawn from the context of the verse. Precedents for Christian action and Biblical citations are used to support his developing definitions. To show the grounds for these economic considerations, Winthrop draws an analogy between the ligaments as bonds of a body and the love that binds Christians together. He defines Christian love through the use of precedents that show the Christian virtues of sympathy, cheerfulness, liberality, love, and mercy. His definition of original sin as selfishness and grace as the force leading men to selflessness is completed by a definition of the exercise of Christian love through analogy and more precedents. From this series of definitions, he infers the proper course for present action according to a principle of necessity. Winthrop's most common kinds of arguments, then, are developed from definition and testimony, with analogy used to a lesser degree. The predominant argument, however, revolves around definition.

As we saw in Chapter I, the habitual use of particular arguments implies a certain view of the world. From Winthrop's preference for definition we can infer that he viewed the world as an eternal unity controlled by the providence of an all-powerful God. Because it was a unity, something of its means of operation could be discovered by man's reason. God was not capricious but operated according to laws comprehensible enough for men to conduct their lives accordingly. Although here we have examined only one piece of evidence, it is representative of Winthrop's thought and conforms to the general picture of the Puritan mind developed by Perry Miller.

Style of persuasion is reflected in language. Winthrop's language has much in common with that used in the Declaration of Independence, where the measured, deliberative statements of what exists, rather than imperative statements of what ought to exist, reveal an argument from definition. Were the Declaration to argue from circumstance, it would have appealed to the "best interests of men and nations," "expedience," "enlightened opinion," and "the strength of our determination and arms." Instead of expressing the wish that everything be regulated according to the desires of men, the Declaration manifests the feeling that men must order their affairs with nature.

Winthrop's language, on the other hand, manifests the feeling that men must order their affairs with God. The difference between ordering life with nature and with God appears in Winthrop's use of a conditional tone, which the Declaration does not have. Nature contains an unalterable set of rules for human affairs that are relatively easy to discover, but God's rules are difficult to interpret and are not everywhere and always the same. Notice the conditional tone in this passage:

> Thus stands the cause between God and vs, wee are entered into Covenant with him for this worke, wee haue taken out a Commission, the Lord hath giuen us leave to draw our owne Articles wee haue professed to enterprise these Accions vpon these and these ends, wee haue herevpon besought him of favour and blessing: Now if the Lord shall please to heare vs, and bring vs in peace to the place wee desire, then hath hee ratified this Covenant and sealed our Commission, [and] will expect a strickt performance of the Articles contained in it, but if wee shall neglect the observacion of these Articles which are the ends wee haue propounded, and dissembling with our God, shall fall to embrace this present world and prosecute our carnall intencions, seekeing great things for our selues and our posterity, the Lord will surely break out in wrathe against vs be revenged of such a periured people and make vs knowe the price of the breache of such a Covenant.

Because it was impossible for Winthrop to know the laws of nature and nature's God through reasoning alone, he had to supplement his definitions with testimony, and because scripture was difficult to interpret, he had to adopt a conditional tone.

Polemical writing poses two special kinds of choices concerning selection of material. For emotional effect, material must be presented so that the audience can identify itself with the problem. This selection determines the rhetorical structure of the discourse. For logical appeal, material must be presented so that the audience can follow the mental progression from underlying assumptions to conclusions drawn from particulars. This selection determines the rational structure of the discourse.

Winthrop, as governor, wished to convince his audience that it would be required to make even greater sacrifices in New England than those that had already been made in order to leave old England. Had he begun his sermon by driving home the point that it would be even harder to live according to God's law in the New World than it had been at home, his stern warning would have been likely to arrest everyone's emotions in fear. After all, the Puritans were leaving England so that they could live more easily according to scripture.

By beginning with the social and economic considerations that must have been on their minds, Winthrop could gradually lead them from the difficulties they were used to, to the new responsibilities they were to face. His long treatment of Christian love in the middle of his sermon gave his audience an emotional foundation for the awful responsibilities of the new covenant. When he came to his final statement, he had led his audience from known difficulties, through a consideration of the way to solve all difficulties, to a mood of heroic response to the greatest difficulties of all:

Now the onely way to avoyde this shipwracke and to provide for our posterity is to followe the Counsell of Micah, to doe Justly, to loue mercy, to walke humbly with our God, for this end, wee must be knitt together in this worke as one man, wee must entertaine each other in brotherly Affection, wee must be willing to abridge our selues of our superfluities, for the supply of others necessities, wee must vphold a familiar Commerce together in all meekness, gentlenes, patience and liberallity, wee must delight in eache other, make others Condicions our owne reioyce together, mourne together, labour, and suffer together, allwayes hauing before our eyes our Commission and Community in the worke, our Community as members of the same body, soe shall wee keepe the vnitie of the spirit in the bond of peace, the Lord will be our God and delight to dwell among vs, as his owne people and will commaund a blessing vpon vs in all our wayes, soe that wee shall see much more of his wisdome power goodness and truthe then formerly wee haue beene acquainted with, wee shall find that the God of Israell is among vs, when tenn of vs shall be able to resist a thousand of our enemies, when hee shall make vs a prayse and glory, that men shall say of succeeding plantacions: the lord make it like that of New England: for wee must Consider that wee shall be as a Citty vpon a Hill, the eies of all people are vppon vs; soe that if wee shall deale falsely with our god in this worke wee haue vndertaken and soe cause him to withdrawe his present help from vs, wee shall be made a story and a by-word through the world, wee shall open the mouthes of enemies to speake euill of the wayes of god and all professours for Gods sake; wee shall shame the faces of many of gods worthy seruants, and cause theire prayers to be turned into Cursses vpon us till wee be consumed out of the good land whether wee are goeing.

Rational structure depends upon the adequacy of premises to conclusions and inferences, the relationship of premises and conclusions, and the kinds of inferences drawn from given particulars. Given Winthrop's assumptions that men are naturally dominated by the selfishness that expresses original sin, it would have been irrational for him to begin with a statement of the necessity for Christian love in order to follow God's laws in the new society they were to build. Nor could he have begun with the penalties for failure to live up to the commission from God that their actions implied. Given his doctrine that God ordains the conditions of men, he had to base his first two reasons on God's providence and continue with the implications of this for economic arrangements. In this sermon, rational structure follows rhetorical structure very closely, because Winthrop, like all Puritans, made every attempt to make rational sense of the world.

Winthrop's deliberate rationality leads into the fourth component of the machine for rhetorical analysis: questions of effect. The deliberative, rational form Winthrop gave his sermon indicates that he believed men to be creatures capable of reasoning. But the conditional tone he used shows that he regarded this capacity as partial. His continual stress on liberality and the good of the whole indicates that most men, for him, were narrow, selfish people. With God's grace, however, Christian love could transform men into true brothers. Because grace was a difficult thing to detect, Winthrop's conclusion shows that he hoped for the best, while he held the worst to be equally possible. This kind of simultaneous hope and fear is the trademark of the Puritan way of thinking. We have seen that his sermon developed its persuasive power through an argument leading up to an heroic passage that held an even balance between hope and fear. Given Puritan theology, this mixture of emotions was the appropriate one for Winthrop's attempt to persuade his followers that, in building their new community, they must truly work together as a band of Christian brothers.

III

A Commonplace to Meet a Crisis

IN CONGRESS

July 4, 1776

*The Unanimous Declaration of the Thirteen
United States of America*

WHEN in the Course of human events, it becomes necessary
for one people to dissolve the political bands which have connected them with another, and to assume among the powers of
the earth, the separate and equal station to which the Laws of
Nature and of Nature's God entitle them, a decent respect to
the opinions of mankind requires that they should declare the
causes which impel them to the separation.—We hold these
truths to be self-evident, that all men are created equal, that
they are endowed by their Creator with certain unalienable
Rights, that among these are Life, Liberty and the pursuit of
Happiness.—That to secure these rights, Governments are instituted among Men, deriving their just powers from the consent of the governed,—That whenever any Form of Government becomes destructive of these ends, it is the Right of the
People to alter or to abolish it, and to institute new Government, laying its foundation on such principles and organizing

its powers in such form, as to them shall seem most likely to effect their Safety and Happiness. Prudence, indeed, will dictate that Governments long established should not be changed for light and transient causes; and accordingly all experience hath shown, that mankind are more disposed to suffer, while evils are sufferable, than to right themselves by abolishing the forms to which they are accustomed. But when a long train of abuses and usurpations, pursuing invariably the same Object evinces a design to reduce them under absolute Despotism, it is their right, it is their duty, to throw off such Government, and to provide new Guards for their future security.—Such has been the patient sufferance of these Colonies; and such is now the necessity which constrains them to alter their former Systems of Government. The history of the present King of Great Britain is a history of repeated injuries and usurpations, all having in direct object the establishment of an absolute Tyranny over these States. To prove this, let Facts be submitted to a candid world.—He has refused his Assent to Laws, the most wholesome and necessary for the public good.—He has forbidden his Governors to pass Laws of immediate and pressing importance, unless suspended in their operation till his Assent should be obtained; and when so suspended, he has utterly neglected to attend to them.—He has refused to pass other Laws for the accommodation of large districts of people, unless those people would relinquish the right of Representation in the Legislature, a right inestimable to them and formidable to tyrants only.—He has called together legislative bodies at places unusual, uncomfortable, and distant from the depository of their public Records, for the sole purpose of fatiguing them into compliance with his measures.—He has dissolved Representative Houses repeatedly, for opposing with manly firmness his invasions on the rights of the people.—He has refused for a long time, after such dissolutions, to cause others to be elected; whereby the Legislative powers, incapable of Annihilation, have returned to the People at large for their exercise; the State remaining in the mean time exposed to all the dangers of invasion from without, and convulsions within.—He has endeavoured to prevent the population of these States; for that purpose obstructing the Laws for Naturalization of Foreigners; refusing to pass others to encourage their migration hither, and raising the conditions of new Appropriations of Lands.—He has obstructed the Administration of Justice, by refusing his Assent to Laws for establishing Judiciary powers.—He has made Judges dependent on his Will alone, for the tenure of their offices, and the amount and payment of their salaries.—He has erected a multitude of New Offices, and sent hither swarms of Officers to harrass our people, and eat out their substance.—He has kept among us, in times of peace, Standing Armies, without the Consent of our legislatures.—He has affected to render the Military independent of and superior to the Civil power. —He has combined with others to subject us to a jurisdiction foreign to our constitution, and unacknowledged by our laws; giving his Assent to their Acts of pretended Legislation:— For quartering large bodies of armed troops among us:—For protecting them, by a mock Trial, from punishment for any Murders which they should commit on the Inhabitants of these States:—For cutting off our Trade with all parts of the world:—For imposing Taxes on us without our Consent:— For depriving us in many cases, of the benefits of Trial by Jury:—For transporting us beyond Seas to be tried for pretended offences:—For abolishing the free System of English Laws in a neighbouring Province, establishing therein an Arbitrary government, and enlarging its Boundaries so as to render it at once an example and fit instrument for introducing the same absolute rule into these Colonies:—For taking away our Charters, abolishing our most valuable Laws, and altering fundamentally the Forms of our Governments:—For suspending our own Legislatures, and declaring themselves invested with power to legislate for us in all cases whatsoever.—He has abdicated Government here, by declaring us out of his Protection and waging War against us.—He has plundered our seas, ravaged our Coasts, burnt our towns, and destroyed the lives of our people.—He is at this time transporting large Armies of foreign Mercenaries to compleat the works of death, desolation and tyranny, already begun with circumstances of Cruelty & perfidy scarcely paralleled in the most barbarous ages, and totally unworthy the Head of a civilized nation.—He has constrained our fellow Citizens taken Captive on the high Seas to bear Arms against their Country, to become the executioners of their friends and Brethren, or to fall themselves by their Hands.—He has excited domestic insurrections amongst us, and has endeavoured to bring on the inhabitants of our frontiers, the merciless Indian Savages, whose known rule of warfare, is an undistinguished destruction of all ages, sexes and conditions. In every stage of these Oppressions We have Petitioned for Redress in the most humble terms: Our repeated Petitions have been answered only by repeated injury. A Prince, whose character is thus marked by every act which may define a Tyrant, is unfit to be the ruler of a free people. Nor have We been wanting in attentions to our British brethren. We have warned them from time to time of attempts by their legislature to extend an unwarrantable jurisdiction over us. We have reminded them of the circumstances of our emigration and settlement here. We have appealed to their native justice and magnanimity, and we have conjured them by the ties of our common kindred to disavow these usurpations, which, would inevitably interrupt our connections and correspondence. They, too, have been deaf to the voice of justice and of consanguinity. We must, therefore, acquiesce in the necessity, which denounces our Separation, and hold them, as we hold the rest of mankind, Enemies in War, in Peace Friends.—

WE, THEREFORE, the REPRESENTATIVES of the UNITED STATES OF AMERICA, in General Congress, Assembled, appealing to the Supreme Judge of the world for the rectitude of our intentions, do, in the Name, and by Authority of the good People of these Colonies, solemnly publish and declare, That these United Colonies are, and of Right ought to be FREE AND INDEPENDENT STATES; that they are Absolved from all Allegiance to the British Crown, and that all political connection between them and the State of Great Britain, is and ought to be totally dissolved; and that as Free and Independent States, they have full Power to levy War, conclude Peace, contract Alliances, establish Commerce, and to do all other Acts and Things which Independent States may of right do.—And for the support of this Declaration, with a firm reliance on the protection of Divine Providence, we mutually pledge to each other our Lives, our Fortunes and our sacred Honor.

A Commonplace to
Meet a Crisis

COMMENTARY

CLASSROOM discussions of the Declaration of Independence rarely get beyond the eighteenth-century background that supposedly gives meaning to the "glittering generalities" of its first two paragraphs. Students are told that this background accounts for the generalities because an argument in polemical writing must be adapted to an audience, and this adaptation produces the rhetoric of the Declaration. As for the Declaration's logic, it is pointed out that historians and political scientists generally question the adequacy of the appeal to "self-evident truths" as justification for the premise that tyranny requires revolution, that they find the bill of indictments against George III inadequate to define a tyrant, and that they assert that the "real causes" of the Revolution are not stated.

The Declaration is actually a somewhat overly formal argu-

ment, based upon an implicit syllogism (an attempt to establish despotism necessitates revolution; George III attempts to
establish despotism; therefore, revolution is necessary). It was
designed to persuade a "candid world" that Americans had
a duty to depose a ruler attempting to establish an "absolute
despotism" and a right to establish any sort of new government assuring their natural rights.

Because polemical writing—if not found fallacious and then
dismissed without further analysis—can be run through the
machine of logic, in which everything follows necessarily from
the premises, the first step in an analysis of expository argument should isolate the assumptions supporting the premises.
Ultimately, all argument depends upon assumptions about the
nature of the universe. At the extremes, men assume the universe to be either ordered or chaotic. The way in which they
understand order or chaos determines the form of their arguments about specific events, actions, or things.

The most striking evidence that a concept of eternal order
formed the Declaration's basis is the ease with which God
appears at each stage of the argument. "Laws of Nature and
of Nature's God," "Creator," "Supreme Judge of the world,"
and "Divine Providence" are the ultimate appeals. Were custom thought to regulate human affairs, the Declaration must
have appealed to the "best interests of men and nations," "expedience," "enlightened opinion," and "the strength of our
determination and arms." Instead of expressing the wish that
everything be regulated according to the desires of men, the
Declaration manifests the feeling that men must order their
affairs with nature.

This feeling accounts for the quiet tone of measured, deliberative statement of what exists: men *are* created; they *are*
endowed; governments *are* instituted. If custom had conditioned the attitudes of the Declaration, the language would

have been imperative: each national group *ought* to have a nation, instead of being *entitled to* a separate and equal station; the people *must* throw off tyranny, instead of saying *it is the right of the people* to alter or abolish arbitrary government.

Men subordinating their concerns to an eternal order naturally choose the syllogism as a form for argument. If there were no order, the invention of principles for action would follow from discussions of probabilities. But the Declaration discovers its first premise—tyranny necessitates revolution—in the concept of God. To justify this premise, the Declaration relies upon an argument from origin. Governments are the products of men, who are the products of God. It is in the nature of things that the product serve some end of the producer. If this end is not served, the producer clearly will destroy or alter the product. The most obvious attribute of God is as creator. As creature, man is sacred. Man's most obvious characteristic is life, to sustain which, liberty is necessary. Happiness, toward which all men aim, life, and liberty constitute the most obvious ends of man's existence. Men created government for these ends. If the creature interferes with the ends of the creator, whose life is sacred because created by God, the creature must be altered to serve these ends. Tyranny is a condition of impiety because God, not the tyrant, is the creator of life. Therefore, tyranny necessitates revolution. The argument is self-evident because it is contained in the most obvious of phenomena: life and creation.

It would be possible for one predisposed to see a chaotic universe to argue from origin, using a concept of final causation just as the Declaration did. But in that argument, "self-evidence" would have to be replaced by "history," for the concept of God would drop from the discussion. Government could be viewed as a convenience established for ends similar to those stated in the Declaration. But the argument would not be likely to establish active revolution in the first premise, because the removal of an order imposed upon chaos would probably appear more inimical to men's ends than tyranny itself. The Declaration safely predicates revolution because it assumes that men will fall back upon the basically benevolent order of nature when the control of custom is removed.

The first premise of the Declaration, then, is not based upon "glittering generalities." Given the preconception of order, applied to the problem of government and revolution, through an argument from origin concerning the relationship of means to ends, the Declaration expresses the "common sense" of the matter. That tyrannical conditions justify revolution is not mere assertion, but the conclusion of sound argument based upon the everyday observations of men viewing the world as an ordered system of relationships.

Before producing evidence for the expected minor premise —we are suffering under tyranny—the Declaration subtly varies the statement to mean that George III *aims* to become a tyrant. This unexpected variation strengthens the case in three ways. First, it allows the characterization of men respectful of others' opinions to include prudence as well. Then, it specifies the time when revolution ought to take place. Finally, it shifts the burden of the bill of indictments from establishing actual conditions to enumerating despotic means by which George III aims to bring about his tyrannic ends. The case strengthened, the assertion, "it is their right," can immediately be elevated to "it is their duty, to throw off such Government."

"The opinions of mankind" have extreme importance for men arguing from predispositions of order. To obtain knowledge of order, men begin with opinions. Although never completely right because they are a part of the order, the opinions of men are never completely wrong. If action has the good opinion of men, there is likely good in the action. Because opinion has it that haste rarely accompanies good action, Congress wished to substantiate its prudence. Independence was not declared for "transient causes"; "repeated petitions" resulted in "repeated injury"; British kin were "deaf to the voice of justice and of consanguinity."

The time for revolution comes before the tyrant obtains despotic powers. Despotism, put into force, puts every man's life at the whim of the tyrant. Not only is it then too late for revolution, but the whole condition is one of disobedience to God, for men should not subject their lives to anyone except their creator. Man's duty to God makes revolution and re-organization of government incumbent when a tyrant's means, "a long train of abuses and usurpations," makes clear his ends.

To convince the "candid world," the Declaration listed eighteen means that George III used to bring about his despotic ends. The first seven deal with attempts to destroy colonial legislative acts and powers; the next two, with attempts to control the colonial judiciary; the next three, with the increase of the Crown's bureaucracy and military powers. Then comes the article most historians argue contained the root of the quarrel: the king had conspired with Parliament so that this carefully unnamed foreign legislative body attempted to impose nine kinds of laws unacknowledged in the colonies. Finally, there are five specifications concerning the manner of war the king was waging upon the colonies.

This bill of indictments is stated in the same measured, deliberative tone as the argument for the first premise of the syllogism. Although the seriousness of the charges progresses, the construction of the statements remains the same. An elevation, and not an inflation, of diction to fit the subject brings out the seriousness of the charges. It is as correct to speak of "Cruelty & perfidy scarcely paralleled in the most barbarous ages, and totally unworthy the Head of a civilized nation" when characterizing the use of foreign mercenaries, the practice of forcing men to fight against their countrymen, and the inciting of slave revolts, as it is to define as "manly firmness" the opposition of the legislators to "invasions on the rights of the people." The tone of the specifications remains constant throughout: "He has" in all cases, except one "He is," as in flat statement of fact.

These "facts," however, have not the concreteness of events. They are facts abstracted. Were the Declaration concerned to establish the material causation of the Revolution, more facts would have been documented, making them come alive as events.

Nor was the Declaration attempting to establish the efficient causes of the Revolution. The question of taxation, which historians from that day to this have in some form regarded as a major "cause" of the Revolution, is stressed no more than the minor issues of the time. A good deal of colonial discussion before the war dealt with a change of form in the British Empire, and much of the acrimony between the colonies and Britain centered in different conceptions of the structure of the empire. The Declaration avoids the question of formal causation by stating that the king "has combined" with Parliament, not that Parliament has destroyed the constitution of the empire by controlling the king. These "facts" listed in the bill of indictments are designed as means used toward King George's despotic ends. The indictments therefore conclude not with statements about men suffering under absolute despotism; or about taxation producing tyranny; or about our place in the empire being destroyed, so that we can no longer remain in it. The indictments instead conclude with: "A Prince, whose character is thus marked by every act which may define a Tyrant, is unfit to be the ruler of a free People." An overriding concern with final causation accounts for the minor premise in the Declaration's syllogism.

The Declaration avoids mentioning any specific form of government. From the theoretical second paragraph we know only that governments should be organized in a manner that the founders believe will ensure the "Safety and Happiness" of the people. The bill of indictments negatively states some of the aspects of this organization. Primarily, some sort of legislative body, which is representative, is essential for government. But the details, even the general type of government thought best, are left vague. The Declaration is quite specific, however, in stating the relationship between God, man, and government. Behind this statement is the notion that good government can be produced only out of man's knowledge of how to subordinate his activities to the laws of nature or, which amounts to the same thing, to God's will. This, together with the Declaration's stress on a representative legislature, leads to the conclusion that government should be a theocracy of all believers: theocracy, because knowledge of God's order is requisite to establishing an institution to insure safety and happiness; all believers, because as God's product every life is sacred and each man should therefore have a voice in what affects his life. The outline drawn, each people entitled by God to a "separate and equal station" fills in the details.

Carl Becker states in *The Declaration of Independence: A Study in the History of Political Ideas* that "in the late eighteenth century [the Natural Rights Philosophy underlying the Declaration] was widely accepted as a commonplace." Confronted with a crisis, it is the commonplace by which men act. By stating the grounds upon which men acted, the Declaration embodied the American Revolution. Our problem has been to understand this commonplace as an argument to meet a crisis.

IV

Tutelage for Self-determination

AN ORDINANCE FOR THE GOVERNMENT OF THE TERRITORY OF THE UNITED STATES NORTHWEST OF THE RIVER OHIO

(1) *Be it ordained by the United States in Congress assembled,* That the said territory, for the purposes of temporary government, be one district, subject, however, to be divided into two districts, as future circumstances may, in the opinion of Congress, make it expedient.

(2) *Be it ordained by the authority aforesaid,* That the estates, both of resident and non-resident proprietors in the said territory, dying intestate, shall descend to, and be distributed among their children, and the descendants of a deceased child, in equal parts; the descendants of a deceased child or grandchild to take the share of their deceased parent in equal parts among them: And where there shall be no children or descendants, then in equal parts to the next of kin in equal degree; and among collaterals, the children of a deceased brother

or sister of the intestate shall have, in equal parts among them, their deceased parents' share; and there shall in no case be a distinction between kindred of the whole and half-blood; saving, in all cases, to the widow of the intestate her third part of the real estate for life, and one-third part of the personal estate; and this law relative to descents and dower, shall remain in full force until altered by the legislature of the district. And until the governor and judges shall adopt laws as hereinafter mentioned, estates in the said territory may be devised or bequeathed by wills in writing, signed and sealed by him or her in whom the estate may be (being of full age), and attested by three witnesses; and real estates may be conveyed by lease and release, or bargain and sale, signed sealed and delivered by the person, being of full age, in whom the estate may be, and attested by two witnesses, provided such wills be duly proved, and such conveyances be acknowledged, or the execution thereof duly proved, and be recorded within one year after proper magistrates, courts, and registers shall be appointed for that purpose; and personal property may be transferred by delivery; saving, however to the French and Canadian inhabitants, and other settlers of the Kaskaskies, St. Vincents and the neighboring villages who have heretofore professed themselves citizens of Virginia, their laws and customs now in force among them, relative to the descent and conveyance, of property.

(3) *Be it ordained by the authority aforesaid,* That there shall be appointed from time to time by Congress, a governor, whose commission shall continue in force for the term of three years, unless sooner revoked by Congress; he shall reside in the district, and have a freehold estate therein in 1,000 acres of land, while in the exercise of his office.

(4) There shall be appointed from time to time by Congress, a

secretary, whose commission shall continue in force for four years unless sooner revoked; he shall reside in the district, and have a freehold estate therein in 500 acres of land, while in the exercise of his office. It shall be his duty to keep and preserve the acts and laws passed by the legislature, and the public records of the district, and the proceedings of the governor in his executive department, and transmit authentic copies of such acts and proceedings, every six months, to the Secretary of Congress: There shall also be appointed a court to consist of three judges, any two of whom to form a court, who shall have a common law jurisdiction, and reside in the district, and have each therein a freehold estate in 500 acres of land while in the exercise of their offices; and their commissions shall continue in force during good behavior.

(5) The governor and judges, or a majority of them, shall adopt and publish in the district such laws of the original States, criminal and civil, as may be necessary and best suited to the circumstances of the district, and report them to Congress from time to time: which laws shall be in force in the district until the organization of the General Assembly therein, unless disapproved of by Congress; but afterwards the Legislature shall have authority to alter them as they shall think fit.

(6) The governor, for the time being, shall be commander-in-chief of the militia, appoint and commission all officers in the same below the rank of general officers; all general officers shall be appointed and commissioned by Congress.

(7) Previous to the organization of the general assembly, the governor shall appoint such magistrates and other civil officers in each county or township, as he shall find necessary for the preservation of the peace and good order in the same: After

the general assembly shall be organized, the powers and duties
of the magistrates and other civil officers shall be regulated and
defined by the said assembly; but all magistrates and other
civil officers not herein otherwise directed, shall, during the
continuance of this temporary government, be appointed by
the governor.

(8) For the prevention of crimes and injuries, the laws to be
adopted or made shall have force in all parts of the district,
and for the execution of process, criminal and civil, the governor shall make proper divisions thereof; and he shall proceed from time to time as circumstances may require, to lay out
the parts of the district in which the Indian titles shall have
been extinguished, into counties and townships, subject however to such alterations as may thereafter be made by the
legislature.

(9) So soon as there shall be five thousand free male inhabitants of full age in the district, upon giving proof thereof to
the governor, they shall receive authority, with time and place,
to elect representatives from their counties or townships to
represent them in the general assembly: *Provided,* That, for
every five hundred free male inhabitants, there shall be one
representative, and so on progressively with the number of
free male inhabitants shall the right of representation increase, until the number of representatives shall amount to
twenty-five; after which, the number and proportion of representatives shall be regulated by the legislature: *Provided,* That
no person be eligible or qualified to act as a representative
unless he shall have been a citizen of one of the United States
three years, and be a resident in the district, or unless he shall
have resided in the district three years; and, in either case,
shall likewise hold in his own right, in fee simple, two hun-

dred acres of land within the same: *Provided, also,* That a
freehold in fifty acres of land in the district, having been a
citizen of one of the states, and being resident in the district,
or the like freehold and two years residence in the district,
shall be necessary to qualify a man as an elector of a representative.

(10) The representatives thus elected, shall serve for the term
of two years; and, in case of the death of a representative, or
removal from office, the governor shall issue a writ to the
county or township for which he was a member, to elect another in his stead, to serve for the residue of the term.

(11) The general assembly or legislature shall consist of the
governor, legislative council, and a house of representatives.
The Legislative Council shall consist of five members, to continue in office five years, unless sooner removed by Congress;
any three of whom to be a quorum: and the members of the
Council shall be nominated and appointed in the following
manner, to wit: As soon as representatives shall be elected, the
Governor shall appoint a time and place for them to meet together; and, when met, they shall nominate ten persons, residents in the district, and each possessed of a freehold in five
hundred acres of land, and return their names to Congress;
five of whom Congress shall appoint and commission to serve
as aforesaid; and, whenever a vacancy shall happen in the
council, by death or removal from office, the house of representatives shall nominate two persons, qualified as aforesaid,
for each vacancy, and return their names to Congress; one of
whom Congress shall appoint and commission for the residue
of the term. And every five years, four months at least before
the expiration of the time of service of the members of council, the said house shall nominate ten persons, qualified as

aforesaid, and return their names to Congress; five of whom Congress shall appoint and commission to serve as members of the council five years, unless sooner removed. And the governor, legislative council, and house of representatives, shall have authority to make laws in all cases, for the good government of the district, not repugnant to the principles and articles in this ordinance established and declared. And all bills, having passed by a majority in the house, and by a majority in the council, shall be referred to the governor for his assent; but no bill, or legislative act whatever, shall be of any force without his assent. The governor shall have power to convene, prorogue, and dissolve the general assembly, when, in his opinion, it shall be expedient.

(12) The governor, judges, legislative council, secretary, and such other officers as Congress shall appoint in the district, shall take an oath or affirmation of fidelity and of office; the governor before the president of congress, and all other officers before the Governor. As soon as a legislature shall be formed in the district, the council and house assembled in one room, shall have authority, by joint ballot, to elect a delegate to Congress, who shall have a seat in Congress, with a right of debating but not of voting during this temporary government.

(13) And, for extending the fundamental principles of civil and religious liberty, which form the basis whereon these republics, their laws and constitutions are erected; to fix and establish those principles as the basis of all laws, constitutions, and governments, which forever hereafter shall be formed in the said territory: to provide also for the establishment of States, and permanent government therein, and for their admission to a share in the federal councils on an equal footing with the original States, at as early periods as may be consistent with the general interest:

(14) It is hereby ordained and declared by the authority aforesaid, That the following articles shall be considered as articles of compact between the original States and the people and States in the said territory and forever remain unalterable, unless by common consent, to wit:

(15) ART. 1. No person, demeaning himself in a peaceable and orderly manner, shall ever be molested on account of his mode of worship or religious sentiments, in the said territory.

(16) ART. 2. The inhabitants of the said territory shall always be entitled to the benefits of the writ of *habeas corpus,* and of the trial by jury; of a proportionate representation of the people in the legislature; and of judicial proceedings according to the course of the common law. All persons shall be bailable, unless for capital offences, where the proof shall be evident or the presumption great. All fines shall be moderate; and no cruel or unusual punishments shall be inflicted. No man shall be deprived of his liberty or property, but by the judgment of his peers or the law of the land; and, should the public exigencies make it necessary, for the common preservation, to take any person's property, or to demand his particular services, full compensation shall be made for the same. And, in the just preservation of rights and property, it is understood and declared, that no law ought ever to be made, or have force in the said territory, that shall, in any manner whatever, interfere with or affect private contracts or engagements, *bona fide,* and without fraud, previously formed.

(17) ART. 3. Religion, morality, and knowledge, being necessary to good government and the happiness of mankind, schools and the means of education shall forever be encouraged. The utmost good faith shall always be observed towards the Indians; their lands and property shall never be taken from

them without their consent; and, in their property, rights, and liberty, they shall never be invaded or disturbed, unless in just and lawful wars authorized by Congress; but laws founded in justice and humanity, shall from time to time be made for preventing wrongs being done to them, and for preserving peace and friendship with them.

(18) ART. 4. The said territory, and the States which may be formed therein, shall forever remain a part of this Confederacy of the United States of America, subject to the Articles of Confederation, and to such alterations therein as shall be constitutionally made; and to all the acts and ordinances of the United States in Congress assembled, conformable thereto. The inhabitants and settlers in the said territory shall be subject to pay a part of the federal debts contracted or to be contracted, and a proportional part of the expenses of government, to be apportioned on them by Congress according to the same common rule and measure by which apportionments thereof shall be made on the other States; and the taxes for paying their proportion shall be laid and levied by the authority and direction of the legislatures of the district or districts, or new States, as in the original States, within the time agreed upon by the United States in Congress assembled. The legislatures of those districts or new States, shall never interfere with the primary disposal of the soil by the United States in Congress assembled, nor with any regulations Congress may find necessary for securing the title in such soil to the *bona fide* purchasers. No tax shall be imposed on lands the property of the United States; and, in no case, shall non-resident proprietors be taxed higher than residents. The navigable waters leading into the Mississippi and St. Lawrence, and the carrying places between the same, shall be common highways and forever free, as well to the inhabitants of the said territory as

to the citizens of the United States, and those of any other States that may be admitted into the confederacy, without any tax, impost, or duty therefor.

(19) **ART.** 5. There shall be formed in the said territory, not less than three nor more than five States; and the boundaries of the States, as soon as Virginia shall alter her act of cession, and consent to the same, shall become fixed and established as follows, to wit: The western State in the said territory, shall be bounded by the Mississippi, the Ohio, and Wabash Rivers; a direct line drawn from the Wabash and Post Vincents, due North, to the territorial line between the United States and Canada; and, by the said territorial line, to the Lake of the Woods and Mississippi. The middle State shall be bounded by the said direct line, the Wabash from Post Vincents to the Ohio, by the Ohio, by a direct line, drawn due north from the mouth of the Great Miami, to the said territorial line, and by the said territorial line. The eastern State shall be bounded by the last mentioned direct line, the Ohio, Pennsylvania, and the said territorial line: *Provided, however,* and it is further understood and declared, that the boundaries of these three States shall be subject so far to be altered, that, if Congress shall hereafter find it expedient, they shall have authority to form one or two States in that part of the said territory which lies north of an east and west line drawn through the southerly bend or extreme of lake Michigan. And, whenever any of the said States shall have sixty thousand free inhabitants therein, such State shall be admitted, by its delegates, into the Congress of the United States, on an equal footing with the original States in all respects whatever, and shall be at liberty to form a permanent constitution and State government: *Provided,* the constitution and government so to be formed, shall be republican, and in conformity to the principles contained

in these articles; and, so far as it can be consistent with the general interest of the confederacy, such admission shall be allowed at an earlier period, and when there may be a less number of free inhabitants in the State than sixty thousand.

(20) Art. 6. There shall be neither slavery nor involuntary servitude in the said territory, otherwise than in the punishment of crimes whereof the party shall have been duly convicted: *Provided, always,* That any person escaping into the same, from whom labor or service is lawfully claimed in any one of the original States, such fugitive may be lawfully reclaimed and conveyed to the person claiming his or her labor or service as aforesaid.

(21) *Be it ordained by the authority aforesaid,* That the resolutions of the 23rd of April 1784, relative to the subject of this ordinance, be, and the same are hereby repealed and declared null and void.

Tutelage for Self-determination

COMMENTARY

WITH the treaty of peace ending the Revolutionary War on
September 3, 1783, the former British colonies in North America definitely became masters of a colonial territory themselves.
The vast area of largely unsettled land lying north of the Ohio
River between the boundary of Pennsylvania and the Mississippi River had already produced problems for the Congress of
the new states. Certain states claimed sections under the authority of colonial charters, while other states argued that the
Northwest Territory was the equal possession of all. Not until
these colonial claims were renounced in 1781 did the states
without claims agree to ratify the Articles of Confederation.

During the spring of 1783, the underfed and unpaid Continental Army had caused Congress trouble before it was dis-

banded. Lacking power of direct taxation, Congress hoped to use the vacant lands in the western territory to meet its promises to the soldiers. At its first meeting in January 1784, a committee on the files of reports and appointments, consisting of Jefferson, Elbridge Gerry, and Hugh Williamson, reported that the first order of business was ratification of the peace treaty, together with some disposition of the western lands. These two matters proceeded together during the winter and spring. The treaty was ratified, January 14, and ratifications were exchanged, May 12. On March 1 a committee on the temporary government of the western lands, composed of Jefferson, Jeremiah Townley Chase, and David Howell, recommended a territorial ordinance to govern all the land west of the mountains. After discussion in committee on April 19, 20, and 21, the Ordinance of 1784 was adopted as amended, on April 23. On April 29, Congress formally resolved to consider the western territory a capital resource, but not until May 20, 1785, did it pass the Basic Land Ordinance governing conditions for selling public land.

Discontent with the Ordinance of 1784 produced a new committee to draw up another plan for temporary government. On September 19, 1786, this committee, composed of William Samuel Johnson, Charles Pinckney, Melancton Smith, Nathan Dane, and William Henry, brought in a new plan that increased Congressional power over the territory. This plan was debated without resolution in May 1787. Finally on July 11, 1787, another committee, composed of Edward Carrington, Nathan Dane, Richard Henry Lee, John Kean, and Melancton Smith, brought in a new report that was approved on July 13, after a clause forbidding slavery was introduced into the Ordinance for the first time since it had been struck out of the draft report on April 19, 1784. The Northwest Ordinance became the basic law regulating the North American territorial colonies of the United States from that time.

All this occurred during a period of continuous discussion of the proper nature and function of government and the proper rights and duties of citizens. After the overthrow of royal and proprietary governments, most of the new republican state constitutions provided for strong bicameral legislatures, weak executives, frequent elections, property qualifications for voting and officeholding, appointive judiciaries with good-behavior tenure, and bills of rights. The Confederation Congress, lacking any real executive branch, was composed of representatives from state governments, not of the people of the states.

While Congress was debating the Northwest Ordinance in New York City, the Constitutional Convention in Philadelphia was trying to work out a balance between branches of a federal government that would have direct power over the people and direct representation of the people in the legislature. In established society, there are many things working against radical changes in government. The establishment of a colony, however, gives men an opportunity to construct government on principles. Careful examination of the Northwest Ordinance can show us answers that the generation of Americans just freed from colonial restrictions gave to fundamental political questions. These answers represent what they thought they had learned about how a government ought to expand its territory without provoking a revolt in its colonies.

Because the Ordinance of 1784 never took effect and was specifically repealed by the Northwest Ordinance, we can regard the three years during which Congress was coming to an agreement as a continuous process. The first committee report on the Ordinance of 1784 was simply a series of statements on how the territory was to be divided, how temporary governments were to be organized (through a process of self-determination that limited them to republican governments subject to Congress in the same degree as the original states), and on how they were to be admitted to the union of states. By the time the final Ordinance of 1784 was adopted, Congress had asserted its authority over colonies whose residents had yet to establish temporary government, had stressed its right to sell lands, and had struck out the clause forbidding slavery. The final form certainly limited the rights of the residents more than the original draft. This process of increasing Congress' power continued, through the discussions of the report presented in 1786, to the final passage of the Northwest Ordinance. Although the clause forbidding slavery was introduced into the final version of the Northwest Ordinance, the act was limited to territory north of the Ohio. Limitations on the rights of the new American colonists were partly prompted by discussions about the rise of "banditti" beyond the mountains, and partly by the need to make a capital resource of the unsettled lands; the limitations also represent a change in attitude toward what ought to be the constitution of government.

The Northwest Ordinance is composed of four sections. Paragraph 1 asserts the authority of Congress over the territory northwest of the Ohio River. Paragraph 2 establishes, in the new colonies, the laws for transfer of property that were being established in the original states. Paragraphs 3 through 12 prescribe the constitution of colonial government. Paragraphs 13–20 contain the articles of compact between the original states and any new state to come from the territory. Paragraph 21 repeals the Ordinance of 1784.

The wording of paragraph 1 clearly implies the absolute authority of Congress over the Northwest Territory. During the war for independence, some suggested that the territory west of the Appalachian Mountains ought to become a series of separate republics. After the war, there was talk of a semi-autonomous military colony occupying the Northwest. The land companies, composed mainly of eastern merchants, exercised a good deal of pressure on Congress in an attempt to gain control over the western lands. Various solutions to the problem of governing the west were entertained because of the widespread opinion that republican government could be effectively maintained only in a small area. In this paragraph, Congress implies its acceptance of the explicit argument, put forth later by the *Federalist*, that republican government was not necessarily limited in area.

Because this is an ordinance for governing the Northwest, it may seem strange that it discusses real and personal property before the actual constitution of government. We have seen, however, that Congress had already specifically stated that it considered the western territory a capital resource. If buyers for the land were to be easily found, they would have to be assured that one of the major results of the Revolution, the abolition of the aristocratic customs of land holding—entail and primogeniture—would be extended to the new colonies. Although congressional decrees could be changed by any government established in the new colonies, initially the settlers could look forward to the same property rights as they enjoyed, for the most part, in the states. Because the principle here was continuation of the established rights of property, Congress specifically did not interfere with the property rights of the French settlers who gave their allegiance to Virginia as a result of the Revolution.

However close to existing practice concerning property rights, the Ordinance reversed the constitutional trend of the original states. The trend had been to weaken executive power while strengthening legislative power. The Ordinance, however, ordained a strong colonial governor, responsible only to Congress.

Not only the governor, but also the judges and secretary of the colonial government, were directly appointed by Congress, and all were assured of an independent income while in office. The governor was appointed for a three-year term with a free-hold estate of 1,000 acres; the secretary, for a term of four years with an estate of 500 acres; and the judges, during good behavior, with estates of 500 acres. All these officials were required to live in the colony, and by this requirement Congress prevented colonial officials from farming out their duties to deputies while they lived at home, as had been common under British colonial rule.

To keep close check on the activities of the colonial government, Congress specified that the secretary report to the Secretary of Congress every six months on every activity of the colonial government. Before the colony was thickly settled enough to warrant a representative assembly, the governor and judges were to adopt whatever laws they thought necessary from the laws existing in the original states. Although Congress could disallow these laws before the colonial legislature was organized and the legislature could change them after its organization, the governor's first initiative and his veto over acts of the assembly gave him great powers. His power also extended to appointment of militia officers below the rank of general, since he was commander-in-chief of the militia. Further, he had the power of appointing all inferior magistrates to districts of his own devising. The powers of the judges did not extend to holding courts of equity, as had been the case in the draft Ordinance of 1786, but were restricted to common-law jurisdiction. The powers of the appointed officials are reminiscent of the theoretic powers of the British colonial officials, although in practice the British officials exercised somewhat less authority.

Only after the residents of the territory presented evidence to the governor that there were "five thousand free male inhabitants of full age in the district," was he authorized to begin proceedings for a general assembly. The qualifications for representatives and electors followed the trend in the original states. Terms of office, however, were to be substantially longer. To insure that property owners moving into the colony were enfranchised, the Ordinance specified that citizenship in one of the states as well as two years' residence in the colony and ownership of specified amounts of land qualified for voting and officeholding.

The power of the representatives was restricted by the composition of the legislature, consisting of governor, legislative council, and house of representatives. The council of five was appointed by Congress from a list of ten nominated by the representatives, each having a substantially larger freehold of land than that required for ordinary representatives. The council's term of office, five years, was much longer than any term common in the United States, except for that of judges. There was no provision that the house originate money bills, as was common in the original states. After the house and council had passed any bill, the governor had an absolute veto, an uncommon power in the original states. The governor had the power to convene and dissolve the legislature at will. Although the council and house, meeting together, had the authority to elect a representative to Congress, he had no vote, but only the right to debate.

Thus far the Ordinance was much less republican than the

Ordinance of 1784. If anything, it was more restrictive than the British colonial governments had been. In its haphazardness, the British colonial system had allowed the colonial houses of representatives more control over the colonial governors than the American colonial system would, especially since the officials appointed by Congress would have greater economic freedom, through their freehold possessions, than had the British governors. Recommendations from the new American colonies were given formal channels through the delegate to Congress, but under the British colonial system such recommendations often had informal channels through members of Parliament, such as Edmund Burke, who served as agents for colonies.

The remainder of the Ordinance, the articles of compact between the original states and the territory, contains pronouncements of civil and religious liberty that have been praised. It is worth noting, however, that, in theory, compacts are agreements between all parties obligated to obey. Congress here is giving the settlers in its colony no opportunity to agree, and therefore these articles are not so much provisions in a compact as commands.

Although these six articles are generally considered a bill of rights for the Northwest Territory, they read more like restrictions upon the activities of America's colonists. Their choices concerning civil relations are narrowly circumscribed. A statement of the aims of Congress' colonial policy preface the articles. Its first aim is to extend "the fundamental principles of civil and religious liberty, which form the basis whereon these republics [i.e., the original states], their laws and constitutions are erected" (paragraph 13). By seeing how Congress meant to accomplish its second goal—establishment of civil and religious liberty in the governments of the colo-

nies (paragraph 13)—the meaning of these principles is clarified. The third goal—to provide for "admission to a share in
the federal councils on an equal footing with the original
States" (paragraph 13)—was obviously the congressmen's way
of preventing what had happened to themselves as colonials.

Article 1, although it insures religious freedom to the "peaceable and orderly," prevents the new colonies from democrat-
ically agreeing upon an established religion and from taking
action against what they might consider socially dangerous
theories masking under religious sentiment. Among the civil
rights enumerated in Article 2—writ of habeas corpus, jury
trial, proportional representation, common-law justice, bail,
moderate fines, no cruel or unusual punishments, nor any
punishment without due process of law—no mention was
made of free speech, press, petition, assembly, or protection
from search; however, property was protected from public
seizure without full compensation, and a statement similar
to the contract clause of the Constitution prevented the colonial legislatures from passing measures relieving debtors during depressions, such as had been passed in many of the original states in the period just ending. The common notion that
the Ordinance provided public support for education is based
on the vague word "encouraged," ending the first sentence of
Article 3, which continues with a statement restricting the
colonists' action concerning the Indians. Although we sympathize today with the statement that the Indians should be
left alone, to the settlers going into the Northwest Territory,
they were a real danger. To have to wait until Congress authorized war could be disastrous, as the coastal states had put
it to the British government when they were colonies themselves.

Article 4 restricted the self-determination of the new American colonies even further. They were to be given no choice about their connection with the original states. As a part of the United States, the new colonies were subject to all federal debts, past, present, and future. Although their taxes were to be levied by their own legislatures, the amounts to be collected were to be apportioned among the colonies, as among the states, by Congress, a body they had no vote in. This solution to the taxation without representation problem is reminiscent of proposals in Lord North's conciliation plan of 1775, which had been rejected by the political body that now proposed this form of taxation for its own colonies. Congress' assertion of its primary right to dispose of the soil in the Northwest was a limitation that the original states found objectionable as colonials themselves, as was the provision in the Ordinance that the new colonies could not tax nonresident owners at a higher rate than residents. The prohibition upon taxing traffic upon the waterways leading into the Mississippi and St. Lawrence prevented the new colonies from using a source of revenue that the original states had been using themselves. This article, thus, placed a heavy financial burden upon the new colonies while it restricted their source of revenue.

Although the geography of the Northwest Territory was imperfectly known at this time, Congress specified, in Article 5, boundaries of not less than three, nor more than five, states to be carved out of it. The new colonists were committed to these boundaries regardless of what their experience of the resources of the territory showed about the economic feasibility of the divisions.

So far, the Ordinance seemed to be building up many of the very complaints that had led to the Revolutionary War. The concluding section of Article 5, concerning the procedure for changing the status of a colony to that of a state, without doubt prevented open revolts in the new American colonies, although there were periods of discontent before the various territories were admitted to the Union. Before a colony could be admitted, the Ordinance specified sixty-thousand free inhabitants, a republican constitution, and conformity to the provisions of the Ordinance. To take care of emergencies, the article concluded by temporizing the population requirement to allow admission of new states when "consistent with the general interest."

The concluding substantive article prohibited slavery in the Northwest Territory, while it included a fugitive-slave provision. There was a good deal of antislavery sentiment during this period, especially in the northern states, and because the territory regulated by this Ordinance was directly west of the states that had already passed laws prohibiting slavery, the Ordinance implicitly expressed the opinion that the emigrants to the new colonies would mostly be from the northern states. With the fugitive-slave provision, the prohibition of slavery in the Northwest actually ratified what Congress took to be the sentiment in the original states.

The Ordinance of 1787 is hardly a document advocating self-determination and the rights of man. Rather, it is a plan for a colonial system that seems very much modeled on the British colonial system. Congress, however, regularized the British procedures and by so doing tightened the home government's control over the colonies. Congress clearly looked upon the colonies, in their first state of development, as a financial asset of the home government. Only after they had passed through a process beginning with absolute government by an appointed official and continuing through a period in which this absolute government was tempered somewhat by an elected house of representatives, were the colonies considered fit to be members of the union of states. Political freedom for colonies, it would seem, could only come after a period of tutelage. In this document, Congress expressed its opinion that untaught men do not form republican governments.

That this opinion was overt and not simply implied in the action of Congress is clear from a letter that Richard Henry Lee, a member of the committee that drafted the Ordinance, wrote to Washington two days after its passage. Although the original states might have "democratic forms," as Lee put it in another letter written at the end of July, the Northwest Territory required "for the security of property among uninformed, and perhaps licentious people, as the greater part of those who go there are, that a strong toned government should exist, and the rights of property be clearly defined."

The feeling that the experience of the original states was necessary for republican government was common among diverse segments of the American revolutionary generation. Writing the history of the American experience from different points of view at the beginning of the nineteenth century, the radical republican, Mercy Otis Warren, and the extreme federalist, John Marshall, agreed upon the experiential basis of the government adopted by the United States. As early as 1781, Jefferson had expressed doubts, in *Notes on Virginia*, about the ability of those who had not lived through the colonial experience and the Revolution to understand republican institutions. European immigrants, he wrote, "will infuse into it [i.e., government] their spirit, warp and bias its direction, and render it a heterogeneous, incoherent, distracted mass." Thus the Americans were quick to adopt the mistrust home governments seem always to have of their colonies. The principles of self-determination they had so proudly proclaimed in their Declaration of Independence were now absorbed in their hopes and fears concerning their own self-determined form of government.

V

The Leader of the Consensus

Thomas Jefferson

FIRST INAUGURAL ADDRESS
AT WASHINGTON, D. C.

March 4, 1801

Friends and Fellow-Citizens.

(1) Called upon to undertake the duties of the first executive
office of our country, I avail myself of the presence of that portion of my fellow-citizens which is here assembled to express
my grateful thanks for the favor with which they have been
pleased to look toward me, to declare a sincere consciousness
that the task is above my talents, and that I approach it with
those anxious and awful presentiments which the greatness of
the charge and the weakness of my powers so justly inspire.
A rising nation, spread over a wide and fruitful land, travers-
ing all the seas with the rich productions of their industry,
engaged in commerce with nations who feel power and forget
right, advancing rapidly to destinies beyond the reach of mor-
tal eye—when I contemplate these transcendent objects, and
see the honor, the happiness, and the hopes of this beloved
country committed to the issue and the auspices of this day, I

shrink from the contemplation, and humble myself before the magnitude of the undertaking. Utterly, indeed, should I despair did not the presence of many whom I here see remind me that in the other high authorities provided by our Constitution I shall find resources of wisdom, of virtue, and of zeal on which to rely under all difficulties. To you, then, gentlemen, who are charged with the sovereign functions of legislation, and to those associated with you, I look with encouragement for that guidance and support which may enable us to steer with safety the vessel in which we are all embarked amidst the conflicting elements of a troubled world.

(2) During the contest of opinion through which we have passed the animation of discussions and of exertions has sometimes worn an aspect which might impose on strangers unused to think freely and to speak and to write what they think; but this being now decided by the voice of the nation, announced according to the rules of the Constitution, all will, of course, arrange themselves under the will of the law, and unite in common efforts for the common good. All, too, will bear in mind this sacred principle, that though the will of the majority is in all cases to prevail, that will to be rightful must be reasonable; that the minority possesses their equal rights, which equal law must protect, and to violate would be oppression. Let us, then, fellow-citizens, unite with one heart and one mind. Let us restore to social intercourse that harmony and affection without which liberty and even life itself are but dreary things. And let us reflect that, having banished from our land that religious intolerance under which mankind so long bled and suffered, we have yet gained little if we countenance a political intolerance as despotic, as wicked, and capable of as bitter and bloody persecutions. During the throes and convulsions of the ancient world, during the agonizing

spasms of infuriated man, seeking through blood and slaughter his long-lost liberty, it was not wonderful that the agitation of the billows should reach even this distant and peaceful shore; that this should be more felt and feared by some and less by others, and should divide opinions as to measures of safety. But every difference of opinion is not a difference of principle. We have called by different names brethren of the same principle. We are all Republicans, we are all Federalists. If there be any among us who would wish to dissolve this Union or to change its republican form, let them stand undisturbed as monuments of the safety with which error of opinion may be tolerated where reason is left free to combat it. I know, indeed, that some honest men fear that a republican government can not be strong, that this Government is not strong enough; but would the honest patriot, in the full tide of successful experiment, abandon a government which has so far kept us free and firm on the theoretic and visionary fear that this Government, the world's best hope, may by possibility want energy to preserve itself? I trust not. I believe this, on the contrary, the strongest Government on earth. I believe it the only one where every man, at the call of the law, would fly to the standard of the law, and would meet invasions of the public order as his own personal concern. Sometimes it is said that man can not be trusted with the government of himself. Can he, then, be trusted with the government of others? Or have we found angels in the forms of kings to govern him? Let history answer this question.

(3) Let us, then, with courage and confidence pursue our own Federal and Republican principles, our attachment to union and representative government. Kindly separated by nature and a wide ocean from the exterminating havoc of one quarter of the globe; too high-minded to endure the degradations of

the others; possessing a chosen country, with room enough for our descendants to the thousandth and thousandth generation; entertaining a due sense of our equal right to the use of our own faculties, to the acquisitions of our own industry, to honor and confidence from our fellow-citizens, resulting not from birth, but from our actions and their sense of them; enlightened by a benign religion, professed, indeed, and practiced in various forms, yet all of them inculcating honesty, truth, temperance, gratitude, and the love of man; acknowledging and adoring an overruling Providence, which by all its dispensations proves that it delights in the happiness of man here and his greater happiness hereafter—with all these blessings, what more is necessary to make us a happy and a prosperous people? Still one thing more, fellow-citizens—a wise and frugal Government, which shall restrain men from injuring one another, shall leave them otherwise free to regulate their own pursuits of industry and improvement, and shall not take from the mouth of labor the bread it has earned. This is the sum of good government, and this is necessary to close the circle of our felicities.

(4) About to enter, fellow-citizens, on the exercise of duties which comprehend everything dear and valuable to you, it is proper you should understand what I deem the essential principles of our Government, and consequently those which ought to shape its Administration. I will compress them within the narrowest compass they will bear, stating the general principle, but not all its limitations. [1] Equal and exact justice to all men, of whatever state or persuasion, religious or political; [2] peace, commerce, and honest friendship with all nations, entangling alliances with none; [3] the support of the State governments in all their rights, as the most competent administrations for our domestic concerns and the surest bulwarks

against antirepublican tendencies; [4] the preservation of the
General Government in its whole constitutional vigor, as the
sheet anchor of our peace at home and safety abroad; [5] a
jealous care of the right of election by the people—a mild and
safe corrective of abuses which are lopped by the sword of revolution where peaceable remedies are unprovided; [6] absolute acquiescence in the decisions of the majority, the vital
principle of republics, from which is no appeal but to force,
the vital principle and immediate parent of despotism; [7] a
well-disciplined militia, our best reliance in peace and for the
first moments of war, till regulars may relieve them; [8] the
supremacy of the civil over the military authority; [9] economy
in the public expense, that labor may be lightly burthened;
[10] the honest payment of our debts and sacred preservation
of the public faith; [11] encouragement of agriculture, and of
commerce as its handmaid; [12] the diffusion of information
and arraignment of all abuses at the bar of the public reason;
[13] freedom of religion; [14] freedom of the press, [15] and
freedom of person under the protection of the habeas corpus,
[16] and trial by juries impartially selected. These principles
form the bright constellation which has gone before us and
guided our steps through an age of revolution and reforma-
tion. The wisdom of our sages and blood of our heroes have
been devoted to their attainment. They should be the creed
of our political faith, the text of civic instruction, the touch-
stone by which to try the services of those we trust; and should
we wander from them in moments of error or of alarm, let us
hasten to retrace our steps and to regain the road which alone
leads to peace, liberty, and safety.

(5) I repair, then, fellow-citizens, to the post you have assigned
me. With experience enough in subordinate offices to have
seen the difficulties of this the greatest of all, I have learnt to

expect that it will rarely fall to the lot of imperfect man to retire from this station with the reputation and the favor which bring him into it. Without pretentions to that high confidence you reposed in our first and greatest revolutionary character, whose preeminent services had entitled him to the first place in his country's love and destined for him the fairest page in the volume of faithful history, I ask so much confidence only as may give firmness and effect to the legal administration of your affairs. I shall often go wrong through defect of judgment. When right, I shall often be thought wrong by those whose positions will not command a view of the whole ground. I ask your indulgence for my own errors, which will never be intentional, and your support against the errors of others, who may condemn what they would not if seen in all its parts. The approbation implied by your suffrage is a great consolation to me for the past, and my future solicitude will be to retain the good opinion of those who have bestowed it in advance, to conciliate that of others by doing them all the good in my power, and to be instrumental to the happiness and freedom of all.

(6) Relying, then, on the patronage of your good will, I advance with obedience to the work, ready to retire from it whenever you become sensible how much better choice it is in your power to make. And may that Infinite Power which rules the destinies of the universe lead our councils to what is best, and give them a favorable issue for your peace and prosperity.

The Leader of the Consensus

COMMENTARY

THE Presidential campaign of 1800 continued the struggle over the proper nature of government. Almost as soon as Congress met under the new Constitution, in the spring of 1789, the parties produced by the ratification controversy saw implications of anarchy or tyranny in each other's proposals. Federalists, led by Secretary of the Treasury Hamilton, advocated governmental aid to industry, commerce, shipping, and finance through management of federal fiscal policies. Led by Secretary of State Jefferson, Republicans opposed these policies while advocating the minimal federal government they thought best for agrarian welfare. In foreign affairs, Republicans wanted to continue ties established with France during the Revolution, while Federalists advocated repeal of the treaties after the execution of Louis XVI and French declarations of war on Britain, Spain, and Holland.

Sides were taken in reaction to the French Revolution, with Federalists picturing French sympathizers as agents of anarchy, and Republicans charging that British sympathizers were transforming the federal government into a tyranny. Late in the decade of the 1790's, the controversy over the Alien and Sedition Acts seemed to substantiate these suspicions. As Vice-President during Adams's administration, Jefferson arranged for the Virginia and Kentucky legislatures to pass resolutions, written by Madison and himself, asserting the right of the states to "interpose" themselves between their citizens and the federal government when it attempted to enforce an "unconstitutional" law. Jefferson's active opposition to the Alien and Sedition Acts confirmed the Federalist view that he was at the head of a movement to reduce the government to anarchy, while these laws themselves confirmed the Republican view that Federalists were bent upon transforming the federal government into an instrument of tyranny.

The campaign of 1800, between Adams and Charles Cotesworth Pinckney as Federalist candidates and Jefferson and Aaron Burr for the Republicans, was particularly bitter. Both sides charged the other with the most heinous acts they could imagine. Adams was charged with fiscal mismanagement for his own advantage and Jefferson with sexual irregularities with his slaves. The real issues revolved around opposing attitudes toward Britain and France, the Alien and Sedition Acts, and increased direct federal taxation, which the administration argued was necessary to cover heavy defense spending required by the unstable conditions in Europe. Although the Republicans had an eight-electoral-vote lead over Adams, because every Republican elector had voted for Burr as well as for

Jefferson, the tie threw the election into the House of Representatives, which Federalists controlled.

Because Federalists regarded Burr as an unprincipled opportunist and Jefferson as a man with dangerous principles, the choice was of the lesser evil. The Federalist caucus first decided to back Burr. Voting by states, as required by the Constitution, resulted in a tie for thirty-five ballots. During this period, there were a great number of complicated plots. Finally, seven days after the count of the Electoral College vote, Hamilton's opinion that Jefferson was preferable to a "profligate" like Burr changed enough votes to elect Jefferson by ten states on February 17, 1801.

In his Inaugural Address, Jefferson faced the necessity of disarming the Federalists, if he intended to unite the country. If he wanted to defeat the Federalists completely, on the other hand, he would have to rally his followers and urge them on to even greater political devotion and sacrifice. This choice was in many ways the most important he would have to make during his presidency. The position and attitude taken at the beginning of an enterprise always becomes the baseline from which all other statements and actions move. Not only does an audience tend to judge by first impressions; anyone tends to govern his own actions by the impressions he thinks he first has made upon his audience. Of course, Jefferson's potential audience already had opinions about his character and political position. His past political statements led all to think of him as a man who would not compromise his principles, but those who remembered his governorship of Virginia during the Revolution might wonder about his courage and efficiency. If he made his inaugural address a rallying cry for the complete victory of Republicanism, the Federalist part of his audience would have its worst fears confirmed. A temporizing speech, on the other hand, would disillusion the more militant Republicans, the group he had to count on for constant support. It would seem that any choice of tone and position for the inaugural address would weaken his position as president.

Jefferson had to address himself to an immediate audience of the assembled federal legislature and to a general audience of Americans that might still be reading his speech after several weeks. He could not offset mistakes in tone with other remarks the next day, as public figures have been able to do since the development of radio. His attempt in the opening paragraph to conciliate the Congress that had elected him was a bow to Federalists that he would have to live with. The humble stance he took in this paragraph, however, was one that could appeal to both Federalists and Republicans. To Republicans, humility was proper because it fit their principles of strong legislature and weak executive. Federalists would have been reassured by Jefferson's humility because they naturally expected the victor in a closely fought contest to exult in his conquest. By picturing his entire audience as members of a "rising nation," Jefferson flatters them and so disarms the skepticism either side might have felt at his humble tone. His statement that his own poor powers would be supported by both the Constitution and other elected members of the government could appeal also to both sides of the political debate. Because the Federalists retained some power in the Supreme Court and in Congress, they could feel that he might find strength in their "wisdom, virtue, and zeal," while the Republicans' principles dictated that a president ought to rely upon the Constitution. Paragraph 1, then, was calculated to disarm both the general and specific audiences and to put them in a frame of mind willing to listen to what he had to say.

Jefferson opened paragraph 2 by answering a question he

assumed to be uppermost in the mind of his audience. Can a country appearing to be as bitterly divided as the United States in the recent election survive? He answered this implied question by appealing to principles of republican government. Only those failing to understand republicanism and Americans could really ask such a question, Jefferson asserted, because Americans were used to settling controversy through means provided by their Constitution. In asserting the principle that majority rule protects minority rights, Jefferson both reassured Federalists and subtly made clear that there would be no repetition of the trials under the Alien and Sedition Acts. The first half of this paragraph concludes with three parallel appeals to the audience that follow from the republican principle of majority rule respecting minority right. Jefferson appealed for what is called consensus today in these three "let us" sentences.

In the latter half of paragraph 2, Jefferson attempted an analysis of the bitterness of the recent election that was designed to show that Americans were in fact united on principles. The mixed metaphor of billowing spasms attempts to show that differences of opinion about governmental operation resulted from different views of European events and not from indigenous American conditions. Jefferson's distinction between opinion and principle allowed him to make the famous statement: "We are all Republicans, we are all Federalists." He believed this to be true because all Americans were (lower case) republicans who had learned from history that republican government was the only reasonable form, since, as Jefferson attempted to demonstrate through the rhetorical questions concluding the paragraph, a republican government could tolerate even those opposed to republicanism. This reliance upon rhetorical questions shows Jefferson's conviction, or hope, that his audience really is united on principles, because such questions can be effective only when there is consensus.

Turning from the past to the future in paragraph 3, Jefferson listed the conditions necessary for the fulfillment of American society, "to make us a happy and a prosperous people." There are three categories of conditions. First, Americans were separated, in a land large enough for them, from the "exterminating havoc" of Europe. Second, there were four felicitous aspects of the American character. Americans are too independent ever to be subjected to others. Each has a sense of the equality of men. The various forms of their "benign religion" inculcate "honesty, truth, temperance, gratitude, and the love of man." Finally, they have a true understanding of God's will for man, which Jefferson defined as happiness here and hereafter. With these advantages, government, the third category, could be narrowly restricted. A "wise and frugal Government" is characterized by three things. First, it restrains men from hurting each other. Then it leaves them alone to develop and regulate their own business. Finally, it taxes lightly. The general description of government Jefferson gave is indeed simple.

Attempting to give the general description specificity, Jefferson, in paragraph 4, listed sixteen "essential principles of our Government." These points can easily be grouped under these heads: civil rights (points [1], [12], [13], [14], [15], [16]), foreign affairs (point [2]), political rights (points [5] and [6]), state's rights (point [3]), and domestic policies (points [4], [7], [8], [9], [10], [11]). The points concerning civil and state's rights follow the first ten amendments to the Constitution, with Jefferson's addition that state governments counteract "antirepublican tendencies" (his audience was free to assume that he meant in the federal government). His one point concerning foreign affairs introduced into American diplomacy the phrase "entangling alliances with none." On political rights, he merely reaffirmed the doctrine of majority decision in elections. His points concerning the domestic policies of the federal government follow closely the provisions of the Constitution. Two points only, [9] and [11], can be considered additions to it. Economy in government had been one of the Republican arguments against Hamilton's fiscal policies in the 1790's, while encouragement of agriculture had been the Republican economic position opposing encouragement of industry that Federalists had advocated. Immediately after listing these points, which at the beginning of the paragraph Jefferson had identified as his own understanding of the principles of American government, he expands them to be the guiding principles of all Americans. Not only do Americans already agree upon these principles, but they ought to continue to test the actions of their government by them. Nothing new needs to be added. These and only these principles will keep the United States on the "road which alone leads to peace, liberty, and safety."

What Jefferson excluded from the "essential principles of our Government" is more indicative of his conception of the nature of government than what he expressly stated. There is no mention of the United States' role in world affairs, except that she should keep free of them. "Encouragement" of agriculture and commerce is far removed from positive concern with the growth of the total economy. There is no mention of government's role in the development of education, science, or the arts. Nor did he mention such governmental concerns as post, public health, highways and harbors. Just as his general description of government was very simple in paragraph 3, the specific concerns he saw fit to mention in paragraph 4 are narrowly circumscribed. In his view, the federal government should function in a largely negative way to preserve the republicanism Americans already possess.

In paragraph 5, Jefferson returned to the humble stance of the opening paragraph. By offering his opinion that he has not the universal confidence placed in him that Washington had, he sought to disarm criticism, again. His piety toward the electorate is expressed in hopes of retaining the confidence of those who voted for him and for conciliating those who opposed him through efforts aimed at the "happiness and freedom of all." In the concluding paragraph, he expanded this piety to include God as well as the people, for it was, after all, Providence that controlled the popular will, in the popular theology of that day. He aims to hold the office only so long as the people cannot make a better choice. This attitude that the president is a representative who follows the will of the people is the outstanding republican principle Jefferson used to organize his First Inaugural Address.

Looking at the development of the speech, we see that Jefferson moved from a humble plea for consensus, through a definition of the American land and people, to a humble plea for confidence. This movement resulted from choices Jefferson made among the almost limitless possibilities open to develop a speech that had to make some reference to the circumstances of his election and had to say something about his plans for the presidency. The choice of the humble stance at beginning and end reflects a general view that largely determined Jefferson's specific choices.

Jefferson's humility is the reverse of an abject pose. Indeed, it might seem that the self-deprecation of paragraphs 1, 5, and 6 is contradicted both by distinctions between the apparent and the real, opinion and principle, and by analysis of the reason for the differences between Federalists and Republicans, in paragraph 2 as well as by the confidence implicit in the definition of American character and the assertion of American principles of government in paragraphs 3 and 4. Arguments from definition and relationship, such as those used in these three paragraphs, imply a constant order in a universe governed by inexorable natural laws. As such, they are favored by men who conclude their arguments with appeals to "an overruling Providence," and "that Infinite Power which rules the destinies of the universe," as did Jefferson in paragraphs 3 and 6. When it is believed that this power expresses itself through the will of the people, then humility before God and the people is the only proper stance. For one who understands something of the nature of the Providential will through understanding the will of the people, as Jefferson believed he did, humility is perfectly compatible with an assertiveness that pronounces on principles of government. The assertiveness is not personal, but is an expression of principles upon which all men will agree when they investigate the situation thoroughly.

The view of the President Jefferson expressed in the First Inaugural Address, then, is of one who both leads and follows the people. The President is a kind of philosopher or teacher, in the sense that Socrates pictured the philosopher as a midwife. He helps the people give birth to their own political ideas, which originate in God's plan for the "happiness of man here and his greater happiness hereafter." Jefferson's speech is couched in general rather than in specific terms because it is the president's job to keep the end of government—"the happiness and freedom of all"—constantly in mind while helping to put into practice ideas that are born in political controversy, such as the election of 1800. In his First Inaugural Address, Jefferson stated a view of republican government that he believed all men would have to agree with, once it was clearly put before them. The form the speech took resulted from the specific need Jefferson felt, as a result of the close election, to appeal for consensus, but this choice depended upon his general view of the nature of God, man, government, and political leadership.

V I

Self-preservation by Strict Construction

John Marshall

WILLIAM MARBURY

v.

JAMES MADISON

Secretary of State of the United States

February, 1803

Opinion of the court.

(1) At the last term on the affidavits then read and filed with
the clerk, a rule was granted in this case, requiring the secretary of state to shew cause why a mandamus should not issue,
directing him to deliver to William Marbury his commission
as a justice of the peace for the county of Washington, in the
district of Columbia.

(2) No cause has been shewn, and the present motion is for a
mandamus. The peculiar delicacy of this case, the novelty of
some of its circumstances, and the real difficulty attending the
points which occur in it, require a complete exposition of the
principles, on which the opinion to be given by the court, is
founded.

(3) These principles have been, on the side of the applicant,

very ably argued at the bar. In rendering the opinion of the court, there will be some departure in form, though not in substance, from the points stated in that argument.

(4) In the order in which the court has viewed this subject, the following questions have been considered and decided.

1st. Has the applicant a right to the commission he demands?

2dly. If he has a right, and that right has been violated, do the laws of his country afford him a remedy?

3dly. If they do afford him a remedy, is it a *mandamus* issuing from this court?

(5) The first object of enquiry is,

1st. Has the applicant a right to the commission he demands?

(6) His right originates in an act of congress passed in February 1801, concerning the district of Columbia.

(7) After dividing the district into two counties, the 11th section of this law, enacts, "that there shall be appointed in and for each of the said counties, such number of discreet persons to be justices of the peace as the president of the United States shall, from time to time, think expedient, to continue in office for five years.

(8) It appears, from the affidavits, that in compliance with this law, a commission for William Marbury as a justice of peace for the county of Washington, was signed by John Adams, then president of the United States; after which the seal of the United States was affixed to it; but the commission has never reached the person for whom it was made out.

(9) In order to determine whether he is entitled to this com-

mission, it becomes necessary to enquire whether he has been appointed to the office. For if he has been appointed, the law continues him in office for five years, and he is entitled to the possession of those evidences of office, which, being completed, became his property.

(10) The 2d section of the 2d article of the constitution, declares, that, "the president shall nominate, and, by and with "the advice and consent of the senate, shall appoint ambas- "sadors, other public ministers and consuls, and all other "officers of the United States, whose appointments are not "otherwise provided for."

(11) The third section declares, that "he shall commission "all the officers of the United States."

(12) An act of congress directs the secretary of state to keep the seal of the United States, "to make out and record, and affix the said seal to all civil commissions to officers of the United States, to be appointed by the President, by and with the consent of the senate, or by the President alone; provided that the said seal shall not be affixed to any commission before the same shall have been signed by the President of the United States."

(13) These are the clauses of the constitution and laws of the United States, which affect this part of the case. They seem to contemplate three distinct operations:

1st, The nomination. This is the sole act of the President, and is completely voluntary.

2d. The appointment. This is also the act of the President, and is also a voluntary act, though it can only be performed by and with the advice and consent of the senate.

3d. The commission. To grant a commission to a person

appointed, might perhaps be deemed a duty enjoined by the constitution. "He shall," says that instrument, "commission all the officers of the United States."

(14) The acts of appointing to office, and commissioning the person appointed, can scarcely be considered as one and the same; since the power to perform them is given in two separate and distinct sections of the constitution. The distinction between the appointment and the commission will be rendered more apparent, by adverting to that provision in the second section of the second article of the constitution, which authorizes congress "to vest, by law, the appointment of such inferior officers, as they think proper, in the President alone, in the courts of law, or in the heads of departments;" thus contemplating cases where the law may direct the President to commission an officer appointed by the courts, or by the heads of departments. In such a case, to issue a commission would be apparently a duty distinct from the appointment, the performance of which, perhaps, could not legally be refused.

(15) Although that clause of the constitution which requires the President to commission all the officers of the United States, may never have been applied to officers appointed otherwise than by himself, yet it would be difficult to deny the legislative power to apply it to such cases. Of consequence the constitutional distinction between the appointment to an office and the commission of an officer, who has been appointed, remains the same as if in practice the President had commissioned officers appointed by an authority other than his own.

(16) It follows too, from the existence of this distinction, that, if an appointment was to be evidenced by any public act,

other than the commission, the performance of such public act would create the officer; and if he was not removeable at the will of the President, would either give him a right to his commission, or enable him to perform the duties without it.

(17) These observations are premised solely for the purpose of rendering more intelligible those which apply more directly to the particular case under consideration.

(18) This is an appointment made by the President, by and with the advice and consent of the senate, and is evidenced by no act but the commission itself. In such a case therefore the commission and the appointment seem inseparable; it being almost impossible to shew an appointment otherwise than by proving the existence of a commission; still the commission is not necessarily the appointment; though conclusive evidence of it.

(19) But at what stage does it amount to this conclusive evidence?

(20) The answer to this question seems an obvious one. The appointment being the sole act of the President, must be completely evidenced, when it is shewn that he has done every thing to be performed by him.

(21) Should the commission, instead of being evidence of an appointment, even be considered as constituting the appointment itself; still it would be made when the last act to be done by the President was performed, or, at furthest, when the commission was complete.

(22) The last act to be done by the President, is the signature of the commission. He has then acted on the advice and consent of the senate to his own nomination. The time for delib-

eration has then passed. He has decided. His judgment, on the advice and consent of the senate concurring with his nomination, has been made, and the officer is appointed. This appointment is evidenced by an open, unequivocal act; and being the last act required from the person making it, necessarily excludes the idea of its being, so far as respects the appointment, an inchoate and incomplete transaction.

(23) Some point of time must be taken when the power of the executive over an officer, not removeable at his will, must cease. That point of time must be when the constitutional power of appointment has been exercised. And this power has been exercised when the last act, required from the person possessing the power, has been performed. This last act is the signature of the commission. This idea seems to have prevailed with the legislature, when the act passed, converting the department of foreign affairs into the department of state. By that act it is enacted, that the secretary of state shall keep the seal of the United States, "and shall make out and record, and "shall affix the said seal to all civil commissions to officers of "the United States, to be appointed by the President:" "Pro-"vided that the said seal shall not be affixed to any commission, "before the same shall have been signed by the President of "the United States; nor to any other instrument or act, with-"out the special warrant of the President therefor."

(24) The signature is a warrant for affixing the great seal to the commission; and the great seal is only to be affixed to an instrument which is complete. It attests, by an act supposed to be of public notoriety, the verity of the Presidential signature.

(25) It is never to be affixed till the commission is signed, because the signature, which gives force and effect to the com-

mission, is conclusive evidence that the appointment is made.

(26) The commission being signed, the subsequent duty of the secretary of state is prescribed by law, and not to be guided by the will of the President. He is to affix the seal of the United States to the commission, and is to record it.

(27) This is not a proceeding which may be varied, if the judgment of the executive shall suggest one more eligible; but is a precise course accurately marked out by law, and is to be strictly pursued. It is the duty of the secretary of state to conform to the law, and in this he is an officer of the United States, bound to obey the laws. He acts, in this respect, as has been very properly stated at the bar, under the authority of law, and not by the instructions of the President. It is a ministerial act which the law enjoins on a particular officer for a particular purpose.

(28) If it should be supposed, that the solemnity of affixing the seal, is necessary not only to the validity of the commission, but even to the completion of an appointment, still when the seal is affixed the appointment is made, and the commission is valid. No other solemnity is required by law; no other act is to be performed on the part of government. All that the executive can do to invest the person with his office, is done; and unless the appointment be then made, the executive cannot make one without the co-operation of others. \

(29) After searching anxiously for the principles on which a contrary opinion may be supported, none have been found which appear of sufficient force to maintain the opposite doctrine.

(30) Such as the imagination of the court could suggest, have been very deliberately examined, and after allowing them all

the weight which it appears possible to give them, they do not shake the opinion which has been formed.

(31) In considering this question, it has been conjectured that the commission may have been assimilated to a deed, to the validity of which, delivery is essential.

(32) This idea is founded on the supposition that the commission is not merely *evidence* of an appointment, but is itself the actual appointment; a supposition by no means unquestionable. But for the purpose of examining this objection fairly, let it be conceded, that the principle, claimed for its support, is established.

(33) The appointment being, under the constitution, to be made by the President *personally,* the delivery of the deed of appointment, if necessary to its completion, must be made by the President also. It is not necessary that the livery should be made personally to the grantee of the office: It never is so made. The law would seem to contemplate that it should be made to the secretary of state, since it directs the secretary to affix the seal to the commission *after* it shall have been signed by the President. If then the act of livery be necessary to give validity to the commission, it has been delivered when executed and given to the secretary for the purpose of being sealed, recorded, and transmitted to the party.

(34) But in all cases of letters patent, certain solemnities are required by law, which solemnities are the evidences of the validity of the instrument. A formal delivery to the person is not among them. In cases of commissions, the sign manual of the President, and the seal of the United States, are those solemnities. This objection therefore does not touch the case.

(35) It has also occurred as possible, and barely possible, that

the transmission of the commission, and the acceptance thereof, might be deemed necessary to complete the right of the plaintiff.

(36) The transmission of the commission, is a practice directed by convenience, but not by law. It cannot therefore be necessary to constitute the appointment which must precede it, and which is the mere act of the President. If the executive required that every person appointed to an office, should himself take means to procure his commission, the appointment would not be the less valid on that account. The appointment is the sole act of the President; the transmission of the commission is the sole act of the officer to whom that duty is assigned, and may be accelerated or retarded by circumstances which can have no influence on the appointment. A commission is transmitted to a person already appointed; not to a person to be appointed or not, as the letter enclosing the commission should happen to get into the post-office and reach him in safety, or to miscarry.

(37) It may have some tendency to elucidate this point, to enquire, whether the possession of the original commission be indispensably necessary to authorize a person, appointed to any office, to perform the duties of that office. If it was necessary, then a loss of the commission would lose the office. Not only negligence, but accident or fraud, fire or theft, might deprive an individual of his office. In such a case, I presume it could not be doubted, but that a copy from the record of the office of the secretary of state, would be, to every intent and purpose, equal to the original. The act of congress has expressly made it so. To give that copy validity, it would not be necessary to prove that the original had been transmitted and afterwards lost. The copy would be complete evidence

that the original had existed, and that the appointment had been made, but, not that the original had been transmitted. If indeed it should appear that the original had been mislaid in the office of state, that circumstance would not affect the operation of the copy. When all the requisites have been performed which authorize a recording officer to record any instrument whatever, and the order for that purpose has been given, the instrument is, in law, considered as recorded, although the manual labour of inserting it in a book kept for that purpose may not have been performed.

(38) In the case of commissions, the law orders the secretary of state to record them. When therefore they are signed and sealed, the order for their being recorded is given; and whether inserted in the book or not, they are in law recorded.

(39) A copy of this record is declared equal to the original, and the fees, to be paid by a person requiring a copy, are ascertained by law. Can a keeper of a public record, erase therefrom a commission which has been recorded? Or can he refuse a copy thereof to a person demanding it on the terms prescribed by law?

(40) Such a copy would, equally with the original, authorize the justice of peace to proceed in the performance of his duty, because it would, equally with the original, attest his appointment.

(41) If the transmission of a commission be not considered as necessary to give validity to an appointment; still less is its acceptance. The appointment is the sole act of the President; the acceptance is the sole act of the officer, and is, in plain common sense, posterior to the appointment. As he may resign, so may he refuse to accept: but neither the one, nor the other, is capable of rendering the appointment a non-entity.

(42) That this is the understanding of the government, is apparent from the whole tenor of its conduct.

(43) A commission bears date, and the salary of the officer commences from his appointment; not from the transmission or acceptance of his commission. When a person, appointed to any office, refuses to accept that office, the successor is nominated in the place of the person who has declined to accept, and not in the place of the person who had been previously in office, and had created the original vacancy.

(44) It is therefore decidedly the opinion of the court, that when a commission has been signed by the President, the appointment is made; and that the commission is complete, when the seal of the United States has been affixed to it by the secretary of state.

(45) Where an officer is removeable at the will of the executive, the circumstance which completes his appointment is of no concern; because the act is at any time revocable; and the commission may be arrested, if still in the office. But when the officer is not removeable at the will of the executive, the appointment is not revocable, and cannot be annulled. It has conferred legal rights which cannot be resumed.

(46) The discretion of the executive is to be exercised until the appointment has been made. But having once made the appointment, his power over the office is terminated in all cases, where, by law, the officer is not removeable by him. The right to the office is *then* in the person appointed, and he has the absolute, unconditional, power of accepting or rejecting it.

(47) Mr. Marbury, then, since his commission was signed by the President, and sealed by the secretary of state, was appointed; and as the law creating the office, gave the officer a

right to hold for five years, independent of the executive, the appointment was not revocable; but vested in the officer legal rights, which are protected by the laws of his country.

(48) To withhold his commission, therefore, is an act deemed by the court not warranted by law, but violative of a vested legal right.

(49) This brings us to the second enquiry; which is,

2dly. If he has a right, and that right has been violated, do the laws of his country afford him a remedy?

(50) The very essence of civil liberty certainly consists in the right of every individual to claim the protection of the laws, whenever he receives an injury. One of the first duties of government is to afford that protection. In Great Britain the king himself is sued in the respectful form of a petition, and he never fails to comply with the judgment of his court.

(51) In the 3d vol. of his commentaries, p. 23, Blackstone states two cases in which a remedy is afforded by mere operation of law.

"In all other cases," he says, "it is a general and indisputable "rule, that where there is a legal right, there is also a legal "remedy by suit or action at law, whenever that right is in-"vaded."

And afterwards, p. 109, of the same vol. he says, "I am next "to consider such injuries as are cognizable by the courts of "the common law. And herein I shall for the present only "remark, that all possible injuries whatsoever, that did not "fall within the exclusive cognizance of either the ecclesiastical, "military, or maritime tribunals, are for that very reason, "within the cognizance of the common law courts of justice; "for it is a settled and invariable principle in the laws of Eng-

"land, that every right, when withheld, must have a remedy, "and every injury its proper redress."

(52) The government of the United States has been emphatically termed a government of laws, and not of men. It will certainly cease to deserve this high appellation, if the laws furnish no remedy for the violation of a vested legal right.

(53) If this obloquy is to be cast on the jurisprudence of our country, it must arise from the peculiar character of the case.

(54) It behoves us then to enquire whether there be in its composition any ingredient which shall exempt it from legal investigation, or exclude the injured party from legal redress. In pursuing this enquiry the first question which presents itself, is, whether this can be arranged with that class of cases which come under the description of *damnum absque injuria* —a loss without an injury.

(55) This description of cases never has been considered, and it is believed never can be considered, as comprehending offices of trust, of honor or of profit. The office of justice of peace in the district of Columbia is such an office; it is therefore worthy of the attention and guardianship of the laws. It has received that attention and guardianship. It has been created by special act of congress, and has been secured, so far as the laws can give security to the person appointed to fill it, for five years. It is not then on account of the worthlessness of the thing pursued, that the injured party can be alleged to be without remedy.

(56) Is it in the nature of the transaction? Is the act of delivering or withholding a commission to be considered as a mere political act, belonging to the executive department alone, for the performance of which, entire confidence is placed by

our constitution in the supreme executive; and for any misconduct respecting which, the injured indvidual has no remedy?

(57) That there may be such cases is not to be questioned;
but that every act of duty, to be performed in any of the great
departments of government, constitutes such a case, is not to
be admitted.

(58) By the act concerning invalids, passed in June, 1794, vol.
3. p. 112, the secretary at war is ordered to place on the pension list, all persons whose names are contained in a report
previously made by him to congress. If he should refuse to do
so, would the wounded veteran be without remedy? Is it to be
contended that where the law in precise terms, directs the
performance of an act, in which an individual is interested,
the law is incapable of securing obedience to its mandate? Is
it on account of the character of the person against whom the
complaint is made? Is it to be contended that the heads of
departments are not amenable to the laws of their country?

(59) Whatever the practice on particular occasions may be, the
theory of this principle will certainly never be maintained.
No act of the legislature confers so extraordinary a privilege,
nor can it derive countenance from the doctrines of the common law. After stating that personal injury from the king to
a subject is presumed to be impossible, Blackstone, vol. 3. p.
255, says, "but injuries to the rights of property can scarcely
"be committed by the crown without the intervention of its
"officers; for whom, the law, in matters of right, entertains no
"respect or delicacy; but furnishes various methods of de-
"tecting the errors and misconduct of those agents, by whom
"the king has been deceived and induced to do a temporary
"injustice."

(60) By the act passed in 1796, authorising the sale of the

lands above the mouth of Kentucky river (vol. 3d. p. 299) the purchaser, on paying his purchase money, becomes completely entitled to the property purchased; and on producing to the secretary of state, the receipt of the treasurer upon a certificate required by the law, the president of the United States is authorised to grant him a patent. It is further enacted that all patents shall be countersigned by the secretary of state, and recorded in his office. If the secretary of state should choose to withhold this patent; or the patent being lost, should refuse a copy of it; can it be imagined that the law furnishes to the injured person no remedy?

(61) It is not believed that any person whatever would attempt to maintain such a proposition.

(62) It follows then that the question, whether the legality of an act of the head of a department be examinable in a court of justice or not, must always depend on the nature of that act.

(63) If some acts be examinable, and others not, there must be some rule of law to guide the court in the exercise of its jurisdiction.

(64) In some instances there may be difficulty in applying the rule to particular case; but there cannot, it is believed, be much difficulty in laying down the rule.

(65) By the constitution of the United States, the President is invested with certain important political powers, in the exercise of which he is to use his own discretion, and is accountable only to his country in his political character, and to his own conscience. To aid him in the peformance of these duties, he is authorized to appoint certain officers, who act by his authority and in conformity with his orders.

(66) In such cases, their acts are his acts; and whatever opinion

may be entertained of the manner in which executive discretion may be used, still there exists, and can exist, no power to control that discretion. The subjects are political. They respect the nation, not individual rights, and being entrusted to the executive, the decision of the executive is conclusive. The application of this remark will be perceived by adverting to the act of congress for establishing the department of foreign affairs. This officer, as his duties were prescribed by that act, is to conform precisely to the will of the President. He is the mere organ by whom that will is communicated. The acts of such an officer, as an officer, can never be examinable by the courts.

(67) But when the legislature proceeds to impose on that officer other duties; when he is directed peremptorily to perform certain acts; when the rights of individuals are dependent on the performance of those acts; he is so far the officer of the law; is amenable to the laws for his conduct; and cannot at his discretion sport away the vested rights of others.

(68) The conclusion from this reasoning is, that where the heads of departments are the political or confidential agents of the executive, merely to execute the will of the President, or rather to act in cases in which the executive possesses a constitutional or legal discretion, nothing can be more perfectly clear than that their acts are only politically examinable. But where a specific duty is assigned by law, and individual rights depend upon the performance of that duty, it seems equally clear that the individual who considers himself injured, has a right to resort to the laws of his country for a remedy.

(69) If this be the rule, let us enquire how it applies to the case under the consideration of the court.

(70) The power of nominating to the senate, and the power of appointing the person nominated, are political powers, to be exercised by the President according to his own discretion. When he has made an appointment, he has exercised his whole power, and his discretion has been completely applied to the case. If, by law, the officer be removable at the will of the President, then a new appointment may be immediately made, and the rights of the officer are terminated. But as a fact which has existed cannot be made never to have existed, the appointment cannot be annihilated; and consequently if the officer is by law not removable at the will of the President; the rights he has acquired are protected by the law, and are not resumable by the President. They cannot be extinguished by executive authority, and he has the privilege of asserting them in like manner as if they had been derived from any other source.

(71) The question whether a right has vested or not, is, in its nature, judicial, and must be tried by the judicial authority. If, for example, Mr. Marbury had taken the oaths of a magistrate, and proceeded to act as one; in consequence of which a suit had been instituted against him, in which his defence had depended on his being a magistrate; the validity of his appointment must have been determined by judicial authority.

(72) So, if he conceives that, by virtue of his appointment, he has a legal right, either to the commission which has been made out for him, or to a copy of that commission, it is equally a question examinable in a court, and the decision of the court upon it must depend on the opinion entertained of his appointment.

(73) That question has been discussed, and the opinion is,

that the latest point of time which can be taken as that at which the appointment was complete, and evidenced, was when, after the signature of the president, the seal of the United States was affixed to the commission.

(74) It is then the opinion of the court,

1st. That by signing the commission of Mr. Marbury, the president of the United States appointed him a justice of peace, for the county of Washington in the district of Columbia; and that the seal of the United States, affixed thereto by the secretary of state, is conclusive testimony of the verity of the signature, and of the completion of the appointment; and that the appointment conferred on him a legal right to the office for the space of five years.

2dly. That, having this legal title to the office, he has a consequent right to the commission; a refusal to deliver which, is a plain violation of that right, for which the laws of his country afford him a remedy.

(75) It remains to be enquired whether,

3dly. He is entitled to the remedy for which he applies. This depends on,

1st. The nature of the writ applied for, and,

2dly. The power of this court.

1st. The nature of the writ.

(76) Blackstone, in the 3d volume of his commentaries, page 110, defines a mandamus to be, "a command issuing in the "king's name from the court of king's bench, and directed to "any person, corporation, or inferior court of judicature "within the king's dominions, requiring them to do some par- "ticular thing therein specified, which appertains to their "office and duty, and which the court of king's bench has pre-

"viously determined, or at least supposes, to be consonant to
"right and justice."

(77) Lord Mansfield, in 3d Burrows 1266, in the case of the
King v. Baker, et al. states with much precision and explicit-
ness the cases in which this writ may be used.

"Whenever," says that very able judge, "there is a right to
"execute an office, perform a service, or exercise a franchise
"(more especially if it be in a matter of public concern, or
"attended with profit) and a person is kept out of possession,
"or dispossessed of such right, and has no other specific legal
"remedy, this court ought to assist by mandamus, upon rea-
"sons of justice, as the writ expresses, and upon reasons of
"public policy, to preserve peace, order and good govern-
"ment." In the same case he says, "this writ ought to be used
"upon all occasions where the law has established no specific
"remedy, and where in justice and good government there
"ought to be one."

(78) In addition to the authorities now particularly cited,
many others were relied on at the bar, which show how far
the practice has conformed to the general doctrines that have
been just quoted.

(79) This writ, if awarded, would be directed to an officer of
government, and its mandate to him would be, to use the
words of Blackstone, "to do a particular thing therein speci-
"fied, which appertains to his office and duty and which the
"court has previously determined, or at least supposes, to be
"consonant to right and justice." Or, in the words of Lord
Mansfield, the applicant, in this case, has a right to execute an
office of public concern, and is kept out of possession of that
right.

(80) These circumstances certainly concur in this case.

(81) Still, to render the mandamus a proper remedy, the officer to whom it is to be directed, must be one to whom, on legal principles, such writ may be directed; and the person applying for it must be without any other specific and legal remedy.

(82) 1st. With respect to the officer to whom it would be directed. The intimate political relation, subsisting between the president of the United States and the heads of departments, necessarily renders any legal investigation of the acts of one of those high officers peculiarly irksome, as well as delicate; and excites some hesitation with respect to the propriety of entering into such investigation. Impressions are often received without much reflection or examination, and it is not wonderful that in such a case as this, the assertion, by an individual, of his legal claims in a court of justice; to which claims it is the duty of that court to attend; should at first view be considered by some, as an attempt to intrude into the cabinet, and to intermeddle with the prerogatives of the executive.

(83) It is scarcely necessary for the court to disclaim all pretensions to such a jurisdiction. An extravagance, so absurd and excessive, could not have been entertained for a moment. The province of the court is, solely, to decide on the rights of individuals, not to enquire how the executive, or executive officers, perform duties in which they have a discretion. Questions, in their nature political, or which are, by the constitution and laws, submitted to the executive, can never be made in this court.

(84) But, if this be not such a question; if so far from being an intrusion into the secrets of the cabinet, it respects a paper,

which, according to law, is upon record, and to a copy of which the law gives a right, on the payment of ten cents; if it be no intermeddling with a subject, over which the executive can be considered as having exercised any control; what is there in the exalted station of the officer, which shall bar a citizen from asserting, in a court of justice, his legal rights, or shall forbid a court to listen to the claim; or to issue a mandamus, directing the performance of a duty, not depending on executive discretion, but on particular acts of congress and the general principles of law?

(85) If one of the heads of departments commits any illegal act, under color of his office, by which an individual sustains an injury, it cannot be pretended that his office alone exempts him from being sued in the ordinary mode of proceeding, and being compelled to obey the judgment of the law. How then can his office exempt him from this particular mode of deciding on the legality of his conduct, if the case be such a case as would, were any other individual the party complained of, authorize the process?

(86) It is not by the office of the person to whom the writ is directed, but the nature of the thing to be done that the propriety or impropriety of issuing a mandamus, is to be determined. Where the head of a department acts in a case, in which executive discretion is to be exercised; in which he is the mere organ of executive will; it is again repeated, that any application to a court to control, in any respect, his conduct, would be rejected without hesitation.

(87) But where he is directed by law to do a certain act affecting the absolute rights of individuals, in the performance of which he is not placed under the particular direction of the

President, and the performance of which, the President cannot lawfully forbid, and therefore is never presumed to have forbidden; as for example, to record a commission, or a patent for land, which has received all the legal solemnities; or to give a copy of such record; in such cases, it is not perceived on what ground the courts of the country are further excused from the duty of giving judgment, that right be done to an injured individual, than if the same services were to be performed by a person not the head of a department.

(88) This opinion seems not now, for the first time, to be taken up in this country.

(89) It must be well recollected that in 1792, an act passed, directing the secretary at war to place on the pension list such disabled officers and soldiers as should be reported to him, by the circuit courts, which act, so far as the duty was imposed on the courts, was deemed unconstitutional; but some of the judges, thinking that the law might be executed by them in the character of commissioners, proceeded to act and to report in that character.

(90) This law being deemed unconstitutional at the circuits, was repealed, and a different system was established; but the question whether those persons, who had been reported by the judges, as commissioners, were entitled, in consequence of that report, to be placed on the pension list, was a legal question, properly determinable in the courts, although the act of placing such persons on the list was to be performed by the head of a department.

(91) That this question might be properly settled, congress passed an act in February, 1793, making it the duty of the secretary of war, in conjunction with the attorney general, to

take such measures, as might be necessary to obtain an adjudication of the supreme court of the United States on the validity of any such rights, claimed under the act aforesaid.

(92) After the passage of this act, a mandamus was moved for, to be directed to the secretary at war, commanding him to place on the pension list, a person stating himself to be on the report of the judges.

(93) There is, therefore, much reason to believe, that this mode of trying the legal right of the complainant, was deemed by the head of a department, and by the highest law officer of the United States, the most proper which could be selected for the purpose.

(94) When the subject was brought before the court the decision was, not that a mandamus would not lie to the head of a department, directing him to perform an act, enjoined by law, in the performance of which an individual had a vested interest; but that a mandamus ought not to issue in that case—the decision necessarily to be made if the report of the commissioners did not confer on the applicant a legal right.

(95) The judgment in that case, is understood to have decided the merits of all claims of that description; and the persons on the report of the commissioners found it necessary to pursue the mode prescribed by the law subsequent to that which had been deemed unconstitutional, in order to place themselves on the pension list.

(96) The doctrine, therefore, now advanced, is by no means a novel one.

(97) It is true that the mandamus, now moved for, is not for the performance of an act expressly enjoined by statute.

(98) It is to deliver a commission; on which subject the acts of Congress are silent. This difference is not considered as affecting the case. It has already been stated that the applicant has, to that commission, a vested legal right, of which the executive cannot deprive him. He has been appointed to an office, from which he is not removable at the will of the executive; and being so appointed, he has a right to the commission which the secretary has received from the president for his use. The act of congress does not indeed order the secretary of state to send it to him, but it is placed in his hands for the person entitled to it; and cannot be more lawfully withheld by him, than by any other person.

(99) It was at first doubted whether the action of *detinue* was not a specific legal remedy for the commission which has been withheld from Mr. Marbury; in which case a mandamus would be improper. But this doubt has yielded to the consideration that the judgment in *detinue* is for the thing itself, *or* its value. The value of a public office not to be sold, is incapable of being ascertained; and the applicant has a right to the office itself, or to nothing. He will obtain the office by obtaining the commission, or a copy of it from the record.

(100) This, then, is a plain case for a mandamus, either to deliver the commission, or a copy of it from the record; and it only remains to be enquired,
Whether it can issue from this court.

(101) The act to establish the judicial courts of the United States authorizes the supreme court "to issue writs of mandamus, in cases warranted by the principles and usages of law, to any courts appointed, or persons holding office, under the authority of the United States."

(102) The secretary of state, being a person holding an office under the authority of the United States, is precisely within the letter of the description; and if this court is not authorized to issue a writ of mandamus to such an officer, it must be because the law is unconstitutional, and therefore absolutely incapable of conferring the authority, and assigning the duties which its words purport to confer and assign.

(103) The constitution vests the whole judicial power of the United States in one supreme court, and such inferior courts as congress shall, from time to time, ordain and establish. This power is expressly extended to all cases arising under the laws of the United States; and consequently, in some form, may be exercised over the present case; because the right claimed is given by a law of the United States.

(104) In the distribution of this power it is declared that "the "supreme court shall have original jurisdiction in all cases af- "fecting ambassadors, other public ministers and consuls, and "those in which a state shall be a party. In all other cases, the "supreme court shall have appellate jurisdiction."

(105) It has been insisted, at the bar, that as the original grant of jurisdiction, to the supreme and inferior courts, is general, and the clause, assigning original jurisdiction to the supreme court, contains no negative or restrictive words; the power remains to the legislature, to assign original jurisdiction to that court in other cases than those specified in the article which has been recited; provided those cases belong to the judicial power of the United States.

(106) If it had been intended to leave it in the discretion of the legislature to apportion the judicial power between the supreme and inferior courts according to the will of that body,

it would certainly have been useless to have proceeded further than to have defined the judicial power, and the tribunals in which it should be vested. The subsequent part of the section is mere surplussage, is entirely without meaning, if such is to be the construction. If congress remains at liberty to give this court appellate jurisdiction, where the constitution has declared their jurisdiction shall be original; and original jurisdiction where the constitution has declared it shall be appellate; the distribution of jurisdiction, made in the constitution, is form without substance.

(107) Affirmative words are often, in their operation, negative of other objects than those affirmed; and in this case, a negative or exclusive sense must be given to them or they have no operation at all.

(108) It cannot be presumed that any clause in the constitution is intended to be without effect; and therefore such a construction is inadmissible, unless the words require it.

(109) If the solicitude of the convention, respecting our peace with foreign powers, induced a provision that the supreme court should take original jurisdiction in cases which might be supposed to affect them; yet the clause would have proceeded no further than to provide for such cases, if no further restriction on the powers of congress had been intended. That they should have appellate jurisdiction in all other cases, with such exceptions as congress might make, is no restriction; unless the words be deemed exclusive of original jurisdiction.

(110) When an instrument organizing fundamentally a judicial system, divides it into one supreme, and so many inferior courts as the legislature may ordain and establish; then enumerates its powers, and proceeds so far to distribute them, as

to define the jurisdiction of the supreme court by declaring the cases in which it shall take original jurisdiction, and that in others it shall take appellate jurisdiction; the plain import of the words seems to be, that in one class of cases its jurisdiction is original, and not appellate; in the other it is appellate, and not original. If any other construction would render the clause inoperative, that is an additional reason for rejecting such other construction, and for adhering to their obvious meaning.

(111) To enable this court then to issue a mandamus, it must be shewn to be an exercise of appellate jurisdiction, or to be necessary to enable them to exercise appellate jurisdiction.

(112) It has been stated at the bar that the appellate jurisdiction may be exercised in a variety of forms, and that if it be the will of the legislature that a mandamus should be used for that purpose, that will must be obeyed. This is true, yet the jurisdiction must be appellate, not original.

(113) It is the essential criterion of appellate jurisdiction, that it revises and corrects the proceedings in a cause already instituted, and does not create that cause. Although, therefore, a mandamus may be directed to courts, yet to issue such a writ to an officer for the delivery of a paper, is in effect the same as to sustain an original action for that paper, and therefore seems not to belong to appellate, but to original jurisdiction. Neither is it necessary in such a case as this, to enable the court to exercise its appellate jurisdiction.

(114) The authority, therefore, given to the supreme court, by the act establishing the judicial courts of the United States, to issue writs of mandamus to public officers, appears not to be warranted by the constitution; and it becomes necessary to enquire whether a jurisdiction, so conferred, can be exercised.

(115) The question, whether an act, repugnant to the constitution, can become the law of the land, is a question deeply interesting to the United States; but, happily, not of an intricacy proportioned to its interest. It seems only necessary to recognise certain principles, supposed to have been long and well established, to decide it.

(116) That the people have an original right to establish, for their future government, such principles as, in their opinion, shall most conduce to their own happiness, is the basis, on which the whole American fabric has been erected. The exercise of this original right is a very great exertion; nor can it, nor ought it to be frequently repeated. The principles, therefore, so established, are deemed fundamental. And as the authority, from which they proceed, is supreme, and can seldom act, they are designed to be permanent.

(117) This original and supreme will organizes the government, and assigns, to different departments, their respective powers. It may either stop here; or establish certain limits not to be transcended by those departments.

(118) The government of the United States is of the latter description. The powers of the legislature are defined, and limited; and that those limits may not be mistaken, or forgotten, the constitution is written. To what purpose are powers limited, and to what purpose is that limitation committed to writing, if these limits may, at any time, be passed by those intended to be restrained? The distinction, between a government with limited and unlimited powers, is abolished, if those limits do not confine the persons on whom they are imposed, and if acts prohibited and acts allowed, are of equal obligation. It is a proposition too plain to be contested, that

the constitution controls any legislative act repugnant to it; or, that the legislature may alter the constitution by an ordinary act.

(119) Between these alternatives there is no middle ground. The constitution is either a superior, paramount law, unchangeable by ordinary means, or it is on a level with ordinary legislative acts, and like other acts, is alterable when the legislature shall please to alter it.

(120) If the former part of the alternative be true, then a legislative act contrary to the constitution is not law: if the latter part be true, then written constitutions are absurd attempts, on the part of the people, to limit a power, in its own nature illimitable.

(121) Certainly all those who have framed written constitutions contemplate them as forming the fundamental and paramount law of the nation, and consequently the theory of every such government must be, that an act of the legislature, repugnant to the constitution, is void.

(122) This theory is essentially attached to a written constitution, and is consequently to be considered, by this court, as one of the fundamental principles of our society. It is not therefore to be lost sight of in the further consideration of this subject.

(123) If an act of the legislature, repugnant to the constitution, is void, does it, notwithstanding its invalidity, bind the courts, and oblige them to give it effect? Or, in other words, though it be not law, does it constitute a rule as operative as if it was a law? This would be to overthrow in fact what was established in theory; and would seem, at first view, an absurdity too gross

to be insisted on. It shall, however, receive a more attentive consideration.

(124) It is emphatically the province and duty of the judicial department to say what the law is. Those who apply the rule to particular cases, must of necessity expound and interpret that rule. If two laws conflict with each other, the courts must decide on the operation of each.

(125) So if a law be in opposition to the constitution; if both the law and the constitution apply to a particular case, so that the court must either decide that case conformably to the law, disregarding the constitution; or conformably to the constitution, disregarding the law; the court must determine which of these conflicting rules governs the case. This is of the very essence of judicial duty.

(126) If then the courts are to regard the constitution; and the constitution is superior to any ordinary act of the legislature; the constitution, and not such ordinary act, must govern the case to which they both apply.

(127) Those then who controvert the principle that the constitution is to be considered, in court, as a paramount law, are reduced to the necessity of maintaining that courts must close their eyes on the constitution, and see only the law.

(128) This doctrine would subvert the very foundation of all written constitutions. It would declare that an act, which, according to the principles and theory of our government, is entirely void; is yet, in practice, completely obligatory. It would declare, that if the legislature shall do what is expressly forbidden, such act, notwithstanding the express prohibition, is in reality effectual. It would be giving to the legislature a

practical and real omnipotence, with the same breath which professes to restrict their powers within narrow limits. It is prescribing limits, and declaring that those limits may be passed at pleasure.

(129) That it thus reduces to nothing what we have deemed the greatest improvement on political institutions—a written constitution—would of itself be sufficient, in America, where written constitutions have been viewed with so much reverence, for rejecting the construction. But the peculiar expressions of the constitution of the United States furnish additional arguments in favour of its rejection.

(130) The judicial power of the United States is extended to all cases arising under the constitution.

(131) Could it be the intention of those who gave this power, to say that, in using it, the constitution should not be looked into? That a case arising under the constitution should be decided without examining the instrument under which it arises?

(132) This is too extravagant to be maintained.

(133) In some cases then, the constitution must be looked into by the judges. And if they can open it at all, what part of it are they forbidden to read, or to obey?

(134) There are many other parts of the constitution which serve to illustrate this subject.

(135) It is declared that "no tax or duty shall be laid on arti-"cles exported from any state." Suppose a duty on the export of cotton, of tobacco, or of flour; and a suit instituted to recover it. Ought judgment to be rendered in such a case? ought the judges to close their eyes on the constitution, and only see the law?

(136) The constitution declares that "no bill of attainder or "*ex post facto* law shall be passed."

(137) If, however, such a bill should be passed and a person should be prosecuted under it; must the court condemn to death those victims whom the constitution endeavours to preserve?

(138) "No person," says the constitution, "shall be convicted of "treason unless on the testimony of two witnesses to the same "overt act, or on confession in open court."

(139) Here the language of the constitution is addressed especially to the courts. It prescribes, directly for them, a rule of evidence not to be departed from. If the legislature should change that rule, and declare *one* witness, or a confession *out* of court, sufficient for conviction, must the constitutional principle yield to the legislative act?

(140) From these, and many other selections which might be made, it is apparent, that the framers of the constitution contemplated that instrument, as a rule for the government of *courts,* as well as of the legislature.

(141) Why otherwise does it direct the judges to take an oath to support it? This oath certainly applies, in an especial manner, to their conduct in their official character. How immoral to impose it on them, if they were to be used as the instruments, and the knowing instruments, for violating what they swear to support!

(142) The oath of office, too, imposed by the legislature, is completely demonstrative of the legislative opinion on this subject. It is in these words, "I do solemnly swear that I will "administer justice without respect to persons, and do equal

"right to the poor and to the rich; and that I will faithfully
"and impartially discharge all the duties incumbent on me
"as   according to the best of my abilities and un-
"derstanding, agreeably to *the constitution,* and laws of the
"United States."

(143) Why does a judge swear to discharge his duties agreeably
to the constitution of the United States, if that constitution
forms no rule for his government? if it is closed upon him, and
cannot be inspected by him?

(144) If such be the real state of things, this is worse than solemn mockery. To prescribe, or to take this oath, becomes
equally a crime.

(145) It is also not entirely unworthy of observation, that in
declaring what shall be the *supreme* law of the land, the
constitution itself is first mentioned; and not the laws of the
United States generally, but those only which shall be made
in *pursuance* of the constitution, have that rank.

(146) Thus, the particular phraseology of the constitution of
the United States confirms and strengthens the principle, supposed to be essential to all written constitutions, that a law
repugnant to the constitution is void; and that *courts,* as well
as other departments, are bound by that instrument.

(147) The rule must be discharged.

Self-preservation by
Strict Construction

COMMENTARY

ONE of the last pieces of legislation enacted during John Adams' term was the Judiciary Act of February 27, 1801. With Jefferson about to take office, Adams continued appointing Federalists to the positions created by the bill until 9 P.M. on March 3, 1801, his last day in office. Jefferson naturally did not like having what he understandably considered to be his appointments made for him, and he instructed the office of Secretary of State to withhold several signed and sealed commissions for justice of the peace in the District of Columbia that John Marshall, acting as Adams' Secretary of State, had neglected to distribute in the confusion of the Federalist administration's last day in office. As he put it in a letter to Henry Knox (March 27, 1801), he thought appointments made by an outgoing President between the date of election of a new President and his inauguration to be "nullities," except for those with life tenure.

Those who had been refused their commissions applied to the Supreme Court at the December term of 1801 for a rule to James Madison, Secretary of State, to show cause why a writ of mandamus should not be issued commanding him to deliver the commissions. The rule was issued and Madison ignored it. Early in March 1802, before the case could be argued, Congress repealed the Judiciary Act of 1801 and passed a new Judiciary Act late in April, which, among other provisions, set one annual term for the Supreme Court.

In the debate on repeal, the Republicans attacked the Federalists for retreating to the judiciary after having been thrown out of the elective offices, while the Federalists countered that the Republicans were violating the Constitution by attempting to remove judges not by impeachment, the only constitutionally sanctioned means, but by abolishing their offices. Judicial review was also questioned, with Republicans arguing that Congress could judge the constitutionality of their own actions as well as could the courts. Federalists countered that, without the check of the courts, government would lose its balance. Just before the next term of the Court, in February 1803, Jefferson sent papers to the House suggesting an impeachment of John Pickering, the federal district judge in New Hampshire. The Republicans were taking every measure to change the political alignment in the federal courts.

The Court that met to hear arguments in *Marbury* v. *Madison* was in a delicate situation, not only because of the general Republican attack on the federal courts, but also because Chief Justice Marshall was particularly obnoxious to Jefferson, as one of those Adams had appointed during the lame-duck period of his term. Republicans feared that Marshall would take any opportunity to rule against the constitutionality of the Judiciary Act of 1802, while Federalists thought that Jefferson would try to find excuses to start impeachment proceedings against the Chief Justice. Whatever the outcome, *Marbury* v. *Madison* would have profound implications for the development of the Federal courts.

Charles Lee, the brother of Light Horse Harry and Richard Bland Lee, as attorney for the group headed by William Marbury, effectively represented the Federalists' legal position, because he had been Attorney General under both Washington and Adams. Supporting his case for the rule to Madison, Lee began by observing that both the basis for holding office as justice of the peace in the District of Columbia and the necessary proceedings for appointment to offices of definite terms not subject to the President's will needed clarification. The facts in this case were obscured by the refusal of the Department of State and the Senate to give any information about the commissions or the proceedings. The first witnesses, two clerks in the Department of State, presented the Republican position by objecting that they were not obliged to reveal any information about the operations of the Department.

To establish the propriety of questioning the witnesses, Lee distinguished between two roles of the Secretary of State. Under the act of July 27, 1789, which established a department of foreign affairs, the Secretary is an agent of the President and therefore not subject to the jurisdiction of the courts. However, the act of September 15, 1789, which redesignated the bureau as the Department of State, delegates to the Secretary certain public duties, such as keeping the great seal and records of the United States. In this capacity, Lee argued, the Secretary is a public officer whose duties can be commanded by the courts, as can any other public officer's. This distinction provided a basis for his argument on the rule.

In an apparent acceptance of this distinction, the Court ruled that the two clerks ought to testify. Their testimony was incomplete on the details of the signing, sealing, and recording of the commissions, but confirmed that some of those requesting the writ of mandamus had been among the names on commissions made out while Adams was still President. The next witness, Attorney General Levi Lincoln, who had been acting Secretary of State when Marbury had called for his commission, also refused to testify, and requested time to consider the balance between his duties to the executive department and to the Court. The Court allowed him until the next day, observing that he was obliged to answer all questions of public fact, such as whether or not the commissions existed, although he was not obligated to give any confidential information. Lincoln testified, the next day, that he had seen commissions in the office, although he did not remember under what names. These particular commissions were superseded by a general commission made out for a list of names he was given. Upon his request, the Court ruled that he did not have to answer what had become of the particular commissions because this information was immaterial to the present case. After introducing the affidavit of James Marshall, brother of the Chief Justice, to the effect that he had picked up about twelve commissions for justice of the peace on March 4, 1801, but had returned a number because he could not carry them, Lee asserted that the existence of the commissions had been established.

Lee concluded his argument for the rule by answering three questions: "1st. Whether the supreme court can award the writ of mandamus in any case. 2d. Whether it will lie to a secretary of state in any case whatever. 3d. Whether in the present case the court may award a mandamus to James Madison, secretary of state."

In answer to his first question, Lee took a broad view of the powers of the Supreme Court. Arguing from the nature of supreme courts, British and American precedent, the Constitution, commentary on the Constitution in the *Federalist* and the Judiciary Act of 1789, Lee concluded that the Supreme Court has the power to issue writs of mandamus. Although by a narrow construction of the Constitution, *Marbury* v. *Madison* could come before the Supreme Court only as the result of appellate jurisdiction, Lee argued that "appellate" does not simply mean an appeal from one court to another. The writ of mandamus is itself a form of appeal for one's rights as he extended the meaning of *appellate*. Section 13 of the Judiciary Act of 1789 specifically gives the Supreme Court power to issue writs of mandamus, and the Court has heard mandamus cases, although it did not find the writs warranted. A writ of mandamus is the proper legal measure for forcing a person to give up something which another has a right to and cannot get through any other specific legal measures.

Lee relied on the distinction made earlier between the two roles of the Secretary of State in developing his second point. Although the President cannot be forced to do anything by mandamus, being responsible to the people only in the manner prescribed in the Constitution, the Secretary of State, when acting as a public official and not merely as an agent of the President, can be forced by the courts to perform his duties as the keeper and recorder of public documents. Even though the President might instruct him to do otherwise, the Secretary, Lee argued, has a legal duty to seal, record, and deliver commissions, patents for land, or other public records where required.

To show that Madison should be awarded a mandamus, his third point, Lee began with a definition of the office of justice of the peace for the District of Columbia. A federal judge is appointed when, after the Senate has advised and consented to his nomination, the President signs the commission and gives it to the Secretary of State to be sealed. The judge then holds office under the Constitution, independent of the President or anyone else. If the Secretary withholds the commission, he does so in contempt of law. Lee argued that although "this case may seem trivial at first view, . . . it is important in principle." The principle involved is the limitation on the power of the Secretary of State. "The citizens of this district have their fears excited," he asserted, "by every stretch of power by a person so high in office as the secretary of state." By an unstated extension, Lee implied that the independence of the entire judicial branch was threatened by Madison's action. He concluded his third point with citation of a number of precedents showing that mandamus is the proper procedure in this case.

Before Marshall delivered his opinion, Lee's case was strengthened by the introduction of an affidavit of Hazen Kimball, a former clerk in the State Department, who specifically remembered commissions signed by Adams for Marbury and Robert T. Hooe, another of the applicants.

Representing Federalist legal views, Lee's argument interpreted the Constitution in a broad way. The Constitution is an instrument allowing the courts to protect the rights of the individual. It is not a document that stands alone; rather it is a continuation of the British legal tradition and British precedents apply under it. Certain powers of the various branches of government are implied by the Constitution simply by virtue of the fact that it establishes these branches. Because the Constitution established a "supreme court," Lee argued, "by reason of its supremacy [it] must have the superintendence of the inferior tribunals and officers, whether judicial or ministerial." By this very supremacy, the Supreme Court of the United States must have powers analogous to the British Court of the King's Bench, even though such powers are not specifically stated in the Constitution.

As the most powerful Federalist remaining in the governmental structure, Marshall was in a position to support Federalist views on the Constitution. From what he wrote about Jefferson and the Republican party in his *Life of Washington*, we know that he regarded them as adherents to outmoded principles that could endanger the existence of the federal government. The power necessary to preserve the liberty and dignity of the United States could not be limited by abstract pronouncements, in his view. Successful government had to be led by men who took a long view of the national interest and who were wise enough to regulate national affairs according to the dictates of changing circumstances. From his service in the Continental Army, Marshall took away strong views of the sanctity of obligations. Congress, he thought, had broken faith with the army when it failed to supply it adequately. A government strong enough to enforce obligations was the primary need of the new United States. For this, there had to be some check on aberrations of public opinion, which had forced legislation opposed to national liberty, dignity, and strict compliance with contracts. These principles, Marshall believed, were embodied in the Constitution.

Although the Constitution does not specifically state that the courts will rule on the constitutionality of legislation, Marshall, together with many other Americans, believed judicial review was implied. Republicans tended to think that the courts ought to rule any legislation unconstitutional that interfered with the political rights of the people, whereas the Federalists were concerned that the courts not uphold legislation that interfered with the rights of property and the obligations of contract. In addition to judicial review, Republicans, in supporting the Virginia and Kentucky Resolutions, asserted the power of individual states to interpose themselves between the federal government and their citizens to protect them from "unconstitutional" measures like the Alien and Sedition Acts. All sides in the American political debate had committed themselves to some check on legislation when they had used as one of the rallying cries of the Revolution that, in the Declaratory Act, Parliament had wrongly asserted its authority to bind the colonies "in all cases whatsoever." When Republicans came out against judicial review in the debates over the repeal of the Judiciary Act of 1801, they were motivated more by their fear of Federalists dominating the courts than by any objection to a check on legislation. Americans' attitudes toward judicial review then, as now, depended upon their opinion of the composition of the courts. And now, as then, their feelings about the independence of the courts depend upon their regard for the party in power. When one party controls the executive and legislative branches, but not the judicial, its adherents tend to feel that the courts thwart the will of the people, whereas when a party controls the courts, but not the legislature, it becomes concerned about judicial independence.

The political implications of judicial independence certainly were on Marshall's mind as he made his choice of how to give his decision in *Marbury* v. *Madison*. Jefferson was out to weaken the courts. If successful in this, there would be no check on that party which Marshall believed did not understand the principles of the Constitution. For the country to survive Republican rule until some wise leader like Washington could gain popular confidence, a strong Supreme Court was necessary. But under the Republican attack, the role of the Court, which had not yet become forceful in national affairs, might dwindle into insignificance. Although the specific issue in *Marbury* v. *Madison* was trivial, the case represented part of the Republican attack. Should he roll with the punch or should he fight back? Such must have been Marshall's dilemma as he contemplated his opinion.

By hearing the case at all, Marshall had already made a partial decision. He might easily have disqualified himself because he already knew a great deal about the circumstances. It was his fault that the commissions were not delivered before Jefferson took office. Or he might just as easily have dismissed the appeal for a rule to Madison with the observation that the Supreme Court could only deal with this matter as appellate jurisdiction. By hearing Lee's argument, he made it difficult for himself not to deal squarely with a case raising the issue of judicial independence.

He would, however, have made it very difficult for the institution of the Supreme Court had he attempted to force Madison to deliver the commissions. The executive department had already ignored the rule to show cause. The Court had no power to force the executive to do anything, except the power of public opinion. To further split an already divided public in the early days of the republic might have resulted in complete dissolution of the union. If he chose to fight out the issue squarely, Marshall could be sure that Jefferson would go even further in his attack on the judiciary. His own position as Chief Justice might become an issue, and Congress could decide to increase or decrease the number of justices so as to render the Court contemptible.

His dilemma involved choosing the proper means to strengthen the Court while at the same time avoiding either open attack upon the executive or capitulation to Jefferson. One of the most striking things about Marshall's opinion is its length, some 10,000 words. If he meant simply to dismiss the rule, he might have done so in a sentence stating that after consideration of the argument he had decided that the Supreme Court had no jurisdiction in the case. If he meant to dismiss the rule by stating that Section 13 of the Judiciary Act of 1789 was unconstitutional, he needed only the final section of the opinion he wrote, from paragraph 100 on, about 3,000 words. Why did he write what seems to be a needlessly long and complicated decision?

By considering the reactions of the audience, the Republicans, which Marshall must have had in mind when writing, we can get a better idea of why he developed his opinion as he did. Expecting Marshall to award mandamus, the Republicans would have viewed the prospect with glee for it would add ammunition to their attack on the courts. They could have then argued that here was a clean-cut example of the Court trying to use its power to abrogate the will of the people. The people did not expect, when they voted Republican in 1800, to see the Federalist Court putting Federalist officials in office by fiat. The Court had invaded the executive branch and the attack had to be resisted by impeachment.

Marshall introduces his opinion, in paragraphs 2 and 3, in a way calculated to justify the Republicans' expectations. The "peculiar delicacy," "novelty," and "difficulty" of the case "require a complete exposition of the principles, on which the opinion to be given by the court, is founded." This certainly sounds like the buildup for a fight. When he goes on to say that his opinion will follow the "substance" of Lee's "very able argument," the Republicans must have been convinced that they had him.

"Having already told us what the conclusion is," the Republicans might well have wondered, "why does Marshall go on in paragraph 4 to divide it up into three headings as though he were actually going to explore the issue dispassionately? He obviously will answer all three questions *yes*, so why bother with all this legal pedantry?" Anxious to get on to the point where Marshall awards mandamus and so invades the executive branch, Republicans in their annoyance would be looking for some place where Marshall steps outside the Constitution or statute law to form a judgment.

Marshall plods on in answer to his first question for some 3,000 words, paragraphs 5 through 48, drawing inferences from the Constitution and positive legislation designed to show that Marbury had a vested right to the commission because he had been justice of the peace allegedly ever since his commission was signed by the President and sealed by the Secretary of State. The Republicans might well have been disturbed by this line of reasoning, because they had taken the commonsense view that an official had to be in possession of his commission before he was empowered to hold office. Lee's argument had also seemed to imply this commonsense point of view, but he had tried to show that commissions cannot be withheld legally, whereas the Republicans had acted as though they could be. The inferences that Marshall drew from the language of the law and from his analysis of will, in paragraphs 22 and 23, revised this commonsense view.

Arguments such as Marshall's were quite familiar to Americans who had lived through the Revolution and had been brought up on complicated arguments about the nature of providence. The notion of covenant and compact was common to these people. They had been long acquainted with complicated arguments about the nature of God's covenant, drawn from inferences from the Bible and from conceptions about the act of will. Their common view was that an act of will involved both deliberation and a last act that committed the decision. During deliberation, there was room for a change of will, but after decision, the will was fixed. Marshall's argument that the President's signature on the commission was the last act that ended deliberation, and confirmed the appointment beyond the power of the President's will to recall it, would have been a difficult one to refute. By going on to examine the nature of sealing a document, which attests merely to the validity of the signature, he made his argument even more unshakable. The delivery of the commissions was merely a duty following appointment, which, as the last act of will, could not be changed by any circumstance. A new appointment might be made if this one was refused, but an appointment once made could not be withdrawn. Republicans might still have objected, at the end of Marshall's explication of the first question, that Adams did not have the power of appointment after his successor was already picked, but they would have had to find Marshall's method of argument and his assessment of the nature of appointments cogent, unless they were to give up their own favorite arguments. Their annoyance would undoubtedly have been increased by finding how cleverly Marshall could use the arguments they themselves were fond of. Instead of finding his assertion of Marbury's right to the commission a source of glee, now perhaps they were embarrassed by their expectation.

Having forced his audience to admit that at the least a case could be made for Marbury's right to the commission, Marshall phrases his second question in such a way that it would be very hard for anyone to answer no: "If he has a right, and that right has been violated, do the laws of his country afford him a remedy?" (paragraph 49) In answer to this, Marshall keeps his audience off-balance by citing British practice and Blackstone's opinion as well as a definition of civil liberty that Americans had fought the Revolution to preserve. A major justification for the Revolution had been that George III had put himself above the laws, as Americans understood them from their own experience as well as from their reading of Blackstone's commentaries on British law. They had intended their government to afford even greater protection of individual rights than did Great Britain's. If Federalists could now show that Republicans had violated the principle of a government not of men but of laws, it would be an embarrassment, indeed.

With his audience on the defensive, Marshall takes up objections to the assertion that Marbury has a right to the commission. Republicans might easily have argued that the case was so trivial that it was an example of "loss without an injury." Instead of picking up the implications of the case that Lee drew about the independency of the judiciary, Marshall expands the issue to involve all offices under the government. His tone in paragraph 55 implies that he finds it incredible that anyone could assume that any office established by Congress could be worthless. In this, he shows himself to be taking acts of Congress more seriously than the Republicans.

One counterargument left to his audience at this point was that appointments are merely political and do not confer property rights, which can be adjudicated by the courts. Marshall develops an argument (paragraphs 57–68), based upon Lee's distinction between the Secretary of State's duties under the law and his acts as an agent of the President, dismissing this objection. His examples of department heads' duties under the law—the Secretary of War's duty to place wounded Revolutionary War veterans on the pension list and the Secretary of State's duty to deliver patents to the purchasers of federal lands—shows that he took the common-law position that government officials have a property in their offices, a view that has not continued in American law. He disarms the Republicans' view that he meant to invade the executive branch by arguing that the courts' power over the heads of departments could, of course, not extend to acts performed by them as agents of the President, but had to include duties imposed by the laws, if the laws were to continue to protect the civil liberty of individuals. Applying this deduction to the case of Marbury (paragraphs 69–73), Marshall repeats his earlier argument concerning the manner of appointments before delivering his opinion on the second part of his argument. Appointments, like facts, he argues, cannot be obliterated.

Although the Republicans would have been embarrassed by Marshall's argument using many of their own positions at this point, they would now be prepared for him to award mandamus to Madison. True, he had obscured his invasion of the executive by clever legal distinctions, but the mere awarding of mandamus would be quite enough for them to make out their case of political influence dominating the decisions of the Court. Everything so far in the argument seemed to indicate that Marshall would go ahead with mandamus, and when he phrased his conclusion to the second part of his decision, "It is then the opinion of the court," (paragraph 74) the Republicans, who no doubt by this time had forgotten that there were to be three questions in the argument, would have returned to their initial emotional state of gleeful expectation. Marshall was about to hang himself.

Everything about Marshall's conclusion to the second part of his argument is designed to lead his audience toward the mandamus. The two parts of the opinion (paragraph 74) sus-

tain Lee's every point. Marshall is almost playful in the
solemnity with which he leads his audience through "1st" and
"2dly" up to "plain violation of that right, for which the laws
of his country afford him a remedy." But instead of "Therefore, this court awards James Madison a writ of mandamus to
deliver William Marbury's commission as justice of the peace
for the District of Columbia," the statement that the audience
expected and had already seen in its mind, it saw on the page,
"It remains to be enquired whether. . . ." "Why does he drag
it out?" would have been the frustrated question in the minds
of Republicans as they began the something over 5,000-word,
repetitious third part of Marshall's decision.

He divides his third heading—whether Marbury "is entitled to the remedy for which he applies"—in two—"1st.
The nature of the writ applied for, and, 2dly. The power of
this court." Then Marshall develops his discussion of the nature of mandamus toward a point where the audience is once
again sure that he will issue the writ (paragraphs 76–100). He
continues to frustrate his audience by quoting British commentary and precedent on the use of mandamus when a person is prevented by a higher authority from occupying a public
office to which he has a legal right. A repetition of Lee's distinction between the two functions of heads of executive departments—as agents of the President and as public officials—
is prefaced by an overly elaborate disclaimer of any attempt
by the Court to act in a political manner. Paragraphs 82 and
83 have a kind of wry tongue-in-cheek tone as Marshall proclaims "it is scarcely necessary for the court to disclaim all
pretensions to . . . jurisdiction" in the political prerogatives
of the President. His audience might well smile at what it no
doubt considered this attempt at ingenuousness, but when
Marshall (paragraph 84) puts the whole case on a man's right

to pay ten cents for a copy of a public document, the humor falls back upon the Republicans for having taken the matter so seriously. In the concluding phrase of this paragraph, Marshall puts the Republicans completely on the defensive through the implication of the question—what prevents the Court from issuing a mandamus? It is the Republicans, through an executive invasion of the legislature, who are unbalancing the federal government.

Marshall's argument becomes more serious (paragraphs 85–87) as he questions the legal authority over actions of members of the executive. No Republican could reply that law did not control the executive, because Republicans had long maintained that the legislature was the more republican branch of government. When Marshall wryly asserts (paragraph 87) that the "President cannot lawfully forbid, and therefore is never presumed to have forbidden" the head of a department to refuse to perform an act, such as delivering a commission, commanded by law, the audience must have felt acute embarrassment, because it was obvious that Jefferson had instructed the office of the Secretary of State to withhold the commissions for justice. The courts' jurisdiction over actions of the executive departments commanded by law, Marshall continues to argue, is established procedure in American law. The example he cites, involving the circuit court's holding unconstitutional an act of Congress directing the circuit courts to report the names of disabled veterans to the Secretary of War, anticipates his final ruling about the constitutionality of part of the Judiciary Act of 1789; but the audience at this point only sees it as a conclusive buildup to his award of mandamus to Madison.

Argument beyond what seems necessary continued to frustrate an audience that would have by this point lost its glee at the prospect of Marshall invading the executive branch and only wanted him to get his opinion over with. The audience would hardly have paid attention to paragraph 99, in which Marshall debates the value of the office to Marbury and concludes that the office can have no value other than itself. Now he must pronounce for mandamus, Republicans undoubtedly thought. The last phrase of paragraph 100, where Marshall questions the jurisdiction of the Supreme Court, comes as a decided anticlimax after he has clearly asserted that Marbury's "is a plain case for a mandamus."

Marshall has now done what was expected of him. He has asserted both Marbury's right and the power of the courts over certain acts of the executive branch. Beginning with paragraph 101, the tone of his opinion changes. Earlier he had been writing directly for his Republican audience. He had teased them, thrown them off balance, and tried to confuse and mislead them about the direction of his argument. All this now changes as he directs his attention toward constant principles and away from the immediate situation.

Marshall divides the second part of question three—whether mandamus can be issued by the Supreme Court—in two parts. Paragraphs 101–114 investigate the constitutionality of Section 13 of the Judiciary Act of 1789, and the rest of the opinion discusses the duties of the courts regarding unconstitutional laws. He makes no attempt to play with his audience here as he had done earlier. Almost immediately, in paragraph 102, he informs his audience through a conditional statement that the Supreme Court cannot issue a mandamus in this case because the legislation authorizing it is unconstitutional. This conditional statement is explored through an analysis of the section of the Constitution on the judiciary.

Marshall construes the Constitution here in a very narrow way. The rule for interpretation he gives in paragraph 110, "adhering to their [i.e., the words'] obvious meaning," allows him to reject both Lee's argument extending the meaning of appellate jurisdiction and Congress's grant of the power to issue mandamus in the Act of 1789. His reasoning here seems strained, however. Section 13 of that act can easily be understood to grant the Supreme Court the power to issue mandamus only where it was exercising its appellate jurisdiction. Marshall did not need to rule the legislation unconstitutional in order to dismiss the plea for mandamus. He could simply have said that the case did not fall within the Court's jurisdiction and referred Marbury to a lower court. By reading Section 13 as a grant of original jurisdiction in cases where the Constitution grants only appellate jurisdiction, Marshall seems to be going out of his way in order to pronounce on the nature of written constitutions.

Beginning with paragraph 115, Marshall asserts principles of a written constitution that justify his contentions about the illegality of withholding the justices' commissions and his pronouncement that Section 13 of the Judiciary Act of 1789 is unconstitutional. These principles are asserted in connection with a discussion of the duties of the courts to rule on the constitutionality of legislation. His pronouncement (paragraph 116) that the government of the United States is based upon an act of will by the people that gives permanent structure to the government, is very much like his earlier analysis of the act of will in a President appointing officials. Because this original act of the people's will has expressed itself in limitations on the various branches of government, these limits cannot be broken without breaking the original will, a revolutionary act. As long as the Constitution lasts, legislative acts that exceed its limits must be void.

Although he asserts that the courts cannot be bound by unconstitutional laws, Marshall begins an examination (paragraph 123) of the effect of such legislation on the courts that develops into his defense for declaring Section 13 of the Judiciary Act of 1789 void. This examination revolves around the nature and function of courts. Because the courts must apply the laws to particular cases, they must, when two laws conflict, be able to judge which law applies under the Constitution and which exceeds constitutional limitations. To those who would argue that it is not the function of the courts to judge legislation but only to apply the laws that are passed, Marshall replies that such a position destroys the whole benefit of written constitutions. He gives several examples of laws, expressly forbidden by the Constitution, whose operation the courts must refuse to carry out even if such were passed by Congress. His general proposition then becomes that the Constitution is not simply a device for setting up the machinery of government, but that it is a law that all other laws must conform to; it is expressly the "supreme" law. The courts, like all branches of government, are bound to uphold it, and judges, as well as other officials, are sworn in that duty.

The rule, issued to James Madison during the December term, 1801, to show cause why a writ of mandamus commanding him to deliver the commissions should not be issued, "must be discharged."

This conclusion was hardly what Republicans had expected from Marshall. It would have been hard for them to use his opinion in *Marbury* v. *Madison* in their attack on the courts even if the Louisiana Purchase had not come up to divert attention from the issue. The precedent for holding acts of Congress unconstitutional was not exercised again until Chief Justice Taney's *Dred Scott* decision in 1857. In his immediate political context, Marshall seems to have evaded an issue in order to protect the Court.

Marshall's decision is a very clever piece of political rhetoric. Instead of directly applying his own principles concerning the duty of government to enforce and maintain agreements and the importance of a wise and active executive in a republic, he turned the Republicans' principles of the sanctity of a written constitution and the priority of the will of the legislature against their immediate political position. He made it appear that Jefferson, by refusing to comply with the act of Congress authorizing justices of the peace for the District of Columbia, had exercised executive prerogative against the legislature. One session of the legislature, moreover, had abrogated the will of the supreme legislature, the will of the people that ratified the Constitution, when it gave unconstitutional powers to the Supreme Court in Section 13 of the Judiciary Act of 1789. By pointing out this error and by refusing to act in error himself, Marshall attempted to show that the Supreme Court was the most republican branch of the three.

To a generation that took argument seriously, Marshall showed himself a very skillful debater. To Republicans, he was perhaps something of a devil who can quote scripture. His construal of the Constitution in *Marbury* v. *Madison* was as strict as any Republican's and certainly far more strict than the construction implied in the Louisiana Purchase. After this decision, Republicans would have to look on Marshall as a man not to be attacked easily. In this, he protected both himself and the courts. The means he used, strict construction of the Constitution, became the standard device of the party out of power in American politics. Most Americans still regard this precedent for the Court declaring legislation unconstitutional and void—though they recognize that it has been abused at times—as one of the devices in American government that protect their freedom.

VII

A Supreme Law?

AN ORDINANCE TO NULLIFY CERTAIN ACTS OF THE CONGRESS OF THE UNITED STATES, PURPORTING TO BE LAWS LAYING DUTIES AND IMPOSTS ON THE IMPORTATION OF FOREIGN COMMODITIES

(1) Whereas the Congress of the United States, by various acts, purporting to be acts laying duties and imposts on foreign imports, but in reality intended for the protection of domestic manufactures, and the giving of bounties to classes and individuals engaged in particular employments, at the expense and to the injury and oppression of other classes and individuals, and by wholly exempting from taxation certain foreign commodities, such as are not produced or manufactured in the United States, to afford a pretext for imposing higher and excessive duties on articles similar to those intended to be protected, hath exceeded its just powers under the Constitu-

tion, which confers on it no authority to afford such protection, and hath violated the true meaning and intent of the Constitution, which provides for equality in imposing the burthens of taxation upon the several States and portions of the confederacy: And whereas the said Congress, exceeding its just power to impose taxes and collect revenue for the purpose of effecting and accomplishing the specific objects and purposes which the Constitution of the United States authorizes it to effect and accomplish, hath raised and collected unnecessary revenue for objects unauthorized by the Constitution:

(2) We, therefore, the people of the State of South Carolina in Convention assembled, to declare and ordain, and it is hereby declared and ordained, that the several acts and parts of acts of the Congress of the United States, purporting to be laws for the imposing of duties and imposts on the importation of foreign commodities, and now having actual operation and effect within the United States, and, more especially, an act entitled "An act in alteration of the several acts imposing duties on imports," approved on the nineteenth day of May, one thousand eight hundred and twenty-eight, and also an act entitled "An act to alter and amend the several acts imposing duties on imports," approved on the fourteenth day of July, one thousand eight hundred and thirty-two, are unauthorized by the Constitution of the United States, and violate the true meaning and intent thereof, and are null, void, and no law, nor binding upon this State, its officers or citizens; and all promises, contracts, and obligations, made or entered into, or to be made or entered into, with purpose to secure the duties imposed by the said acts, and all judicial proceedings which shall be hereafter had in affirmance thereof, are and shall be held utterly null and void.

(3) And it is further ordained, that it shall not be lawful for any of the constituted authorities, whether of this State or of the United States, to enforce the payment of duties imposed by the said acts within the limits of this State; but it shall be the duty of the Legislature to adopt such measures and pass such acts as may be necessary to give full effect to this ordinance, and to prevent the enforcement and arrest the operation of the said acts and parts of acts of the Congress of the United States within the limits of this State, from and after the 1st day of February next, and the duty of all other constituted authorities, and of all persons residing or being within the limits of this State, and they are hereby required and enjoined, to obey and give effect to this ordinance, and such acts and measures of the Legislature as may be passed or adopted in obedience thereto.

(4) And it is further ordained, that in no case of law or equity, decided in the courts of this State, wherein shall be drawn in question the authority of this ordinance, or the validity of such act or acts of the Legislature as may be passed for the purpose of giving effect thereto, or the validity of the aforesaid acts of Congress, imposing duties, shall any appeal be taken or allowed to the Supreme Court of the United States, nor shall any copy of the record be permitted or allowed for that purpose; and if any such appeal shall be attempted to be taken, the courts of this State shall proceed to execute and enforce their judgments, according to the laws and usages of the State, without reference to such attempted appeal, and the person or persons attempting to take such appeal may be dealt with as for a contempt of the court.

(5) And it is further ordained, that all persons now holding any office of honor, profit, or trust, civil or military, under

this State, (members of the Legislature excepted,) shall, within such time, and in such manner as the Legislature shall prescribe, take an oath well and truly to obey, execute, and enforce, this ordinance, and such act or acts of the Legislature as may be passed in pursuance thereof, according to the true intent and meaning of the same; and on the neglect or omission of any such person or persons so to do, his or their office or offices shall be forthwith vacated, and shall be filled up as if such person or persons were dead or had resigned; and no person hereafter elected to any office of honor, profit, or trust, civil or military, (members of the Legislature excepted,) shall, until the Legislature shall otherwise provide and direct, enter on the execution of his office, or be in any respect competent to discharge the duties thereof, until he shall, in like manner, have taken a similar oath; and no juror shall be empannelled in any of the courts of this State, in any cause in which shall be in question this ordinance, or any act of the Legislature passed in pursuance thereof, unless he shall first, in addition to the usual oath, have taken an oath that he will well and truly obey, execute, and enforce this ordinance, and such act or acts of the Legislature as may be passed to carry the same into operation and effect, according to the true intent and meaning thereof.

(6) And we, the people of South Carolina, to the end that it may be fully understood by the Government of the United States, and the people of the co-States, that we are determined to maintain this, our ordinance and declaration, at every hazard, do further declare that we will not submit to the application of force, on the part of the Federal Government, to reduce this State to obedience; but that we will consider the passage, by Congress, of any act authorizing the employment of a military or naval force against the State of South

Carolina, her constituted authorities or citizens; or any act abolishing or closing the ports of this State, or any of them, or otherwise obstructing the free ingress and egress of vessels to and from the said ports, or any other act on the part of the Federal Government, to coerce the State, shut up her ports, destroy or harrass her commerce, or to enforce the acts hereby declared to be null and void, otherwise than through the civil tribunals of the country, as inconsistent with the longer continuance of South Carolina in the Union: and that the people of this State will thenceforth hold themselves absolved from all further obligation to maintain or preserve their political connexion with the people of the other States, and will forthwith proceed to organize a separate Government, and do all other acts and things which sovereign and independent States may of right to do.

(7) Done in Convention at Columbia, the twenty-fourth day of November, in the year of our Lord one thousand eight hundred and thirty-two, and in the fifty-seventh year of the declaration of the independence of the United States of America.

A Supreme Law?

COMMENTARY

GOVERNMENT revolves around the basic question: who shall judge? The answer implies other questions, such as: What economic policy should a country follow? What political rights should citizens have? How should diplomacy be conducted? Can laws prescribe social behavior? What is property and how is it possessed? Depending upon who is to judge answers to questions like these, the nature of governments differ.

The basic answer the revolutionary generation gave was that law should determine correct answers to questions of government. They did not mean the everyday statute law, however, for particular legislatures might err in pursuit of selfish interests, as had the British Parliament after the French and

Indian War. There must be a supreme law setting forth the general principles to which laws meeting particular situations had to conform. Reasoning in this way, the new American states adopted written constitutions during the Revolution. These basic laws not only set up the mechanics of government, but also established limits and directions. The Constitutional Convention followed the state precedents in drafting a new plan for union during the summer of 1787. By adopting a basic law establishing limits and direction for government, Americans were turning from the practice of vesting the supreme power in an executive or a legislature toward the view that law, itself, was sovereign.

Such a view solves certain problems. When law is sovereign, an executive cannot follow his whims, but must direct his policy according to established procedures. Unless there is a written constitution, a supreme law, however, the legislature can follow its whims and become as arbitrary as any despot. As a minority in the British Empire, Americans had seen their rights, as they regarded them, invaded by a legislature concerned only with the majority's interests. A written constitution limiting the powers of government was the way to preserve the essential rights of all citizens, Americans reasoned.

This way of reasoning, however, leads to as many problems as it solves. In the seventeenth century, English Puritans had rejected both tradition and episcopacy in favor of the text of the Bible as a rule for church government. No text is unambiguous, however, and those that seem the clearest can be argued into contradictory meanings. Contrary to their assumption that men would agree upon the essential texts for church government, Puritans in both Britain and America found their movement splintering. Either they had to tolerate divergent opinion and movements, as in England, or enforce conformity, as in New England. Their experience, however, did not force them to give up the notion that the text was a more reliable guide than the opinions of those in particular positions. Following in this Puritan tradition, late eighteenth-century Americans, perhaps regarding political matters as being easier to solve than religious ones, relied upon the text of the law to preserve individual rights. When pushed as to who interprets the law, they replied, "the courts."

This was an easy answer when it applied to the courts of the particular states. These states considered themselves sovereign powers with all the rights of any independent nation. When members of the revolutionary generation spoke of their "country," they more frequently meant Virginia, New York, or Georgia than the United States. The states had different social and political traditions and their economic conditions were not the same. The class and sectional differences in a state were small compared to the differences between states, especially states as geographically separated as those in New England and the South. The Revolution had brought them together in agreement upon what they were against, but positive agreements were harder to achieve.

Constitutional limits on the domestic power of the federal government, especially after the first ten amendments, expressed this situation. The designation "federal" was itself carefully chosen to distinguish the union of states from a national government. As a compromise between those who wanted national government with power over all political matters and those who wanted strictly federal government limited to the regulation of the foreign affairs of the union, the Constitution became the issue in American political quarrels. All sides agreed that the Constitution was the supreme law, but it was impossible to agree upon interpretations of this law. Federalists, wishing to extend national power under their doctrine of powers implied in the Constitution, regarded the national government and especially the judicial branch of it as the proper authority on the meaning of the supreme law. Republicans, feeling that individual rights could best be protected by political bodies closer to the people, countered by arguing that, because no one could judge his own case, the states had to determine when the national government had violated the limits set by the Constitution.

The doctrine that a state has the right to interpose its sovereignty between an unconstitutional federal law and its own citizens developed until Chief Justice Chase asserted in *Texas v. White* (1869) that "the victory of the North killed State sovereignty." Although a state's right to interpose is thought of as a uniquely southern doctrine, it has been exercised by all who felt the rights of a minority were being violated. The Federalist decision in *Chisholm* v. *Georgia* (1793) that a state could be sued in the federal courts without its consent provoked the Eleventh Amendment, which overruled a portion of the Constitution giving federal courts jurisdiction (Art. III, Sec. 2). The Kentucky and Virginia Resolutions (Nov. 16, 1798 and Nov. 22, 1799) asserted both the unconstitutionality of the Alien and Sedition Acts and the duty of the sovereign states to judge infractions, to interpose, and to nullify legislation that threatened the political rights of individuals. In the Hartford Convention (Dec. 15, 1814–Jan. 5, 1815), the New England states asserted their discontent with Madison's foreign policy by reaffirming the doctrine of the Kentucky and Virginia Resolutions and called for revisions of the Constitution. Personal Liberty Laws passed in the Free States after 1840 prevented state officials from enforcing either the fugitive slave clause in the Constitution or federal laws regarding fugitive slaves. But the most famous case of state interposition was South Carolina's Ordinance of Nullification.

This Ordinance was the result of a long debate over the constitutionality of a protective tariff, which began in 1789 when the first Congress passed a tariff act "for the support of government, for the discharge of the debts of the United States, and the encouragement and protection of manufactures." Whether or not Congress had the power to pass a protective tariff depended upon the construction of Article I, Section 8, which enumerates congressional powers beginning with "Congress shall have Power To lay and collect Taxes, Duties, Imposts and Excises, to pay the Debts and provide for the common Defense and general Welfare of the United States; but all Duties, Imposts and Excises shall be uniform throughout the United States." Federalists followed Hamilton's argument in *Federalist* 30 and 34 that the phrase "the general welfare" allowed the national government to do anything required by unforeseen circumstances. Republicans, however, accepted Madison's contention in *Federalist* 41 that Congress had only the power to do those things enumerated in the remainder of Section 8. Until the 1820's, controversy over the tariff was only a subordinate issue in the debate between strict and broad constructionists of the Constitution. With the definite development of manufacturing restricted to the northern states, while the South became dependent upon the export of staple crops, the continuing American debate over the meaning of the Constitution focused on the legality of protective tariffs.

Strict constructionists found an issue in Henry Clay's definition of the "American system" as a combination of protective tariff with internal improvements to develop domestic commerce at the expense of overseas trade. In this defense of the Tariff of 1824, they found an invasion of constitutional limits in both the protective aspects of the tariff and the provision that its revenue go to internal improvements, neither of which they found in the express delegation of powers to Congress in the Constitution. When the northern woolen interests demanded further increase in the tariff to eliminate British competition in 1827, South Carolina, thinking that her economy depended upon free trade with Great Britain, bitterly opposed the new proposals. Party maneuvering in the 20th Congress, designed to discredit the Adams administration, resulted in the passage of a bill that, although it reduced the tariff on woolens, seemed to the southern free-trade adherents to make a protective tariff part of established national policy. Several southern states issued formal protests concerning the 1828 "Tariff of Abominations," and the South Carolina legislature issued Calhoun's anonymous *Exposition and Protest,* which asserted a theory of state sovereignty as the protection of minority rights. Nothing more was done, however, as the South waited for action by Jackson when he took office as President in March 1829. When Jackson affirmed protectionism and the Tariff of 1828 in his annual message of 1830, those opposed to the tariff in South Carolina began to build a political following, which captured the legislature in the state election of October 1832, following the passage of yet another tariff bill decreasing the rates but retaining protection. The assembly called for a state convention to take action regarding the tariff. An election for delegates was held and the convention met on November 19, 1832 at Columbia.

This convention was obviously a well-planned meeting. In six days, from Monday, November 19, to Saturday, November 24, four documents were reported: "Report of the Committee of Twenty-one, to the Convention of the People of South Carolina, on the subject of the several acts of Congress imposing duties for the Protection of Domestic Manufactures, with the Ordinance to Nullify the same"; "An Ordinance to Nullify certain acts of the Congress of the United States, purporting to be laws laying duties and imposts on the importation of foreign commodities"; "Address to the People of South Carolina, by their delegates in Convention"; and "Address to the People of the United States. To the people of Massachusetts, Virginia, New York, Pennsylvania, North Carolina, Maryland, Connecticut, Vermont, New Hampshire, Maine, New Jersey, Georgia, Delaware, Rhode Island, Kentucky, Tennessee, Ohio, Louisiana, Indiana, Mississippi, Illinois, Alabama, and Missouri." Passed on the final day of the convention by a vote of 136 to 26, the Ordinance became, with the state's constitution, a part of the fundamental law of the state. It was signed in a solemn ceremony with seven Revolutionary War veterans signing first, followed by the others in alphabetical order.

The three documents accompanying the Ordinance were designed to support it both legally and emotionally. They are a mixture of rational argument about the nature of the federal Union, appeals for justice, and romantic *Götterdämmerung* sentiments. Although they are addressed to different audiences, the emotional progression of each from deliberation through indignation to defiance indicates attention more to the position taken than to the audience. In these documents, the convention is really talking to itself.

In the "Report of the Committee of Twenty-one," an investigation of the history of the protective tariff attempts to show that it is a conspiracy of the manufacturing states to further their economic interests at the expense of the South.

The tariff, however, is only the entering wedge in a movement to reduce the federal nature of the union to a consolidated government. Such a government not only would violate the intentions of the members of the Constitutional Convention, but also would be an impossibility because the variations of geography and population between the states prevent common economic, political, and social institutions. To prevent the revolution and dissolution of the union that would necessarily result from consolidated government, South Carolina is nullifying the tariff acts and calling for a convention of the states that can work out a system for effective protection of minority rights. Extensive quotation of the Virginia and Kentucky Resolutions substantiates the legality of this action.

A definition of the Constitution as a "compact between sovereign States" opens the justification for the Ordinance in the "Address to the People of South Carolina." Because the compact was ratified by states, "there is not now, nor has there ever been, such a relation existing as that of a citizen of New Hampshire and a citizen of South Carolina, bound together in the same *social* compact." Citizens owe their allegiance to their states and are bound by actions taken by the people of a state in convention. Because the Constitution is a compact between states, there is no power or body that can judge disputes between a state and the federal government except the state itself. The federal government is a mere agent of the states and not a sovereign power itself. When the federal government presumes to act in areas not delegated to it by the states, any state has the right to judge the nature of the infraction and take actions to remedy it. The proper action under the Constitution is interposition or nullification until all the states acting together in convention can revise the Constitution to prevent further infractions. This is not only a right, it is a duty, if the states are to carry out their obligations to defend the Constitution against all attacks, even from the federal government itself. The address ends with an appeal and a command to the citizens of South Carolina. They must do their duty to their country (South Carolina), "AND LEAVE THE CONSEQUENCES TO GOD."

The revolutionary tone ending this document is taken up in a conciliatory way in the "Address to the People of the United States." A full paragraph states the convention's theory of the Federal compact more succinctly than previously:

> We hold, then, that, on their separation from the Crown of Great Britain, the several colonies became free and independent States, each enjoying the separate and independent right of self-government; and that no authority can be exercised over them, or within their limits, but by their consent, respectively given as States. It is equally true, that the Constitution of the United States is a compact formed between the several States acting as sovereign communities; that the Government created by it is a joint agency of the States, appointed to execute the powers enumerated and granted by that instrument; that all its acts, not intentionally authorized, are themselves essentially null and void, and that the States have the right, in the same sovereign capacity in which they adopted the Federal Constitution, to pronounce, in the last resort, authoritative judgment on the usurpations of the Federal Government, and to adopt such measures as they may deem necessary and expedient to arrest the operation of the unconstitutional acts of that Government within their respective limits. Such we deem to be the inherent rights of the States— rights, in the very nature of things, absolutely inseparable from sovereignty. Nor is the duty of a State, to arrest an unconstitutional and oppressive act of the Federal Government less imperative, than the right is incontestable. Each State, by ratifying the

Federal Constitution, and becoming a member of the confederacy, contracted an obligation to "protect and defend" that instrument, as well by resisting the usurpations of the Federal Government, as by sustaining that Government in the exercise of the powers actually conferred upon it. And the obligation of the oath which is imposed, under the Constitution, on every functionary of the States, to "preserve, protect, and defend" the Federal Constitution, as clearly comprehends the duty of protecting and defending it against the usurpations of the Federal Government, as that of protecting and defending it against violation in any other form, or from any other quarter.

An attempt is made to show what South Carolina considers to be oppression in terms as simple as possible: "If the protecting duties were repealed, one hundred bales of cotton or one hundred barrels of rice would purchase as large a quantity of manufactures as one hundred and fifty will now purchase." This oppression of the federal government, acting as the agent of the manufacturing interests, is seen as analogous to the oppression of Great Britain before the Revolution. Just as representation in the British Parliament then would have been vain, so South Carolina's representatives in Congress could do nothing against the majority. The tone of indignity and the underlying threat of rebellion is tempered by a proposal that the tariff either be repealed or domestic manufactures be taxed at the same rate as imports. Either this or a national convention to revise the Constitution is necessary if South Carolina be not driven out of the union. The threat becomes explicit as the address closes with the assertion that if South Carolina goes, so will the rest of the South. Defiance is the final note as the convention asserts that its members "will cling to the pillars of the temple of our liberties, and if it must fall, we will perish amidst the ruins."

The delegates having argued for their position in three slightly different ways, the actual Ordinance of Nullification needed only seven paragraphs. Paragraph 1 states the situation in abstract, legal language. Under the cover of the first clause of Section 8, Article I of the Constitution, the sectional majority in Congress has enacted import duties designed not to "pay the Debts and provide for the common Defense and general Welfare of the United States," nor to "regulate commerce with foreign Nations," but to protect manufacturing restricted to the region of the majority, a function not authorized by the Constitution. Furthermore, the economy of the United States differs so as to impose the payment of these duties on the South, a consequence violating the Constitution's provision that "all Duties, Imposts and Excises shall be uniform throughout the United States." Nor has the revenue from these duties been used in ways enumerated in Section 8 or elsewhere in the Constitution, but it has been spent upon internal improvements, which are in effect bounties to the manufacturing region of the Union.

It is easy enough to dismiss this statement of the situation as a minority's selfish rationalization. South Carolina was simply acting like the small boy who takes his bat and goes home. There was, of course, something of the small boy's attitude in South Carolina's self-righteous attitude, but there is a real ambiguity in the language of Article I, Section 8. It is not clear from the way this section is written, punctuated, and indented whether the specific powers listed in the clauses following the first are *examples* of ways Congress may "provide for the common Defense and general Welfare," or an exhaustive list of all the means that Congress can use to do this. South Carolina obviously takes the second meaning. "General" to them applies to the welfare of each state at the present time. Just as they would argue that "common Defense" could not mean that the Union might sacrifice any one state in a war so that the rest might be saved, so they cannot admit that a protective tariff, which might be advantageous for most of the Union, but disadvantageous for one state, could be in the interest of the "general Welfare." This interpretation of the language of the Constitution depends upon a conception of the nature of the Constitution.

It might seem that in declaring the tariff "null and void" in paragraph 2 of the Ordinance, South Carolina refused to recognize the legally binding nature of ratifying the Constitution. This, however, is too easy a way to dismiss the action. Had South Carolina regarded the Constitution as nothing more than a treaty, she would merely have had to point out a reason of state for breaking it. A short statement that the treaty called the Constitution was no longer in the interest of South Carolina would have been sufficient. Statements in paragraph 1, charging Congress with violating the Constitution, make it clear that this is not what the Ordinance did. By asserting that Congress had violated the Constitution, South Carolina implicitly recognized that the Constitution is the "supreme law." It is not, however, the supreme law of an organic state. If the Union was an organic state in which the interests of the parts could not in reality conflict with the interest of the whole, then the reading of "general Welfare" would imply that the enumeration of the powers of Congress was merely illustrative and not definitive. South Carolina took a strict-constructionist view of the Constitution because she assumed that it was the states who were organic unities, and not the Union of States. In this view, Congress was merely an agent for the states in certain restricted areas. When the agent overstepped these bounds, its authority was no longer valid and it became necessary for one of the principals, one of the states, to correct it. A majority decision among representatives to the agent of the organic states, that is, Congress, could only commit the principals to actions of a kind they had previously agreed to. Without prior agreement to a category of action, no action could be legally binding, in South Carolina's theory of the Constitution. The Constitution was a supreme law in this theory, but a supreme law restricted to certain definite ends.

The restrictions, in paragraphs 3, 4, and 5, upon the minority of South Carolina's own citizens who might want to follow the tariff regulations are, therefore, not contradictory. It might seem that South Carolina's position—a minority can nullify the will of the majority—would have forced them to recognize the right of their own minority to nullify this Ordinance. This inference, however, ignores the whole basis of nullification. South Carolina, considering itself to be a sovereign state, is an organic unity. As such, the will of the majority rules, in a republican state. There cannot be a power over an organic unity capable of judging the interest of that unity. Therefore, the federal Supreme Court cannot be an adequate judge of South Carolina's actions implementing the Ordinance. Only the state's own judiciary can judge the state's own laws. The Supreme Court's jurisdiction is restricted to judgment of issues arising only out of activities delegated to its agent (the federal government) by the states in the compact (the Constitution). Any organic unity has the right and the duty to enforce majority decisions for the good of the whole. Therefore, South Carolina's refusal to allow an outside agency to judge the case of those who may oppose the Ordinance is consistent with the theory that led to the convention and nullification.

The threat to leave the Union should the federal government attempt force might also seem to imply failure to recognize the Constitution as a supreme law. Given the kind of supreme law South Carolina thought the Constitution was, however, this is not so. As one of the principals delegating power to the federal government as agent, South Carolina obviously would not have delegated the power to use military force against itself. Any attempt to do so would obviously violate what South Carolina thought to be the purpose of the Union. With its purpose destroyed, the Union would cease to exist. South Carolina would resume the powers delegated to the federal government. Self-protection being obviously one of the main powers of any organic unity, South Carolina as a sovereign state would have to resist by force any attempt to interfere with her decisions as an organic unity.

The final paragraph of the Ordinance appears to be a standard formula. The concluding phrase, "in the fifty-seventh year of the declaration of the independence of the United States of America," however, might appear odd given the militancy of the previous paragraph. Why didn't the Ordinance conclude with something like "in the fifty-seventh year of the independence of the sovereign state of South Carolina?" There seem to be at least two reasons. First, as written, the phrase has rhetorical effectiveness in showing South Carolina's attachment to the United States. But, second, "United States" to South Carolina does not mean a unified state, but a union of states. In their theory, the Declaration asserted the independence of thirteen sovereign states fighting for a common cause. So long as this cause continued to be common, so long as South Carolina received from the Union what she believed it was the Union's purpose to give, common defense, her attachment was sincere. When this purpose was destroyed, how-

ever, the union was destroyed. The independence of South
Carolina, however, would still date from the Declaration, be-
cause she was one of the principals that had directed the
Continental Congress as an agent to proclaim independence.

The Ordinance, then, is based upon a clear and consistent
theory. A society is a group of individuals bound together for
the pursuit of common goals. They support their lives through
the use of their property in a unified economy. To preserve
their community of interests, they must be free from outside
interference. In order to support the life, liberty, and property of its citizens, a society must resist anything that tends
to destroy their community of interest, whether it is a force
outside the society or a minority within. A minority, of course,
has the right of revolution, and because God controls the
destinies of men and nations, violent conflicts are trials by
combat. The American Revolution was successful because the
colonies had a right to be free and independent states. So
long as a society exists, however, majority interest must rule,
because a society is an organic unity in which minority interests must be either absorbed or cast out.

Just as individuals come together in a social compact, so
societies can join each other for mutual protection. Each
association is limited by the nature of the bond. A society
existing to protect the life, liberty, and property of its citizens
cannot, by the very nature of things, presume to instruct an
individual's will in matters not pertaining to the aims of society. The government of a society is an agent for the citizens
in matters that they, as the sovereign voice, have delegated
to it. Should the agent exceed the will of the principals, they
will obviously discharge him. Revolution obviously follows
when government oversteps the bounds delegated to it by the
majority will.

In an association between societies, it is the societies that retain the sovereign voice. A majority of these societies cannot direct their agent to perform actions not delegated by all the societies because the association of societies does not make up an organic whole; it is not a society in itself. If the majority should attempt to direct the agent to perform an action which one member feels against its interest, that member must either seek a new understanding of the powers of the association's agent or withdraw from the association. Withdrawal from such an association can only be considered revolution when the society refuses an obligation delegated by all the societies in their original compact. In any other case, if the agent of the association, or other members of the association, attempts to prevent the society from withdrawing, aggression is committed.

In the Ordinance of Nullification, South Carolina followed this theory. She regarded the federal government as her agent for a limited number of functions. Because a protective tariff and internal improvements were not among these functions, they could be nullified until a convention of all the States reached a new understanding of the Constitution. Any State that did not agree with this new understanding would of course withdraw from the Union, just as the states were free not to ratify the Constitution in the first place. According to South Carolina's theory, however, the state government was not competent to judge such an important matter as a violation of the limits of the Constitution by the federal government. Just as the federal government was South Carolina's agent, so the South Carolina government was agent for the people of the State. A convention elected independently was the only body competent to judge the issue. The sovereign power, the people of the state, had to judge basic decisions, according to the South Carolina theory.

Whether or not South Carolina's theory of the nature of

government, the American union, and the sovereign states was generally understood, the action of nullifying a federal law was generally condemned. Jackson's proclamation on the subject asserted that the compact, which formed the federal union, was a binding agreement. As President, he must and would enforce the law by whatever means necessary.

State governments backed Jackson's views about nullification. No state regarded it as proper. Georgia and Alabama recommended a general convention of all the states, while Alabama and Virginia asked South Carolina to suspend the Ordinance until Congress could modify the tariff. South Carolina kept up a militant front as newly elected governor Robert Y. Hayne issued a counter-proclamation to Jackson's. The Ordinance, however, was suspended on January 21, 1833, while Congress considered reduction of the tariff. After the new tariff act was passed, South Carolina's convention reassembled and rescinded the Ordinance. The Force Bill, which had passed along with the compromise tariff, was declared null and void, but the action was merely face-saving.

Each side in the controversy had asserted a power which neither exercised. South Carolina suspended its Ordinance before it took effect. The federal government, by asserting its power to force South Carolina while reducing the tariff, ensured that there was nothing left to force. Congress made sure that it would not have to perform what it claimed to be able to do. The nullification controversy was like a Cold War "battle" in which, after probe and counter-probe, both sides pull back to their original positions. The question—"Who shall judge?"—was as unsettled as before.

VIII

The Measure of an Underdeveloped Nation

Chap. CXXX

AN ACT DONATING PUBLIC LANDS TO THE SEVERAL STATES AND TERRITORIES WHICH MAY PROVIDE COLLEGES FOR THE BENEFIT OF AGRICULTURE AND THE MECHANIC ARTS

July 2, 1862.

Be it enacted by the Senate and House of Representatives of the United States of America in Congress assembled, That there be granted to the several States, for the purposes hereinafter mentioned, an amount of public land, to be apportioned to each State a quantity equal to thirty thousand acres for each senator and representative in Congress to which the States are respectively entitled by the apportionment under the census of eighteen hundred and sixty: *Provided,* That no mineral lands shall be selected or purchased under the provisions of this act.

Public lands, not mineral, to be given to each State.

SEC. 2. *And be it further enacted,* That the land aforesaid, after being surveyed, shall be apportioned to the several States in sections or subdivisions of sections, not less than one quarter of a section; and whenever there are public

How apportioned.

To be selected from those subject to sale at private entry, &c. if any.

225

lands in a State subject to sale at private entry at one dollar and twenty-five cents per acre, the quantity to which said State shall be entitled shall be selected from such lands within the limits of such State, and the Secretary of the Interior is hereby directed to issue to each of the

Where there rea no such lands, scrip to be issued. States in which there is not the quantity of public lands subject to sale at private entry at one dollar and twenty-five cents per acre, to which said State may be entitled under the provisions of this act, land scrip to the amount in acres for

Scrip may be sold. the deficiency of its distributive share: said scrip to be sold by said States and the proceeds thereof applied to the uses and purposes prescribed in this act, and for no other use or purpose what-

Proviso. soever: *Provided,* That in no case shall any State to which land scrip may thus be issued be allowed to locate the same within the limits of any other State, or of any Territory of the United States, but their assignees may thus locate said land scrip upon any of the unappropriated lands of the United States subject to sale at private entry at one dollar and twenty-five cents, or less, per acre: *And provided, further,* That not more than one million acres shall be located by such assignees in any one of the States: *And provided, further,* That no such location shall be made before one year from the passage of this act.

Expenses of management, &c. to be paid by States. SEC. 3. *And be it further enacted,* That all the expenses of management, superintendence, and taxes from date of selection of said lands, previous to their sales, and all expenses incurred in the management and disbursement of the moneys which may be received therefrom, shall be paid by the States to which they may belong, out of the treasury of said States, so that the entire proceeds of the sale of said lands shall be applied without any diminution whatever to the purposes hereinafter mentioned.

SEC. 4. *And be it further enacted,* That all moneys derived from the sale of the lands aforesaid by the States to which the lands are apportioned, and from the sales of land scrip hereinbefore provided for, shall be invested in stocks of the United States, or of the States, or some other safe stocks, yielding not less than five per centum upon the par value of said stocks; and that the moneys so invested shall constitute a perpetual fund, the capital of which shall remain forever undiminished, (except so far as may be provided in section fifth of this act,) and the interest of which shall be inviolably appropriated, by each State which may take and claim the benefit of this act, to the endowment, support, and maintenance of at least one college where the leading object shall be, without excluding other scientific and classical studies, and including military tactics, to teach such branches of learning as are related to agriculture and the mechanic arts, in such manner as the legislatures of the States may respectively prescribe, in order to promote the liberal and practical education of the industrial classes in the several pursuits and professions in life.

SEC. 5. *And be it futher enacted,* That the

Side notes:

Moneys from sales of such lands to be invested;

to constitute a perpetual fund;

interest to be applied to support one college for agriculture and the mechanic arts.

Conditions of this grant. grant of land and land scrip hereby authorized shall be made on the following conditions, to which, as well as to the provisions hereinbefore Assent of States. contained, the previous assent of the several States shall be signified by legislative acts:

Diminution of fund to be made up by State. First. If any portion of the fund invested, as provided by the foregoing section, or any portion of the interest thereon, shall, by any action or contingency, be diminished or lost, it shall be replaced by the State to which it belongs, so that the capital of the fund shall remain forever un- Annual interest to be applied regularly. diminished; and the annual interest shall be regularly applied without diminution to the purposes mentioned in the fourth section of this act, except that a sum, not exceeding ten per centum upon the amount received by any State under the provisions of this act, may be expended for the purchase of lands for sites or experimental farms, whenever authorized by the respective legislatures of said States.

No portion to be applied to buildings. Second. No portion of said fund, nor the interest thereon, shall be applied, directly or indirectly, under any pretence whatever, to the purchase, erection, preservation, or repair of any building or buildings.

Any State claiming the benefits of this act, to provide college within five years. Third. Any State which may take and claim the benefit of the provisions of this act shall provide, within five years, at least not less than one college, as described in the fourth section of this act, or the grant to such State shall cease; and said State shall be bound to pay the United States the amount received of any lands previously sold, and that the title to purchasers under the State shall be valid.

Fourth. An annual report shall be made regarding the progress of each college, recording any improvements and experiments made, with their cost and results, and such other matters, including State industrial and economical statistics, as may be supposed useful; one copy of which shall be transmitted by mail free, by each, to all the other colleges which may be endowed under the provisions of this act, and also one copy to the Secretary of the Interior.

Annual report of college.

Fifth. When lands shall be selected from those which have been raised to double the minimum price, in consequence of railroad grants, they shall be computed to the States at the maximum price, and the number of acres proportionally diminished.

If lands are selected from those at double minimum price, computation how made.

Sixth. No State while in a condition of rebellion or insurrection against the government of the United States shall be entitled to the benefit of this act.

States in rebellion not to have benefit of this act.

Seventh. No State shall be entitled to the benefits of this act unless it shall express its acceptance thereof by its legislature within two years from the date of its approval by the President.

Assent of State to be given within two years.

SEC. 6. *And be it further enacted,* That land scrip issued under the provisions of this act shall not be subject to location until after the first day of January, one thousand eight hundred and sixty-three.

Land scrip not to be located until after January 1, 1863.

SEC. 7. *And be it further enacted,* That the

Fees of land officers.

land officers shall receive the same fees for locating land scrip issued under the provisions of this act as is now allowed for the location of military bounty land warrants under existing laws; *Provided,* their maximum compensation shall not be thereby increased.

Governors of States to report annually to Congress.

SEC. 8. *And be it further enacted,* That the Governors of the several States to which scrip shall be issued under this act shall be required to report annually to Congress all sales made of such scrip until the whole shall be disposed of, the amount received for the same, and what appropriation has been made of the proceeds.

APPROVED, July 2, 1862.

The Measure of an
Underdeveloped Nation

COMMENTARY

ALMOST every statement about public higher education in the
United States contains some reference to the Morrill Act of
1862—"An Act donating Public Lands to the several States
and Territories which may provide Colleges for the Benefit of
Agriculture and the Mechanic Arts." Speaking at the University of Illinois centennial celebration of the Morrill Act, Allan
Nevins asserted that the Act "was remarkable as a profession
of faith in the future in the midst of civil war; but it was still
more memorable as an embodiment of the whole democratic
dream of the time and the conviction that the nation must
move fast to avoid a betrayal of its imminent needs." And a
former president of the University of Minnesota, James Lewis
Morrill, has written that "the land-grant philosophy has been

America's most fundamental contribution to higher education. . . ."

Such statements are made by virtue of hindsight, for when the bill became law in 1862, after Buchanan had vetoed an earlier version in 1859, there was little reason to expect the development of 69 land-grant institutions over the next century. Although there are no accurate statistics before 1870 on higher education in the United States, there were around 250 colleges at the time of the Civil War, only 17 of which were public institutions. Perhaps 700 colleges had failed before the war. Most of these were on the model of Harvard, founded to furnish ministers for the great variety of American denominations.

Even at the few public institutions, the classical curriculum was designed for the development of men who were to enter the professions of their fathers—law, medicine, and the ministry—not public service, which has come to be identified with the "land-grant philosophy of education." The study of Greek and Latin took up most of a curriculum designed to develop the mental discipline thought necessary for gentlemen. No attention was paid to the development of vocational skills, which, since the rise of the land-grant institutions, came to be thought the purpose of public as well as private institutions of higher learning. The American system of higher education, consisting of 1,316 private and 721 public schools in 1962, in which the public schools enrolled more than twice as many students as the private, has completely changed its character in the century since the Morrill Act.

In the century before the Morrill Act, higher education was financially impoverished and intellectually rigid. Today, although the intellectual quality may be doubted, higher education's quantity staggers the imagination. In 1960, institutions of higher education had a total income of $5.7 billion and expended $5.6 billion. This was a little over 1 percent of the gross national product. Higher education's income exceeded the mining industry's, and was not far behind the telephone and telegraph industry's. By 1962, public institutions alone were expending $3.9 billion annually, while private institutions spent a little over $3 billion. In 1862, all the colleges in the country could have failed and it would have made little difference to the economy. Today, higher education is vital to the economy of large areas of every state simply as an employer of clerks, gardeners, and maintenance men. It has taken over from the apprentice system the function of training recruits for business; its laboratories develop new techniques for industry and the military; while professors of political science and sociology advise government agencies and individual politicians. Before the Civil War, higher education in America was not really a part of the economic and political life of the country. Today, it could not withdraw from politics and business even if it tried.

Both those regarding this change as good and those regarding it as bad look at the Morrill Act as a causal factor. Actually, it was a symptom in a changing attitude toward the function of higher education. Before the Civil War, mental discipline and piety had been the aims of a college education. Between the Civil War and World War I, universities such as Johns Hopkins (1876) and the University of Chicago (1892) were founded to carry out what Americans thought to be the German university ideal of research and the advancement of knowledge. This ideal, combined with the stress placed on social utility by new universities like Cornell (1868), and old institutions like Harvard, under the forty-year presidency of C. W. Eliot (1869–1909), produced a complete change in the aims of education and the role of higher education in the United States. Institutions of higher education were deliberately made into instruments serving society.

Such a change would have been impossible without the dramatic expansion of the American economy. The earliest estimates available on per-capita income and gross national product, for the five years of 1869–1873, set the gross national product at $6.71 billion and per-capita income at $165. The poorest country in Western Europe in 1963, Portugal, had a per-capita income of $321 with a gross national product of $2.9 billion. In 1870, there were 563 institutions of higher learning in the United States enrolling 52,000 students. By 1910, there were 951 colleges and universities enrolling 355,000 students, while the per-capita income had gone up to an estimated $349, with a gross national product of $31.6 billion. It was not until World War II, however, when personal income for the first time went over $1,000 in 1942 and the income of institutions of higher education rose to over a billion dollars a year in 1944 (a year the federal government contributed $308 million as opposed to $58 million two years before) that higher education in the United States could be regarded as financially sound. By 1962, the income of higher education, $7.4 billion, far exceeded the receipts of the federal government at any time in American history up to and including 1941. A century after the Morrill Act, Americans had a per-capita income of $2,980, with a gross national product of $556.2 billion, and could well afford an even more extensive system of higher education.

In 1862, the United States, in the currently fashionable phrase, was an underdeveloped country. Based on the Frickey index of manufacturing production, which takes 1899 as equal to 100, the figure for 1862 is only 15. Lacking an adequate base for taxation, the federal government had long before 1862 turned to its only resource, the public domain, to support projects for the general welfare. The policy of giving away land instead of money to pay a government's debts originates in feudalism. Colonial charters had the character of feudal grants, and the American understanding of them as such was one of the main points in the dispute with Parliament that developed into the Revolution. During the Revolution, both Congress and states with western land voted military bounties in land. Although it quickly became evident that the veterans would sell their land scrip to speculators for a fraction of its worth, this method of inducing enlistment was continued in the War of 1812 and the Mexican War.

As early as the spring of 1784 the Continental Congress had passed a resolution considering the western lands a "capital resource." Provisions for selling the land were made in the Land Ordinance of 1785, which provided for rectangular surveys dividing the area into 6-square-mile townships of 36 sections of 640 acres each. One section in each township was set aside for the support of a public school. After the inauguration of the federal government in 1789, a debate developed between advocates of large sales to speculators, which would immediately contribute to federal revenue, and those who favored a policy of small sales to actual farmers. Never really decided, this debate continued in various forms throughout most of the nineteenth century.

With the admission to the union of the first public-land state, Ohio, the federal government had to decide whether to transfer title to the land to the states or to keep it as a capital resource. The Ohio Enabling Act of 1802 continued federal ownership of the land except for one section in each township granted to the state for educational purposes. This set the policy to be followed with all the new states, except that the land grant for education was raised to two sections with the admission of states west of the Mississippi. As it became necessary, grants were made to the states for internal improvements such as canals, roads, and the drainage of swamps. In 1819, Connecticut was given a township for the support of a school for the deaf and dumb, as was Kentucky in 1826. In 1854, the Dix bill, for the establishment of insane asylums supported by land grants in proportion to the size and population of the states, was passed, but vetoed by Pierce. The first of a long line of land-grant railroads, the Illinois Central, was chartered in 1851. The grants for internal improvements were justified as increasing the value of the remaining land, while the grants given Connecticut and Kentucky were anomalies until the passage of the Morrill Act. Land in one state had not normally been granted for the use of another, because under the federal system the conflict of sovereignty would have produced impossible problems.

As the Union expanded, the conflict over disposition of the public lands centered around eastern desires to realize as much revenue as possible from sales, western demands for both cheap lands and preemption (legal confirmation of squatters' claims), and southern desires to balance any new free states with new slave states. During the Jacksonian era, the theory grew up in the eastern urban centers that free homesteads for eastern surplus labor would relieve growing social problems. Throughout the forties and fifties, there was increasing discussion of a homestead bill as well as of agricultural colleges with federal help. Before 1850, the East resisted any attempts to reduce the potential revenue from the public domain, but in exchange for western support on such measures as high tariffs, favorable immigration laws, a national banking system, and ship subsidies, eastern politicians became willing to support land grants and a homestead act. In the debates on the homestead bills of 1852–1853, the eastern Whig capitalists commanded enough support in Congress to defeat the proposal in both houses, but after the breakup of the Whig organization in the election of 1856, the mood of the majority in Congress began to shift toward a changed land policy.

On December 14, 1857, Justin Smith Morrill (1810–1898), who had been elected to the House as an antislavery Whig in 1854, introduced his bill to grant public lands for the support of "colleges for the benefit of agriculture and the mechanic arts." The bill ran into immediate opposition when, instead of being referred to the friendly Committee on Agriculture, as Morrill proposed, it was shifted to the Committee on Public Lands, where a majority of southern representatives opposed grants for the benefit of particular states as unconstitutional. After a negative report from the Committee, Morrill managed to keep the bill on the floor and, on April 20, 1858, he gave his only sustained speech in its support.

Morrill based his argument on a definition of national purpose:

> The prosperity and happiness of a large and populous nation depend:
> 1. Upon the division of the land into small parcels.
> 2. Upon the education of the proprietors of the soil.

Such language is reminiscent of pious phrases from the revolutionary generation. The South Carolina politician and physician David Ramsay, in his *History of the United States,* drew the moral for his fellow citizens that, "from the great excess of the number of independent farmers in these states, over

and above all other classes of inhabitants, the long continuance of your liberties may be reasonably presumed." The underlying feeling here is that welfare depends upon "natural"
activities, such as farming. Men, however, have to be educated
as to what is natural. Soil exhaustion, which Morrill cited as
existing in all states, resulted from improper activity: "Our
agriculturists, as a whole, instead of seeking a higher cultiva-
tion, are extending their boundaries; and the education, on
the contrary, is limited to the metes and bounds of their forefathers." Unless corrected, this circumstance would lead to
national decline.

Progress, in Morrill's argument, depends upon scientific
specialization. Agricultural decline can only be reversed
through the systematic collection of many experiments in different situations. Such experiments can only be made at the
"thoroughly scientific institutions" that the bill envisions. In
his view, science is "a rational induction of principles" from
a widely gathered set of facts; "and the more widely gathered
are the facts, the sounder the science."

To conduct experiments and to deduce principles requires
specialized education, in Morrill's argument. "How," he asks,
"are we to expect one to solve all the scientific relations of
earth, water, air, and vegetable and animal life, who has only
explored reading, writing, and arithmetic?" Rather than a
set of statements common to all human activity, he regards
principles as specific to the activity in question. "It is plainly
an indication that education is taking a step in advance," he
argues, "when public sentiment begins to demand that the
faculties of young men shall be trained with some reference to
the vocations to which they are to be devoted through life."
His assumption is that mental activity is separated into a
number of more or less exclusive faculties, which do not de-

pend upon each other for their development. The purpose of nineteenth-century American education—intellectual discipline—he argues, "can be obtained under more than one mode, and, if the primary education sought for this purpose can be afterwards applied to practical use in the destined occupation, it is a point clearly gained." Progress, which depends upon scientific specialization, implies educational specialization as well.

Morrill's predictions for the effects of the bill were extravagant:

> If this bill shall pass, the institutions of the character required by the people, and by our native land, would spring into life, and not languish from poverty, doubt, or neglect. They would prove (if they should not literally, like the schools of ancient Sparta, hold the children of the state) the perennial nurseries of patriotism, thrift, and liberal information—places "where *men* do not decay." They would turn out men for solid use, and not drones. It may be assumed that tuition would be free, and that the exercise of holding the plow and swinging the scythe—every wit as noble, artistic, and graceful, as the postures of the gymnastic or military drill—would go far towards defraying all other expenses of the students.

Such a piece of rhetoric is designed to appeal to assumptions about the natural virtues of an agrarian way of life. Although natural, a life devoted to hard work for immediate practical goals, rather than pleasure, must be "turned out" by an educational process and not left to chance. This distinction between directed development and individual development implies that the citizen should be devoted to public welfare, not personal gain.

Morrill used two additional arguments for the bill. First,

he cited European agricultural schools in the argument that America ought to be keeping up with the old world. Then he argued that land grants for colleges in all the states would be a *quid pro quo* for the eastern states: "now by this bill the old states, by whose blood and treasure the public domain was so largely acquired, will be allowed some direct share, but not greater than that of others, in the distribution." Realizing that there was some constitutional question, Morrill went on to ask, "What clause in the constitution interposes any barriers to this?"

Led by southerners and westerners, opposition to the bill developed around the constitutional issue of the balance between state and federal power. On April 22, 1858, the day the bill passed the House, Representative Cobb, of Alabama, chairman of the Committee on Public Lands, spoke against the bill. In his view, land grants could only be constitutional when they made the value of the remaining land greater. Such had been the effects of the land granted to railroads, because without means of convenient transportation the land was of little value. Although he objected to the proportional means of distribution—New York, for example, would get far more than any other state—his main objection was that the bill would set a precedent for altering federal-state relations. Once the federal government became responsible for state welfare, the states would ask for everything.

Referred to the Senate Committee on Public Lands on April 23, 1858, the bill was not debated until the winter of 1858–1859. The constitutional issue was raised by southerners, and westerners complicated the issue through their fears that the bill would increase speculation. The conflict between the land-grant colleges bill and the homestead principle, an issue debated more extensively when the bill was taken up again in 1862, was raised in a passionate way by Rice of Minnesota:

If you wish to establish agricultural colleges, give to each man a college of his own in the shape of one hundred and sixty acres of land, where he and his children can learn how to make it yield the fruits of the earth in the greatest abundance; but do not give lands to the states to enable them to educate the sons of the wealthy at the expense of the public.

On the day the bill passed the Senate, February 7, 1859, Clay of Alabama forcefully put the constitutional argument against it. The bill would fundamentally alter the Constitution because it "treats the states as agents instead of principals, as the creatures, instead of the creators of the Federal government; proposes to give to them their own property, and to direct them how to use it. . . ." The Constitution had created a union in which "the States may do whatever is not forbidden by the Constitution; the Federal Government can do nothing that is not authorized by its charter, or letter of attorney, the Federal Constitution." If the legal basis of the Union could be changed, "if Congress may provide for and direct the education of the people of the State, why not supply all their physical as well as moral wants?" Clay asked.

In his message of February 24, 1859, vetoing the bill, Buchanan argued that it was "both inexpedient and unconstitutional." Its inexpediency was argued in five points. First, the bill would deprive the federal treasury of a large sum at a time when the support of the federal government was difficult. Second, by a grant to meet state expenses, the bill would create a dangerous precedent, for "should the time ever arrive when the State governments shall look to the Federal Treasury for the means of supporting themselves and maintaining their systems of education and internal policy, the character of both Governments will be greatly deteriorated." The means of making the land grants through scrip that must be sold to private individuals and organizations would, third, "operate greatly to the injury of the new States." Buying up the scrip at low prices, speculators would hold it until "men who desire to cultivate the soil will be compelled to purchase these very lands at rates much higher than the price at which they could be obtained from the Government." Recognizing the value of the advancement of agriculture and the mechanic arts, Buchanan, in a fourth point, expressed doubts of the bill's ability to achieve its object. Because the federal government has no power to enforce compliance with the terms of the bill, it would be helpless should the states use the funds from the land grants for any other purpose. Fifth, by forcing the creation of new institutions in each state, the bill would seriously injure the already existing colleges. Rivalries between colleges and between congressional districts for new colleges would strain the available funds. Far better would be grants to existing colleges for professorships of agriculture, because the federal government could enforce compliance with its aims through the courts; but money donated to State governments cannot be overseen.

All these objections, however, are not as important as the sixth, constitutional objection. Buchanan begins by assuming that all are agreed that the Constitution allows appropriations from the federal treasury only for the purposes enumerated. Should Congress exceed its powers by appropriating money raised by taxes for education in the states, the separation of state and federal governments would be violated. The public domain is part of the federal government's source of revenue. When the Constitution specifies that Congress has the power to "dispose of . . . the territory, or other property belonging to the United States," "dispose of" can only mean sell to provide funds for the purposes enumerated in the document itself. To use funds realized from sales of public lands for purposes other than those specified in the Constitution is as clearly a violation of its intent as to give away lands for purposes other than to raise the value of the lands remaining. Educational grants to a public-land state increase the land's value, but "it cannot be pretended that an agricultural college in New York or Virginia would aid the settlement or facilitate the sale of public lands in Minnesota or California."

Morrill's only reply to the reading of Buchanan's veto message was to move that it be printed and to observe, on what he called a "provocative" occasion, that the object of his bill had been to prevent further decline in American agriculture and to give a free education to farmers and mechanics. Because nothing could be done until a president with a different reading of the Constitution was in office, Morrill did not reintroduce the bill until ten months after Lincoln took office. On December 16, 1861, a time when it was reasonable to assume the union could not last, Morrill again introduced his agricultural colleges bill in the House.

As introduced, it differed little from the version of 1858. In section 1, the figure for the total amount of land to be granted was dropped, while the amount for each congressman was raised from 20,000 to 30,000 acres. The census of 1860 was to be used as a standard. A renewed controversy, at the beginning of the Civil War, over the status of mines in the public domain no doubt accounts for the exclusion of mineral lands from the grants. Because the provision that governors determine the value of public lands in their states had been opposed, it did not appear in section 2 of the new draft bill. The introduction of "and including military tactics" in section 4 was obviously the result of the war. Paragraph 4 of section 5 was strengthened by the addition of "State industrial and economic statistics" to the other material for the annual report, which was to be sent only to the Secretary of Interior instead of to both the Smithsonian and the agricultural department of the Patent Office, debate on the earlier version having charged that the bill would create an agricultural department. Paragraph 6 of section 5 was an obvious necessity during civil war.

As before, the bill was referred to the Committee on Public Lands, which delayed reporting "that it do not pass" until May 29, 1862. In the meantime, Wade of Ohio had introduced the bill in the Senate on May 2 and the Committee on Public Lands reported it with amendments on May 16. For the reading in section 2, "and whenever there are public lands in a State worth $1.25 per acre, the quantity to which that State shall be entitled shall be selected from these lands," the committee proposed, "and whenever there are public lands in a State the minimum price of which has not been reduced under the graduation laws below one dollar and twenty-five cents per acre, the quantity to which said State shall be entitled shall be selected from such lands." Agreed to, this amendment was changed, after the Senate had voted to repeal the Graduation Act, to read, in the final bill, "and whenever there are public lands in a State subject to sale at private entry at one dollar and twenty-five cents per acre, the quantity to which said State shall be entitled shall be selected from such lands within the limits of such State." The amendment and final reading were obviously designed to prevent states from assigning a lower value to their public lands than that assigned by the land office, so that they could claim scrip for more valuable lands elsewhere. Also, the phrase, "subject to sale at private entry," limited state selection to lands that had been offered for public sale by the land office. Earlier land grants to the states were not so limited. Lands for sale at $1.25 were often worth a good deal less, and it had been the object of the Graduation Act of 1854 to set the sale price progressively lower the longer lands were unsold. The second amendment—a change in paragraph 5, section 5 from "When lands shall be selected from those which have been raised to double the minimum price, in consequence of railroad grants, they shall be computed to the States at double the quantity," to "When lands shall be selected from those which have been raised to double the minimum price, in consequence of railroad grants, they shall be computed to the States at the maximum price, and the number of acres proportionally diminished"—clarified the language of the bill, so as to reduce the potential amount of the grant.

Opponents of the Morrill bill in 1858–1859 looked at the public domain as a source of revenue for the federal treasury and had based their case on the issue of constitutionality. Without southerners, Congress in 1862, as a collective body, had changed from a strict to a loose constructionist view of the Constitution. Although northeastern urban interests still regarded the public domain as a capital source, the fact that the Homestead Act had passed earlier that year indicated that easterners had learned to accept, and perhaps to use, free soil sentiments such as this one:

> I am one of those who believe that God never designed or intended that this Government should receive one single cent for her public lands. I believe that God has made her the guardian, and that she is to hold that land and part with it for no other purpose than for homes for her citizens. . . .

This was Senator Lane of Kansas speaking against the Morrill Act on May 30, 1862.

Earlier, on May 21, Lane had begun debate by expressing his fear that speculators would take up all the land left in his state, effectively preventing the state government from taxing it, for taxes could not be collected from nonresidents, and thereby keep his state a wilderness without means for building roads or schools. Pomeroy, Lane's colleague from Kansas, recognizing that the bill was a *quid pro quo* for eastern support on the Homestead Act, expressed his willingness to give something to the old states, but he wanted Kansas to keep her public lands. Searching for ways to guard against what he thought would be the pernicious effects of the bill, Lane could only come up with one small amendment in section 2: the insertion of a clause prohibiting State governments with scrip from locating it themselves within either territories or states.

The next day Lane continued his attack on the bill. It would, he argued,

> brand us with inconsistency in passing a homestead bill, and then passing this bill and saying to the poor white man, "you shall have land provided you build an agricultural college in every congressional district in the United States." There never has been a bill introduced into the Congress of the United States more inconsistent and more iniquitous so far as the western states are concerned.

This bill, he went on, could do nothing to prevent the slave states from returning to the Union, giving their scrip to the ex-slaves, and sending them all to Kansas. On May 24, Lane proposed two amendments to section 2 limiting the land taken up in any one state and postponing action under the bill until at least some settlers had been able to take advantage of the Homestead Act: *"And provided, further,* That not more than one million acres shall be located by such as-

signees in any one of the States: *And provided, further,* That
no such location shall be made before one year from the passage of this act." Lane's later attempt to force a State to take
up all its public lands below $1.25 before it could be issued
scrip failed, but his amendments to section 2 were accepted
in the final debate before passage on June 10, 1862.

On the last day of debate, Pomeroy attempted to limit potential speculation by another addition to section 2: *"And
provided, further,* That the land scrip authorized to be issued
by the Secretary of the Interior shall state upon its face that
the issue was by virtue of this law; and shall contain the name
of the assignee; and no assignment to any one person shall be
valid for more than one section of six hundred and forty
acres." Although passed, this amendment was later rescinded.
Three western senators, Howe of Wisconsin, Wilkinson of
Minnesota, and Harlan of Iowa, joined the attempt to amend
so as to prevent speculation. Wilkinson offered an amendment
preventing the bill from taking effect until July 1, 1864, but
this was rejected because Lane had already inserted a post-
ponement in section 2. Harlan, attempting to achieve a similar
effect, succeeded in introducing paragraph 7 in section 5: "No
State shall be entitled to the benefits of this act unless it shall
express its acceptance thereof by its legislature within two
years from the date of its approval by the President."

As debate continued on the tenth, Harlan added the meaningless sections 6 and 7. Section 6, providing "That land scrip
issued under the provisions of this act shall not be subject to
location until after the first day of January, one thousand
eight hundred and sixty-three," was meaningless because section 2 already prohibited location until a year after passage
of the bill. The sponsors of the bill were by this time anxious
to get it through and gave Harlan's section 7, providing for

land officer's fees, little difficulty. Earlier in the day Howe's proposal that the bill be changed to give $30,000 for each congressman from the sale of public lands had been quickly rejected with the observation that it would take too long for the land to be sold, but when he introduced section 8 requiring the governors to account for the sales of scrip and the appropriations of the proceeds, it was approved. The bill was finally passed, thirty-two to seven, with some westerners such as Pomeroy voting for it, although Lane voted against. Nine days later, June 19, after no substantial debate, the House approved the measure ninety to twenty-five, and it was enrolled on July 1, 1862.

Although we tend to think that those who supported the beginnings of what has come to be must necessarily have been in the right, it is the case that the Morrill bill had many of the effects its opponents predicted. It interfered with the operation of the Homestead Act, increased speculation, and provided little financial support for the colleges; and, at least for the first two decades, agricultural and mechanical education was not increased or improved by it. Such results seem almost inevitable given a bill stating in its title that land is to be given to both States and Territories, and then, in its text, proceeding to neglect any means of handling the donation to the territories.

The ambiguous machinery for transferring land from federal to state government and from state government to college seems responsible for the failure of the Morrill bill. West of the Mississippi, States with large tracts of public land could directly locate their grant on land that had been open to entry. The land could then be sold and the proceeds invested as an endowment for any college designated by the legislature as the agricultural and mechanical college. Such a procedure obviously limited the effectiveness of the Homestead Act. Paul Wallace Gates, writing on "The Homestead Law in an Incongruous Land System," cited the experience of Kansas: "Settlers arriving in Kansas—to consider a typical state—between 1868 and 1872 were greeted with advertisements announcing that the choicest lands in the state had been selected by the State Agricultural College, which was now offering 90,000 acres for sale on long-term credits." This land sold for an average price of $4.78 per acre, more than four times its price from the public land office. But even in the public-land states, location under the Morrill bill was limited by grants to the railroads, for, as soon as railroad land was granted, all land surrounding the area through which the road would run was removed from entry to prevent speculators getting hold of it.

States obliged to take the land scrip were even less able to raise an endowment for their agricultural colleges. Ambiguity in the bill's language created a situation preventing the colleges from realizing anything near the $1.25 per acre that the land was nominally worth. Although Brown University successfully challenged a ruling from the General Land Office and located some of the scrip that Rhode Island had assigned it, and the University of Illinois directly located about 5 percent of its scrip, it was generally assumed that both states and colleges could only sell the scrip and use the proceeds for endowment.

In effect, the scrip provision of the bill created a land-bank currency in denominations of 160 acres. Land paper had always sold at a discount for negotiable paper in the open market because of the cost of finding the land and entering it at the land office. Having little experience with this market, most states sold their scrip to professional dealers in land paper. In a complicated market depressed by the Civil War and the "free" land available under the Homestead Act, the college scrip sold badly. Vermont, selling its scrip to New York dealers in the spring of 1864, realized an average of 81.8 cents. Two years later, the price had fallen to just over 50 cents. By this time one dealer, Gleason F. Lewis of Cleveland, was becoming the expert on college scrip, and eventually most of it passed through his hands. Some of the southern states, who did not receive their scrip until after coming back into the Union, were able to get a better price for it, but of the northern colleges only Cornell, as a result of clever management by Ezra Cornell and because New York had received so much more than the other states, received anything like a workable endowment.

Although the actual return to colleges from the scrip sometimes appears to be the result of fraud, Thomas LeDuc, who traced the history in "State Disposal of the Agricultural College Land Scrip," concluded that "the states derived from their scrip exactly what their short-sighted policies entitled them to: the going market value." Even at retail prices, Lewis was offering 160-acre lots at only $1.00 an acre in the summer of 1871. The scrip market, just as opponents of the Morrill bill had predicted, increased speculation without profit to the colleges. "Probably no other scrip or warrant act," Professor Gates reckoned, "was used so extensively by speculators to build up large holdings as was this Agricultural College Act."

A financial failure, the Morrill Act could do little for agricultural education. Even the money available was more than could be spent for anything reasonable. There was hardly anyone in the United States capable of teaching anyone anything about agriculture. The best the University of Minnesota could do by 1877 was three courses: "How Crops Grow,"

"How Crops Feed," and "Farm Drainage." At the University of California, Professor Ezra Carr's idea of agricultural education was a course that began with a discussion of the fruit grown in the Garden of Eden. In addition, almost every land-grant institution experienced intense quarrels over the amount of financial support given to various departments. In many states, the agriculture department at the land-grant college became a political issue. These quarrels expressed the frustration of a people lacking sufficient intellectual or financial resources.

Only with the passage of the Hatch Act (1887), providing annual appropriations of $15,000 to each state for agricultural research and experimentation in each land-grant college, followed by the second Morrill Act three years later, did agricultural education become financially possible. Profiting from the sad experience of the first bill, the second Morrill bill provided cash grants from the sales of public lands for instruction only in "agriculture, the mechanic arts, the English language and the various branches of mathematical, physical, natural and economic science, with special reference to their applications in the industries of life. . . ." At the end of the 1880's, per-capita income reached $200 a year. This indicates that only then had the national financial picture improved enough to support higher education. The first Morrill Act, viewed in retrospect, becomes an expression of the attempt by an underdeveloped nation to pull itself into the nineteenth century.

IX

High Priest in a Holy War

Abraham Lincoln

SECOND INAUGURAL ADDRESS

March 4, 1865

Fellow-Countrymen:

(1) At this second appearing to take the oath of the Presidential office there is less occasion for an extended address than there was at the first. Then a statement somewhat in detail of a course to be pursued seemed fitting and proper. Now, at the expiration of four years, during which public declarations have been constantly called forth on every point and phase of the great contest which still absorbs the attention and engrosses the energies of the nation, little that is new could be presented. The progress of our arms, upon which all else chiefly depends, is as well known to the public as to myself, and it is, I trust, reasonably satisfactory and encouraging to all. With high hope for the future, no prediction in regard to it is ventured.

(2) On the occasion corresponding to this four years ago all thoughts were anxiously directed to an impending civil war.

All dreaded it, all sought to avert it. While the inaugural address was being delivered from this place, devoted altogether to *saving* the Union without war, insurgent agents were in the city seeking to *destroy* it without war—seeking to dissolve the Union and divide effects by negotiation. Both parties deprecated war, but one of them would *make* war rather than let the nation survive, and the other would *accept* war rather that let it perish, and the war came.

(3) One-eighth of the whole population were colored slaves, not distributed generally over the Union, but localized in the southern part of it. These slaves constituted a peculiar and powerful interest. All knew that this interest was somehow the cause of the war. To strengthen, perpetuate, and extend this interest was the object for which the insurgents would rend the Union even by war, while the Government claimed no right to do more than to restrict the territorial enlargement of it. Neither party expected for the war the magnitude or the duration which it has already attained. Neither anticipated that the *cause* of the conflict might cease with or even before the conflict itself should cease. Each looked for an easier triumph, and a result less fundamental and astounding. Both read the same Bible and pray to the same God, and each invokes His aid against the other. It may seem strange that any men should dare to ask a just God's assistance in wringing their bread from the sweat of other men's faces, but let us judge not, that we be not judged. The prayers of both could not be answered. That of neither has been answered fully. The Almighty has His own purposes. "Woe unto the world because of offenses; for it must needs be that offenses come, but woe to that man by whom the offense cometh." If we shall suppose that American slavery is one of those offenses which, in the providence of God, must needs come, but which, hav-

ing continued through His appointed time, He now wills to remove, and that He gives to both North and South this terrible war as the woe due to those by whom the offense came, shall we discern therein any departure from those divine attributes which the believers in a living God always ascribe to Him? Fondly do we hope, fervently do we pray, that this mighty scourge of war may speedily pass away. Yet, if God wills that it continue until all the wealth piled by the bondsman's two hundred and fifty years of unrequited toil shall be sunk, and until every drop of blood drawn with the lash shall be paid by another drawn with the sword, as was said three thousand years ago, so still it must be said "the judgments of the Lord are true and righteous altogether."

(4) With malice toward none, with charity for all, with firmness in the right as God gives us to see the right, let us strive on to finish the work we are in, to bind up the nation's wounds, to care for him who shall have borne the battle and for his widow and his orphan, to do all which may achieve and cherish a just and lasting peace among ourselves and with all nations.

High Priest in a Holy War

COMMENTARY

WHEN Lincoln delivered the second inaugural address, March 4, 1865, the outcome of the Civil War was no longer in doubt. The Confederate government and army were crumbling like poorly baked cornbread. During the summer and fall of 1864, Sherman's army had marched through Georgia to the sea and then, during the winter of 1865, the Union army had turned north to move through South Carolina and, by March, into North Carolina. Although Grant's army was still held up by Lee before Petersburg, 20 miles south of Richmond, the badly outnumbered Confederates obviously could not withstand much longer the siege that had been going on since June 1864. Cut off from transportation facilities to the lower south, the Confederate government at Richmond was losing control.

South Carolina had virtually nullified, on December 23, 1864, an act of the Confederate Congress authorizing impressment of badly needed goods and services. Although Johnston was blocking Sherman's advance in North Carolina, the pockets of resistance to Union power could not last much longer. At the Hampton Roads peace conference a month earlier, February 3, Jefferson Davis had instructed the southern delegates to insist on independence as the price for peace, but the Union's power was so great by this time that its delegates would not even listen to such talk.

The situation had been much more obscure when the election campaign began, with Lincoln's nomination at the Baltimore convention on June 7, 1864. During that summer, caught between Copperheads and radicals, Lincoln's defeat seemed certain. Heavy losses at Cold Harbor, Grant's failure to take Petersburg, Sherman's defeat at Kenesaw Mountain, and Confederate General Jubal A. Early's raid into Maryland, all between June 1 and July 15, resulted in defeatist pressures for immediate peace. In Chicago at the end of August, the Democratic Convention called for immediate cessation of hostilities and restoration of the federal Union. Having pocket-vetoed a radical reconstruction bill on July 4, Lincoln lost for a time the support of the radicals, who began to consider calling a second Republican Convention to replace him as nominee. By the end of July, political managers, like Thurlow Weed, were telling Lincoln that his election was impossible.

On August 23, six days before the Democratic Convention, Lincoln pledged his cooperation with the President-elect in a memorandum based on the observation that "it seems exceedingly probable that this Administration will not be re-elected." To undercut charges that he was continuing the war solely to abolish slavery, Lincoln instructed Henry J. Raymond, on August 24, to attempt a peace conference with Davis or his representatives, and to propose peace "upon the restoration of the Union and the national authority, . . . all remaining questions to be left for adjustment by peaceful modes." This instruction was in response to Raymond's suggestion, two days earlier, that Davis' rejection of a peace offer would squelch Copperhead criticism. With Sherman's occupation of Atlanta, September 2, sentiment began to swing toward Lincoln's reelection. By October 13, Lincoln was estimating an electoral college vote of 120–114 in favor of the Republican ticket. Voting on November 8 resulted in an overwhelming victory in electoral votes, 212–21, but the popular majority out of 4 million votes was only 400,000.

Viewed in the light of Lincoln's assassination thirty-six days later, the second inaugural address has taken on symbolic qualities as an archetypical example of charity, especially because its complete statement is usually thought of as the last of the speech's four paragraphs. In the dramatic framework we give the Civil War, these seventy-four words become the last utterance of the tragic hero. Failure and success, victory and defeat become one in the emotion represented by these words that lift the actor from the context of the play into the eternal present. The sentence becomes a goal for moral action. All that is left is for some Horatio to tell the story. The full address, however, is both something more and something less than the master playwright's finest lines projected in a dying gasp by the masterful actor.

Taken from this popular dramatic context, the speech has some peculiarities. Why did Lincoln put it in general terms? Most speeches as general as this one, although they may be effective at first, seem trite later. Why hasn't the speech become trite? Why do its generalities retain their power? Faced with the immediate problem of what to do with the defeated South, why did Lincoln choose not to specify steps toward reconstruction? Although his power was cresting with military victory, the close popular vote checked his potential authority. Why did he avoid talking about the election or the office of President? These peculiarities can be understood by a close look at the implications of the speech's development.

Instead of beginning with a review of his administration's past accomplishments, moving through a discussion of its present problems to their solution, and concluding with an appeal for support, as it would seem that the circumstances of the speech's delivery called for, Lincoln began with the present, jumped to the past in paragraph 2, moved from the past through the present to the future in paragraph 3, and concluded with a plea for action in a particular emotional vein. This order must be designed to bring out something not immediately obvious.

One way of understanding the purpose of a speech is to look for the picture the speaker tries to project of himself. Lincoln initially presents himself as a man whose mind is so well known that another discussion of his policies as President would be redundant. He is a cautious man, finishing one project before attempting another. Completely identified with "the progress of our arms," his "high hope" does not justify "prediction."

In paragraph 2, Lincoln changes his stance from that of a participant in events to that of commentator on them. Through his construction in the third sentence—"while the inaugural address was being delivered," instead of "while I was delivering the inaugural address"—he achieves a distance from events that allows him, in the rest of paragraph 2 and the first half of paragraph 3, to show, with apparent impartiality, conjunctions and distinctions between the parties. With the observation, "it may seem strange that any men should dare to ask a just God's assistance in wringing their bread from the sweat of other men's faces . . . ," this impartiality is broken. Instead of identifying himself as a Union partisan, however, he presents himself, in the rest of paragraph 3, as an instrument of providence. He takes on the character of a priest as he queries his audience's conception of God's attributes. The four lines of verse—"Fondly do we hope,/ fervently do we pray,/ that this mighty scourge of war/ may speedily pass away"—are the official prayer, but the citation of the second half of verse nine from Psalm 19, which concludes the paragraph, affirms God's majesty. In the concluding one-sentence paragraph, he becomes the theocratic priest directing the action of his charges through a formal prayer. The picture Lincoln projected was not that of the leader of a democracy, but that of the high priest in a holy war. The second inaugural address, therefore, is much closer in its form to a sermon than to a piece of political rhetoric.

Sermons that Lincoln would have been familiar with tended to follow the standard formula of doctrine, reasons, uses. A text from the Bible was selected for explication as a doctrine, which was defended by logical and textual arguments, then applied to individual action. Underlying this formula is the argument that because God absolutely directs the course of events, men should direct their actions by God's revealed will, which may be discovered through analysis of either revealed word in the Bible or the course of events. Both text and events are likely to be paradoxical, initially, and it is the priest's function to unravel the paradox.

In the second inaugural, Lincoln avoids the formula to

begin, after an introductory paragraph, with the paradox that
although neither side wanted war, it came. In paragraph 2
and the first half of paragraph 3, this paradox is developed
through comparison of similarity and difference between what
Lincoln carefully calls the "parties" in the conflict. In drawing
the comparison, he builds toward the definition that resolves
the paradox. The parties were similar because neither wanted
war, but they differed in that one side would "make" war to
dissolve the Union while the other would "accept" war to
preserve it. The parties were similar in that both knew that
the circumstance of slavery, "localized in the southern part"
(Lincoln initially wrote "half"), was the "cause" of the war.
They differed in that the "insurgents" wished to extend
slavery, while the "Government" desired to restrict it. Both
parties similarly expected easy victory. Neither expected total
war or fundamental change. In drawing his last comparison
—"Both read the same Bible and pray to the same God, and
each invokes His aid against the other"—the change from
past to present tense indicates the approaching resolution of
the paradox. The following observation of the "strangeness"
of the southern position, contradicted immediately by the
well-known injunction against human judgment, begins the
process of resolving the paradox through an implied definition of the nature of God. First, however, the paradox is explicitly stated: "The prayers of both could not be answered.
That of neither has been answered fully."

The paradox is resolved through the theory of providence.
The face of God is dark and his purposes are obscure to
human reason. The text Lincoln uses to illustrate providence,
Matthew 18:7, comes from Jesus' discussion of humility with
his disciples. Lincoln's quotation, a familiar one to his audience, is immediately followed in the Bible by Jesus' statement

that "wherefore if thy hand or thy foot offend thee, cut them off, and cast *them* from thee: it is better for thee to enter into life halt or maimed, rather than having two hands or two feet to be cast into everlasting fire." This context gives Lincoln's subjunctive about the role of the Civil War in providence frightful meaning, which in turn raises the question of the correctness of man's attribution of benevolent qualities to God. The revealed word of Psalm 19:9, however, allows no question of the righteousness of God's judgments shown through history. Men cannot do other than assume God's benevolence, whatever result his sovereign control over events produces.

The paradox of human will and divine guidance resolved, the concluding paragraph gives the "uses" implicit in the resolution. Whatever the will of men, history is God's will. It is thus for men to conform their wills to God's as far as they can know it. The cardinal virtue revealed in God's word is charity, and thus charity must inform all human action. The northern states, nearing the end of a long civil war brought on by the seeming willfulness of the South, must be reminded by the priest that events result from God's will, that no party to a dispute completely conforms to God's will because no party completely achieves its end, and that victory must not result in vengeance, but in charity.

The second inaugural address, in spite of its general appearance, was directed toward the immediate situation brought on by the approaching end of the war. Lincoln evidently pictured his audience as impatient, and anxious, now that it was winning, to crush the South completely. Had he developed his speech as one expected from a war leader, he could not have resisted his followers' natural desires for vengeance. Only by putting distance between himself and the situation, only by taking on the character of priest could he make a convincing plea for charity. This charity, however, is pointedly not of the variety that excuses abuses. The victors should care for the needs of the defeated, but there is no indication that the former ought to forgive or forget. Rather, charity is the duty of the victors exactly because their victory will be the result of their use as God's agents.

This picture of his audience accounts for Lincoln's less logical and more emotional presentation than is usual in his better speeches. The audience needs not so much to be persuaded rationally to accept certain positions or take certain actions as it needs to be forced emotionally to adopt a certain frame of mind. To prevent the normal consequences of military victory, Lincoln calls upon one of the most powerful of human emotions, fear of God. He does not contradict his audience's attitude toward slavery or the South; he forcefully reminds it of a theory of providence that all more or less accept. Because success or failure in this theory depends not upon human exertion but upon divine will, men deserve neither praise nor blame for the results of their actions. Results being beyond human control, men can only conduct themselves in a spirit conforming to what they could know of God's will from the Bible and from the outcome of events. Not pride but humility, not vengeance but charity, were the emotions Lincoln attempted to arouse in his audience.

The reason for the curious lack of specific details seems accounted for, then, by Lincoln's attempt to change not what his audience thought about the Civil War, but what it felt toward the object of its thought. With this effect in mind, there is no reason for specific detail about a situation already adequately known by the audience. To change emotions, however, there is need for a new perspective from which to understand the situation. Lincoln took the perspective toward all events officially accepted in a Christian nation, and forced his audience to view emotionally the immediate situation in the larger context. The fact that this larger context was a clearly defined relationship between providence and the results of human action prevents the general nature of the speech from becoming trite. Although men rarely act in a humble and charitable spirit, they continue to think that they should, because the virtues of humility and charity are the implications for human action of a traditional and well-defined theory of providence. Thus Lincoln used the second inaugural address as a means to force men to make their actions conform with their principles.

X

The Absorption
of Protest

POPULIST PARTY PLATFORM

July 4, 1892

(1) Assembled upon the 116th anniversary of the Declaration of Independence, the People's Party of America, in their first national convention, invoking upon their action the blessing of Almighty God, put forth in the name and on behalf of the people of this country, the following preamble and declaration of principles:

PREAMBLE

(2) The conditions which surround us best justify our co-operation; we meet in the midst of a nation brought to the verge of moral, political, and material ruin. Corruption dominates the ballot-box, the Legislatures, the Congress, and touches even the ermine of the bench. The people are demoralized; most of the States have been compelled to isolate the voters at the polling places to prevent universal intimi-

dation and bribery. The newspapers are largely subsidized or muzzled, public opinion silenced, business prostrated, homes covered with mortgages, labor impoverished, and the land concentrating in the hands of capitalists. The urban workmen are denied the right to organize for self-protection, imported pauperized labor beats down their wages, a hireling standing army, unrecognized by our laws, is established to shoot them down, and they are rapidly degenerating into European conditions. The fruits of the toil of millions are boldly stolen to build up colossal fortunes for a few, unprecedented in the history of mankind; and the possessors of these, in turn, despise the Republic and endanger liberty. From the same prolific womb of governmental injustice we breed the two great classes—tramps and millionaires.

(3) The national power to create money is appropriated to enrich bond-holders; a vast public debt payable in legal-tender currency has been funded into gold-bearing bonds, thereby adding millions to the burdens of the people.

(4) Silver, which has been accepted as coin since the dawn of history, has been demonetized to add to the purchasing power of gold by decreasing the value of all forms of property as well as human labor, and the supply of currency is purposely abridged to fatten usurers, bankrupt enterprise, and enslave industry. A vast conspiracy against mankind has been organized on two continents, and it is rapidly taking possession of the world. If not met and overthrown at once it forebodes terrible social convulsions, the destruction of civilization, or the establishment of an absolute despotism.

(5) We have witnessed for more than a quarter of a century the struggles of the two great political parties for power and plunder, while grievous wrongs have been inflicted upon the

suffering people. We charge that the controlling influences dominating both these parties have permitted the existing dreadful conditions to develop without serious effort to prevent or restrain them. Neither do they now promise us any substantial reform. They have agreed together to ignore, in the coming campaign, every issue but one. They propose to drown the outcries of a plundered people with the uproar of a sham battle over the tariff, so that capitalists, corporations, national banks, rings, trusts, watered stock, the demonetization of silver and the oppressions of the usurers may all be lost sight of. They propose to sacrifice our homes, lives, and children on the altar of mammon; to destroy the multitude in order to secure corruption funds from the millionaires.

(6) Assembled on the anniversary of the birthday of the nation, and filled with the spirit of the grand general and chief who established our independence, we seek to restore the government of the Republic to the hands of the "plain people," with which class it originated. We assert our purposes to be identical with the purposes of the National Constitution; to form a more perfect union and establish justice, insure domestic tranquillity, provide for the common defence, promote the general welfare, and secure the blessings of liberty for ourselves and our posterity.

(7) We declare that this Republic can only endure as a free government while built upon the love of the people for each other and for the nation; that it cannot be pinned together by bayonets; that the Civil War is over, and that every passion and resentment which grew out of it must die with it, and that we must be in fact, as we are in name, one united brotherhood of free men.

(8) Our country finds itself confronted by conditions for which

there is no precedent in the history of the world; our annual agricultural productions amount to billions of dollars in value, which must, within a few weeks or months, be exchanged for billions of dollars' worth of commodities consumed in their production; the existing currency supply is wholly inadequate to make this exchange; the results are falling prices, the formation of combines and rings, the impoverishment of the producing class. We pledge ourselves that if given power we will labor to correct these evils by wise and reasonable legislation, in accordance with the terms of our platform.

(9) We believe that the power of government—in other words, of the people—should be expanded (as in the case of the postal service) as rapidly and as far as the good sense of an intelligent people and the teachings of experience shall justify, to the end that oppression, injustice, and poverty shall eventually cease in the land.

(10) While our sympathies as a party of reform are naturally upon the side of every proposition which will tend to make men intelligent, virtuous, and temperate, we nevertheless regard these questions, important as they are, as secondary to the great issues now pressing for solution, and upon which not only our individual prosperity but the very existence of free institutions depend; and we ask all men to first help us to determine whether we are to have a republic to administer before we differ as to the conditions upon which it is to be administered, believing that the forces of reform this day organized will never cease to move forward until every wrong is righted and equal rights and equal privileges securely established for all the men and women of this country.

PLATFORM

We declare, therefore—

First.—That the union of the labor forces of the United States this day consummated shall be permanent and perpetual; may its spirit enter into all hearts for the salvation of the Republic and the uplifting of mankind.

Second.—Wealth belongs to him who creates it, and every dollar taken from industry without an equivalent is robbery, "If any will not work, neither shall he eat." The interests of rural and civil labor are the same; their enemies are identical.

Third.—We believe that the time has come when the railroad corporations will either own the people or the people must own the railroads; and should the government enter upon the work of owning and managing all railroads, we should favor an amendment to the constitution by which all persons engaged in the government service shall be placed under a civil-service regulation of the most rigid character, so as to prevent the increase of the power of the national administration by the use of such additional government employes.

FINANCE.—We demand a national currency, safe, sound, and flexible issued by the general government only, a full legal tender for all debts, public and private, and that without the use of banking corporations; a just, equitable, and efficient means of distribution direct to the people, at a tax not to exceed 2 per cent, per annum, to be provided as set forth in the sub-treasury plan of the Farmers' Alliance, or a better system; also by payments in discharge of its obligations for public improvements.

1. We demand free and unlimited coinage of silver and gold at the present legal ratio of 16 to 1.

2. We demand that the amount of circulating medium be speedily increased to not less than $50 per capita.

3. We demand a graduated income tax.

4. We believe that the money of the country should be kept as much as possible in the hands of the people, and hence we demand that all State and national revenues shall be limited to the necessary expenses of the government, economically and honestly administered.

5. We demand that postal savings banks be established by the government for the safe deposit of the earnings of the people and to facilitate exchange.

TRANSPORTATION.—Transportation being a means of exchange and a public necessity, the government should own and operate the railroads in the interest of the people. The telegraph and telephone, like the post-office system, being a necessity for the transmission of news, should be owned and operated by the government in the interest of the people.

LAND.—The land, including all the natural sources of wealth, is the heritage of the people, and should not be monopolized for speculative purposes, and alien ownership of land should be prohibited. All land now held by railroads and other corporations in excess of their actual needs, and all lands now owned by aliens should be reclaimed by the government and held for actual settlers only.

EXPRESSION OF SENTIMENTS

Your Committee on Platform and Resolutions beg leave unanimously to report the following:

Whereas, Other questions have been presented for our consideration, we hereby submit the following, not as a part of the Platform of the People's Party, but as resolutions expressive of the sentiment of this Convention.

1. RESOLVED, That we demand a free ballot and a fair count in all elections, and pledge ourselves to secure it to every legal voter without Federal intervention, through the adoption by the States of the unperverted Australian or secret ballot system.

2. RESOLVED, That the revenue derived from a graduated income tax should be applied to the reduction of the burden of taxation now levied upon the domestic industries of this country.

3. RESOLVED, That we pledge our support to fair and liberal pensions to ex-Union soldiers and sailors.

4. RESOLVED, That we condemn the fallacy of protecting American labor under the present system, which opens our ports to the pauper and criminal classes of the world and crowds out our wage-earners; and we denounce the present ineffective laws against contract labor, and demand the further restriction of undesirable emigration.

5. RESOLVED, That we cordially sympathize with the efforts of organized workingmen to shorten the hours of labor, and demand a rigid enforcement of the existing eight-hour law on Government work, and ask that a penalty clause be added to the said law.

6. RESOLVED, That we regard the maintenance of a large standing army of mercenaries, known as the Pinkerton system, as a menace to our liberties, and we demand its abolition; and we condemn the recent invasion of the Territory of Wyoming by the hired assassins of plutocracy, assisted by Federal officers.

7. RESOLVED, That we commend to the favorable consideration of the people and the reform press the legislative system known as the initiative and referendum.

8. RESOLVED, That we favor a constitutional provision limiting the office of President and Vice-President to one term,

and providing for the election of Senators of the United States by a direct vote of the people.

9. RESOLVED, That we oppose any subsidy or national aid to any private corporation for any purpose.

10. RESOLVED, That this convention sympathizes with the Knights of Labor and their righteous contest with the tyrannical combine of clothing manufacturers of Rochester, and declare it to be a duty of all who hate tyranny and oppression to refuse to purchase the goods made by the said manufacturers, or to patronize any merchants who sell such goods.

The Absorption of Protest

COMMENTARY

AMERICAN mythology explains politics by asserting that all men are divided by nature into two parties. Where one party exists, this signifies tyranny. The existence of more than two parties often expresses a kind of anarchy. In the natural state, government consists of a party in power and an opposition. Once in power, a party tries to stay in power, while the opposition devotes itself to getting into power. This struggle constitutes good government in the American myth. Where we see no struggle for power we conclude that the tyranny this implies suggests a threat to our ideal of world order. More than two parties struggling for power also implies danger to our security because such anarchy is the very antithesis of natural processes.

In our myth, there is no room for the notion that a political party could be a group held together by similar intellectual interests. If a party can be an intellectual community, then consensus in a country would mean that more than one party, the group expressing the intellectual consensus as their goal, would be a nuisance. When there is no consensus, it seems obvious that there will be a number of parties, certainly more than two. Underlying our myth that two is the natural number is the assumption that politics is simply the machinery through which a universal human desire for power is expressed and controlled.

The slightest reflection ought to reveal that our two-party myth obscures political realities. That Alexander Hamilton and John Adams belonged to the same political party is ludicrous, but we continue to insist that they were both Federalists. When we assert, in *Time* fashion, that the South is really making progress now because a Republican Party, which, if anything, is more racist than the old Democratic Party, is becoming a political power, our political mythology shows its sinister interior. The reality that the myth conceals was shown in a remark from Richard Nixon to John Kennedy, during their TV "debate," in the fall of 1960, to the effect that their disagreement was about means rather than ends. If such a distinction can have any meaning, it can only be that they quarreled over whether the Republicans or the Democrats should control the execution of national power. These vast amorphous organizations are merely coalitions for grasping the means to divide the spoils of power.

Parties that aim at anything else upset our national sense of rightness. Organizations that have specific ideological aims, such as Americans for Democratic Action or the John Birch Society, are strongly resisted by party stalwarts; and the implication that such a group controls or could control one of the parties is quickly contradicted by press and party alike. One of the main objections Americans seem to have to a Communist Party among them is that it aims to gain political power and use it as a means toward an intellectual goal. Power in our mythology is an end in itself. There seems to be something impious about using power. It is rather to be exercised with the relish of someone like John Kennedy; Americans, however, withhold their love from those too obviously in pursuit of power, as many viewed Robert Kennedy before he began to question the administration's Vietnam policy and the national welfare practice.

Our attitude toward power explains the curious sense of shocked decency greeting attempts to form political organizations representing groups and expressing goals unrepresented and unexpressed by the two major parties. The very fact that "third-party movements" is an American idiom expresses this attitude. *The Oxford Companion to American History* assesses third parties in this way: they "have usually been short-lived, and rarely has a third party succeeded in winning a large number of electoral votes. But third parties have occasionally influenced the outcome of elections, and often their programs have later been incorporated in the planks of one or the other of the two major parties." It is sometimes argued that third parties actually win when they go out of existence because their goals have been absorbed by the amoeboid major parties.

Looking backward, the Populist Party seems the first real threat to the struggle for political power. The shifting political alliances of the first half of the republic's history ossified after the Civil War into our familiar Democrats and Republicans. Although Greenback, Prohibition, and Union Labor became major parties in the presidential elections between

1876 and 1888 by polling over 10,000 votes (the test of the Bureau of the Census), the first of the third parties to poll over a million votes and to show strength in the electoral college (the popular test for a major party) was the Populist, or People's Party in 1892 with 22 electoral and 1,029,846 popular votes. Since then there have been three other presidential elections in which a third party has passed the test: 1912, when Theodore Roosevelt, polling over 4,000,000 popular and 88 electoral votes on the Progressive ticket, ran ahead of Taft on the Republican ticket; 1924, when Robert LaFollette ran third as a Progressive with 13 electoral and 4,800,000 popular votes; and 1948, when two third-party candidates, Strom Thurmond of the States Rights' and Henry Wallace of the Progressive ticket, polled over 1,000,000 votes, but only Thurmond showed electoral college strength, with 39 votes. We tend to think, however, of the election of 1892 as the only significant threat to the two-party struggle for power. The third-party strength in the other three elections is passed off as criticism of the other parties, mere rhetorical tricks for correcting unliked tendencies.*

This feeling, perhaps, is best accounted for by the existence of the Populist Party platform. Platforms have generally been made up of broad pious platitudes. They are, in the popular phrase, "not something you stand on, but something you get in." By attempting radical criticism of the existing situation and specific proposals to change it, the Populists upset the national expectation.

The platform of July 4, 1892, was the result of about three years of meetings among farmers of the West and South. Following the Civil War, the Wholesale Price Index shows a long

---

* At this writing, it is too early to anticipate how George Wallace's American Party will affect the traditional view of party politics.

decline until a slight rise in 1890. Four per cent higher than in 1889, the index for wholesale farm prices in 1890 stood at the same level as in 1850. While prices declined, the amount of currency declined. With low prices and tight money, farmers, who had borrowed heavily to get started in the West after the Civil War, defaulted on their mortgages. Long organized in regional associations, the various farmer organizations met in St. Louis with representatives of the Greenback party and the Knights of Labor in December 1889. This meeting issued a list of "demands" that became the first in a series of platforms for political action. In June 1890, the Kansas People's Party was organized; it set off a series of political meetings throughout the summer that resembled religious revivals. The agrarian ticket in Kansas, Nebraska, South Dakota, Minnesota, and Indiana showed considerable strength, and attempts in the South to capture the Democratic Party were successful in the elections of 1890. This success led to the meeting held in Ocala, Florida, in December 1890. Here southerners argued for capture of the existing parties, partly from fear of possible Negro power, but also because they had managed to control the Democratic Party in the election just past. The northerners, however, wished to establish a third party. The Ocala meeting issued another, similar, set of demands. A national convention to consider third-party action was held in Cincinnati in May 1891. Attended by more than 1,400 delegates from 32 states, this meeting reasserted the earlier "demands" and issued a call for a People's Party of the United States of America. Formally organized at a meeting in St. Louis in February 1892, the party held its national convention in Omaha at the beginning of July 1892. Here a presidential candidate, James B. Weaver of Iowa, and a vice-presidential candidate, James G. Field of Virginia, were nominated, and a platform, drawing together the previous demands, was approved.

The preamble—written by Ignatius Donnelly of Minnesota, a leader in almost every reform and third-party movement since the founding of the Republican Party, author of numerous utopian stories and two books arguing for Bacon's authorship of Shakespeare's plays—expanded upon the preamble of the St. Louis platform. With an eye on the dramatic, which many of the Populists seemed to share, Donnelly recast parts of the statement that played up the fact that it was being presented to the Washington's Birthday convention in St. Louis with references to the Fourth of July date for the Omaha meeting. He also added four paragraphs (7–10) and deleted several statements from the earlier document. Usually thought to be a mere repetition of the St. Louis preamble, the Omaha statement has a different impact. Although the preamble superficially sounds something like the Communist Manifesto, Donnelly's attempt to identify the party with the past rather than the future, and his analysis of recent history as the process of a unique conspiracy make his pronouncements very un-Marxist, indeed.

The introductory paragraph, a bit of prefabricated prose, is nevertheless interesting for two points. First, dating the convention on the anniversary of the nation's origin identifies the participants as patriots. Second, the wording attempts to embrace all the "people." In the St. Louis preamble, no nationalistic appeal had been made. Rather, the meeting had been termed "the first great labor conference of the United States, and of the world," and the platform had been addressed "to and for the producers of the nation."

The preamble proper opens with a statement of apparently socialistic sentiment. Grammatically, "us" and "our" refer to "the people of this country." Because there was no substantial change from the wording of the St. Louis platform in the paragraph that follows, however, the actual reference is to the "producers of the nation." The large, and rather vague, list of charges that form the body of the paragraph are designed to substantiate the contention that the nation is on "the verge of moral, political, and material ruin" (given the seriousness of the charges, one wonders why the country was only on the "verge"). It is this, in turn, that "justifies" the "cooperation," not some universal principle of human nature. The image this paragraph seems to reveal is that of a group of small animals huddled together, while a few large predators pick off the outer ring.

Through its list of outrages, paragraph 2 identifies the cause, vehicle, and consequence of this "unprecedented" turn in "the history of mankind." Unlike a Marxist analysis, which views historical developments "scientifically" as the results of necessary changes in the means of production, the recent history of the United States is viewed here as the product of the unnatural concentration of wealth in "the hands of capitalists." By definition corrupt, these capitalists have used the "prolific womb of governmental injustice" (a peculiar image) to produce almost universal corruption. The state governments, apparently, have been curiously spared, because most of them have found ways "to isolate the voters at the polling places to prevent universal intimidation and bribery." A typical American xenophobia is expressed in the predicted consequences. Industrial labor is "rapidly degenerating into European conditions," a situation that is anathema to the American way of life. The final result will be "two great classes—tramps and millionaires." Capitalists charge what the market will bear; tramps take everything they can get for free; logically, what is the difference in their positions? In the earlier version, this had read "paupers and millionaires." The substitution strengthens the distaste. Paupers are the victims of circumstances, but tramps choose a corrupted life.

Paragraphs 3 and 4 identify the symptom of the social disease produced by conspiracy among capitalists: government monetary policy. The phrase, "national power to create money," may even now shock some, but to Populists, many of whom had been members of the Greenback Labor Party (James B. Weaver also ran for President on the Greenback ticket in 1880), belief in fiat money was a cardinal principle. They were committed to the quantity theory of money, which asserts a direct proportion between prices and the quantity of money in circulation. When the quantity of money increases, prices increase to the same degree, and when the stock of money decreases, prices follow. Implicit in this theory is the assumption that the total value of money in a financial system remains constant regardless of the number of monetary units. When the stock of money is large, prices rise, and money is distributed widely throughout the population. A small quantity of money, however, produces low prices and wages, restricts circulation, and concentrates money in the hands of a few. Opposed to this is the mercantilist theory, which regards money as identical with wealth. Money in the quantity theory is a convenience for trade, whereas in the mercantilist theory, trade exists for the accumulation of gold, which is "real," as opposed to merely fiat, money. Fiat money in the mercantilist theory is a trick of the poor, whereas to the Populists, holding to the quantity theory, money tied to gold expressed a conspiracy of the rich. Creating money in the mercantilist theory is an impossibility. The Populists, on the other hand, regarded its creation as a necessity for trade.

Although the legal tender cases—*Hepburn* v. *Griswold* in
1870 and *Knox* v. *Lee, Parker* v. *Davis* (in 1871), together with
Julliard v. *Greenman* (1884)—had resulted in the Supreme
Court's ratification of Congress' power to make notes legal
tender, popular opinion even today seems to hold that notes
must be backed by gold reserves. The Populist position implies that value of monetary units in a financial system ought
to have nothing to do with such things as international rates
of banking exchange, much as the ruble is today. Instead,
these units should be tied to the needs for exchanging goods
and services within the system.

Events since the Civil War seemed to substantiate the Populist theory. In an era of Treasury surplus, the excess was used
to pay off the Civil War debt, represented by the greenbacks
in circulation. The debt was funded into long-term bonds,
while the greenbacks were redeemed. The resulting shortage
of currency raised interest rates. The combination seemed disastrous to farmers depending upon short-term credits. Looking back in 1892 upon what appeared to them as a consistent
financial policy pursued for a quarter of a century, the charges
in paragraphs 3 and 4—that the policy had been deliberately
adopted and followed for the benefit of the bondholding class
—seemed specific to the Populists.

In recent years, it has been popular to view the Populists as
precursors of the reactionaries who have gained attention in
the United States since World War II. Before the war, the
democratic and reformist aspects of the Populists had been
stressed by historians like John Hicks. In the late 1950's, it
became fashionable to follow Richard Hofstadter's lead, in
The Age of Reform, and be "drawn to that side of Populism
and Progressivism—particularly of Populism—which seems
very strongly to foreshadow some aspects of the cranky pseudo-

conservatism of our time." A major shared aspect is the conspiratorial theory of history. As the reactionaries of our day see an international Communist conspiracy, so the Populists saw an international conspiracy of bankers and bondholders. Distinguishing between the view that conspiracies do exist and the theory that the whole of the historical process is explicable as the result of conspiracy, Hofstadter argued that "there is a great difference between locating conspiracies *in* history and saying that history *is*, in effect, a conspiracy, between singling out those conspiratorial acts that do on occasion occur and weaving a vast fabric of social explanation out of nothing but skeins of evil plots." Surveying a range of Populist expression, he found that "populist thought showed an unusually strong tendency to account for relatively impersonal events in highly personal terms." The causal mechanism for this, he suggested, perhaps lay in the circumstances of agrarian life, for "it is the city, after all, that is the home of intellectual complexity."

American liberal intellectuals, understandably, have developed a strong distaste for conspiratorial views of events since World War II. Their existence as viable members of society has been menaced by the absurd charges of reactionaries. The ease with which they accepted the one-man-acting-alone theory of John Kennedy's assassination is evidence for this distaste. Anomalies in the handling of the case were initially attributed to bungling brought on by psychological stress. Only after considerable criticism of the evidence by leftists have liberal intellectuals come to doubt the essential validity of the official explanation. In 1968, it is much easier to see events as the product of conspiracy than it was a decade ago.

Hofstadter's case for the naiveté of the Populists seems quite convincing when he summarizes plots of novels and quotes examples of their extravagant rhetoric. It is easier, however, to see them as naive than it is to understand why they saw things as they did. Their attitude toward money, a subject at least as many people become hysterical toward as sex, was not nearly as naive as Hofstadter's view of them would indicate; nor was their conspiratorial view, as evinced by the platform, as universal as he implies. In paragraph 4, the statements about silver and gold, the currency supply, and the conspiracy against mankind are not nearly so vague as they seem when looked at outside the context of the experience of those to whom the platform was presented.

The single gold standard was a relatively recent thing in 1892. Great Britain in 1821 had been the first country to substitute gold for silver. No other country followed until Germany did, in 1871–1873, followed by the Latin Monetary Union (France, Italy, Belgium, and Switzerland), in 1873–1874, the Scandinavian Union (Denmark, Norway, and Sweden) and The Netherlands, in 1875–1876. What appeared by this time to be a concerted movement was completed when the United States resumed specie payments in gold on January 1, 1879. During this period, a series of actions by the federal government appeared to have prepared for the single gold standard. The Public Credit Act of March 18, 1869, provided for payment of government obligations in gold. The Coinage Act, through what is now thought to be an oversight, omitted to provide for coinage of the silver dollar, and so the bill became the "Crime of '73." In 1875, the Specie Resumption Act, providing for the resumption of gold payments as of January 1, 1879, and the reduction of greenbacks to $300 million, seemed to reveal the intention of the Coinage Act. Although the Bland-Allison Act of 1878 required the Secretary of the Treasury to purchase between $2 million and $4 million worth of silver per month and convert it into standard dollars, the conservative policy followed by the Treasury did not produce the inflationary effect that agrarian forces wanted. When specie payment was resumed in 1879, the fact that the greenbacks did not go out of circulation was an indication that paper currency had appreciated to a par with gold. Continued attempts to achieve cheaper currency were unsuccessful. A compromise between the hard- and soft-money advocates in 1890 produced the Sherman Silver Purchase Act, but its effects increased the redeemable paper currency just enough to further frustrate those who had been suffering for years from what they analyzed as a money shortage.

For us it is easy to see these developments as a series of steps to meet immediate problems. Prone to look at events in what is popularly termed a "pragmatic" way, we would at the worst call the movement to the gold standard bungling. To men responsible for international payments, it is obviously much easier to conduct business with some standard of exchange. Perhaps these men had been unthinking, but we would be loath to call them conspiratorial.

To Populists, however, such an explanation would not satisfy. To a generation familiar with the manipulations of financiers such as Jay Gould and James Fisk, the Tweed Ring, Crédit Mobilier, the Whiskey Ring, the scandal surrounding the impeachment of Belknap, and the disputed election of 1876, individual responsibility could be fixed. Bankers dealing with international payments obviously had excellent means of communication. It was clearly to their advantage to reduce currency and to operate on the single gold standard. If this had been done unthinkingly through a desire for efficiency and not through self-seeking motives, so much the worse for them. Their actions, in any case, expressed lack of concern for the general welfare. If the effect of such actions was the same as if there had been a conscious conspiracy, then the only remedy was to treat those involved as though they were in collusion.

Recently, moreover, Paul M. O'Leary has argued that the author of the Coinage Act of 1873, H. R. Linderman, who was appointed first director of the Bureau of the Mint when the Coinage Act took effect on April 1, 1873, was fully aware that the shortage of silver—which had kept its price so high that silver dollars had not circulated since 1836—was about to end. Linderman, in O'Leary's argument, deliberately excluded silver dollars from the coinage to prevent a silver standard from developing when specie payments were resumed. The fact that the report recommending dropping the silver dollar was submitted in 1870, before the price of silver had begun to fall (in 1872 after new mines were opened in the West), may be a weakness in O'Leary's argument. Nevertheless, that an historian in 1960 could seriously argue for a crime of 1873 indicates that the Populists were not as conspiracy-mad as they have appeared to be in the writings of Hofstadter.

Paragraph 4 in the St. Louis platform was followed by two short paragraphs asserting the "union and independence" of "intelligent working people and producers," which was necessary to meet "this crisis of human affairs." By deleting this and by adding the first sentence of paragraph 5, the Omaha platform broadened its audience, while pinning down the time during which the conspiracy had been developing to "more than a quarter of a century," that is, since the Civil War. Further, the added sentence gives force to the "charge" in the second sentence of paragraph 5. The "we" who have "witnessed" for such a long time—a "we" that includes not only those responsible for the platform and the participants in the convention, but the larger audience of the "people" as well—obviously do not make the charge intemperately. In a government controlled by two political parties, the conditions that have made this convention necessary could not have developed if either party had made a "serious effort" to prevent it. The third sentence, another addition, indicates that the Populists still retain their temperate view. What happened could be forgotten, but the parties still do not "promise us any substantial reform." The fact that the tariff is the only question debated by the two parties indicates that they must have, at least implicitly, agreed to ignore the basic issue of the entire financial system. Although today, we might easily find the cause for this in a failure to understand so complex a thing as the entire financial system, and in a belief that the tariff was a key to fiscal complexities, before we dismiss the Populist charge, we should consider such things as the Bobby Baker case. Political parties need money. The most convenient source is, obviously, the rich. No one is anxious to destroy his source of supply. A final sentence in this paragraph as it stood in the St. Louis version, asserting the necessity of a political organization to "redress the grievances," was deleted because the organization was now in existence.

Two paragraphs in the St. Louis version were combined to make paragraph 6. The earlier version had been presented on Washington's birthday and the Populists had used the occasion to assert their identification with the past. Presented on July 4, the Omaha version retained the reference to Washington and the identification of the revolutionary generation as "plain people." Deleted, however, was a reference to "the first great revolution on this continent against oppression." The introduction to the quote from the preamble of the Constitution was toned down from "in order to restrain the extortions of aggregated capital, to drive the money changers out of the temple," to the straightforward assertion of identical purposes. An appeal for the aid of all was deleted here to be expanded upon in paragraph 10. This paragraph expresses prefabricated Independence Day sentiment, but the changes from the St. Louis version represent an attempt to tone down the revolutionary content of the rhetoric, perhaps to increase the range of the audience.

Paragraph 7, the first of four paragraphs added to this section of the document, continues the attempt to increase the audience. In the St. Louis platform an appeal to forget the bitterness of the Civil War was included in the "Resolutions," which were not part of the platform, but were the general feelings of the convention. The earlier expression had been maudlin with its references to "men who wore the gray and the men who wore the blue," "last smoldering embers," and "tears of joy." By moving this expression from resolutions to preamble, it was, obviously, greatly strengthened. By casting it in a straightforward way, it became a far more powerful expression. The appeal here is made on principle, not on sentiment, as it was in the earlier version. The country must become "in fact" what it is "in name." The image of bayonets attempting to pin a nation together is a powerful one. By introducing this image with the principle that "free government" depends upon "the love of the people for each other and for the nation," the picture provoked is that of bayonets thrust through hearts. Since the southern agrarians were reluctant to leave the Democratic Party, the primary appeal of this paragraph is directed toward them. Secondarily, however, the image is directed toward the northerners, because it was they who had attempted to use the bayonets.

Having dealt with the cause (an international conspiracy of the moneyed), the vehicle (control over government), and the consequences (social confusion) of the existing situation, the preamble turns, in paragraph 8, to the solution. Although the first clause is too sweeping for support, the remainder of the sentence states the existing agricultural situation accurately to people basing their analysis on the quantity theory of money. If there is naiveté here, it is in the faith that "wise and reasonable legislation" can correct the situation, rather than in the analysis of the circumstances. The identification, in paragraph 9, of the "power of government" with the power "of the people" explains this faith. The Americans are "an intelligent people" capable of using "the teachings of experience." The role of government, here, is assumed to be that of providing common services, which lead toward "the end that oppression, injustice, and poverty shall eventually cease in the land." The surprising thing about these two paragraphs, given the previous description of circumstances, is the circumspection of the suggested solution. An appeal for violent revolution might more easily be expected. If the federal government has become the vehicle of an international conspiracy, the Populists' faith in normal democratic procedures can only be understood as a product of their belief in the uniqueness of the United States. The last quarter of a century would have been viewed as an accident, by them. The essential character of the country would have been, in their view, one that coincided with their own definitions. Patience could be reasonable only in such a case.

The final paragraph of the preamble appeals for aid from "all men." Populists, however, will restrict action to the "great issues now pressing," financial questions, because they will "determine whether we are to have a republic to administer."

Issues not directly bearing upon the financial, such as prohibition, alluded to in the "sympathies" expressed for proposals that "tend to make men intelligent, virtuous, and temperate," or woman's suffrage, alluded to in the final phrase of the paragraph, cannot be solved until the basic question is solved. Proper handling of financial questions, it seems, would place everything else in perspective.

The ten paragraphs of the preamble provide the basis for the specific proposals in the platform proper. Paragraph 1 identifies the occasion. The circumstances necessitating the meeting are listed in paragraph 2. Paragraphs 3–5 discuss the causes producing these circumstances. The steps necessary to rectify them are presented in paragraphs 6–10. The preamble identifies its audience, Americans, as a unique people. Their situation is also unique. But due to an unprecedented conspiracy, they are being drawn into the circumstances of Europeans. To correct this, they must return to their own uniqueness. Underneath the inflated language, there is an attempt to argue from relationships. The preamble wishes to identify the causes and probable effects of the circumstances. If we see an effect, such as falling prices, there must be a cause, contraction of currency. Who benefits from contracting currency? Those who control the supply of money, the bankers, and their customers, the bondholders. If government controlled the supply of money, then the situation would be corrected. All questions must, therefore, wait on the money question.

The platform proper in the Omaha version shows three additions, a substitution, and one rearrangement from the St. Louis statement. The third declaration, "per annum" after the interest on currency in the sub-treasury plan, and the ratio for silver coinage are new (the earlier version had merely specified unlimited silver coinage with no mention of gold), while the planks on land and transportation were reversed. Moving transportation ahead of land indicates a change in priorities. The additions give a more "conservative" tone to the proposals. The substitution of "civil" for "urban" in the second declaration broadens the audience for the platform.

The first declaration is another of the prefabricated sentences in this document. The "spirit" it refers to is made explicit in the second declaration, which might also appear prefabricated. The first phrase of this declaration states a version of the labor theory of value, a theory common to all sides of the debate over economics in the nineteenth century. The theory that an item's monetary worth is related to the labor that went into its production can obviously be challenged by the observations that some things are sold for whatever they will bring, which depends upon fashion, and that the price of other things depends upon their use-value. First formulated by Adam Smith, the labor theory of value, as worked out by David Ricardo, ignored interest and regarded capital as stored-up labor. In this form, it was adopted by Marx. Ricardo believed that capital could be ignored in determining value, because his studies seemed to show that the normal price of goods tended to be proportional to the amount of labor required to produce them. As stated in the Populist platform, the theory is moral proscription rather than economic description.

The "spirit" that will uplift mankind is the recognition of this proscription. Money accumulated through selling above a necessary minimum for processing represents gain from robbery. The labor implied here seems to be only that productive of sweat. The change from "urban labor" in the St. Louis version to "civil labor" in the Omaha indicates a recognition of this narrow restriction. Clerks who handle the work necessary for transporting and selling goods are, after all, not the necessary enemies of manual labor. It is bankers and employers of large labor forces who could be considered "uncivil."

The third declaration might be seen as contradicting paragraph 9 of the preamble. If the Populists really believed in the expansion of government power, why should a civil-service amendment be asked for? Because both points were additions from the St. Louis version, there must be some connection between them.

The connection was the operation of party government in the United States. Patronage was a primary source of party power from the beginning of the federal government. To ignore the spoils system was to lose political power, as John Quincy Adams discovered during his single term as President after he declared his refusal to have anything to do with patronage. To fight it, as Rutherford B. Hayes did in attempting to clean up the New York Customs House, was, in this case, to see the Port Collector, Chester A. Arthur, become the next Vice-President. In 1871, Congress had authorized a Civil Service Commission. But after no appropriations had been made, the commissioner resigned in 1875 and the Commission died. The Pendleton Act, passed in 1883 under the impact of the assassination of Garfield by a self-proclaimed disappointed office-seeker, set up the existing Civil Service Commission, but it affected only about 10 percent of the patronage jobs throughout the remainder of the century. Unless patronage could be eliminated, it was obvious to the Populists that more government employees would mean, in effect, greater taxes to support the party in power. Because Congress seemed incapable of passing adequate legislation to control the spoils system, a constitutional amendment would have seemed the only peaceful way.

Because all questions for the Populists revolved around money, the first plank in their platform would obviously be on finance. It is not easy for most of us to conceive of the complicated financial transactions that were commonplace to Americans in 1892. About the only similar experience we might have would be traveling across Europe and finding our pockets stuffed with bills and coins of different sizes and colors. Before the financial structure was stabilized in the early 1930's, Americans had had to deal with different sorts of currencies whose relationships to each other fluctuated. In 1892, a man's stock of money might consist of gold and silver coin and certificates, greenbacks, and national banknotes. The greenbacks were not redeemable in coin and the banknotes were issued by national banks on their investments in United States securities. The most common form of currency, greenbacks and banknotes, were liable to fluctuate in value at any time. Furthermore, the value of gold and silver was tied to a market economy. In times of economic panic, the national banks were liable to suspend payments or fail altogether, and they were at any time able to contract the currency so as to bring down prices, according to the quantity theory of money. Complete federal control of currency, the solution finally arrived at in the early 1930's, appeared to be the only solution for the Populists.

But all this was minor compared to the difficulties of an inadequate supply of currency. Paragraph 8 of the preamble had stated the problem and it was up to the Populists to present a solution here that would inspire confidence in the voters. The total currency in the United States, currently held in the treasury and outside the treasury in circulation, had risen to over $1 billion for the first time in 1863, but after a modest contraction in 1866, the total fell to $888 million in

1868. It did not reach the billion mark again until 1879. As of June 30, 1892, the total was $1,752 million. In 1863, the estimated population of the United States had been just over 34 million. It increased by around a million a year, until by July 1, 1892, it was estimated at 65,666,000. Increase in currency was obviously not keeping up with growth of population. The two most popular means of dealing with the situation among Populists were free and unlimited coinage and the sub-Treasury plan.

The sub-Treasury plan had been first proposed at the December 1889 meeting of the Southern Alliance in St. Louis. Essentially, it suggested:

That the system of using certain banks as United States depositories be abolished, and in place of said system, establish in every county in each of the States that offers for sale during the one year five hundred thousand dollars worth of farm products; including wheat, corn, oats, barley, rye, rice, tobacco, cotton, wool and sugar, all together; a sub-treasury office, which shall have in connection with it such warehouses or elevators as are necessary for carefully storing and preserving such agricultural products as are offered it for storage, and it should be the duty of such sub-treasury department to receive such agricultural products as are offered for storage and make a careful examination of such products and class same as to quality and give a certificate of the deposit showing the amount and quality, and that United States legal-tender paper money equal to eighty percent of the local current value of the products deposited has been advanced on same on interest at the rate of one percent per annum, on condition that the owner or such other person as he may authorize will redeem the agricultural product within twelve months from the date of the certificate or the trustee will sell same at public auction to the highest bidder for the purpose of satisfying the debt. Besides the one percent interest the sub-treasurer should be allowed to charge a trifle for handling and storage, and a reasonable amount for insurance, but the premises necessary for conducting the business should be secured by the various counties donating to the general government the land and the government building the very best modern buildings, fireproof and substantial. With this method in vogue the farmer, when his produce was harvested, would place it in storage where it would be perfectly safe and he would secure four-fifths of its value to supply his pressing necessity for money at one percent per annum. He would negotiate and sell his warehouse or elevator certificates whenever the current price suited him, receiving from the person to whom he sold, only the difference between the price agreed upon and the amount already paid by the sub-treasurer. When, however, these storage certificates reached the hand of the miller or factory, or other consumer, he to get the product would have to return to the sub-treasurer the sum of the money advanced, together with the interest on same and the storage and insurance charges on the product.

Although this plan did not appear in either the St. Louis demands of the Southern Alliance or the separately issued platform of the Northern Alliance, the official proclamations of the December 1889 meeting, it was picked up by the Ocala demands of December 1890, where real estate was added to nonperishable farm products and the interest was increased to 2 percent per annum; and it was repeated in the same fashion by the Cincinnati platform of May 1891. Intense opposition to the sub-Treasury as "class legislation" that would expand and contract the currency in a wild, uncontrollable fashion and could do nothing for farmers raising perishable products, such as fruit and livestock, accounted for its absence from the Omaha resolutions of the Northern Alliance in January 1891. Instead, this meeting suggested "the abolition of national banks, and that the surplus funds be loaned to individuals upon land security at a low rate of interest." But it remained part of the Populists' suggestions as the price northerners paid southerners for the principle of government ownership of the railroads. The phrase, "or a better system," first following the statement of the sub-Treasury plan in the St. Louis platform of February 1892, indicates the uneasiness about the plan. By mentioning neither produce nor land, the two platforms of 1892 attempted to slide over the difficulties. Payment for public improvements was the only other system the Populists had thought of to get more currency directly into the hands of the people without going through the banks.

Earlier Populist statements about coinage had been restricted to the demand for "free and unlimited coinage of silver." The change in point 1 of the finance plank of the platform of July 1892 was in a conservative direction. To call for free and unlimited coinage of silver is in effect to propose fiat currency. Since the middle of the 1870's, the supply of American silver was so great that had it all been minted, the increased money supply would have been truly inflationary. The ratio proposed—16 ounces of silver worth 1 ounce of gold—was taken from the definition given the silver dollar in 1792. Although silver had been worth more than this during the years before the new discoveries of silver deposits, the price then fell until it was greater than 20 to 1 in 1892. The mountain states whose economy depended upon mining would have been given handsome profits indeed had their entire production of silver been bought by the federal government at a price that much greater than the market value of the metal. To Populists, who accepted the quantity theory of money, the debates over silver and gold were irrelevant. However, because their main aim was to increase the supply of money in circulation, they were willing to support any means of doing so, and the support of the silver states was necessary for the election. The specification of a price for silver was a device for gaining wider support, as was any proposal for silver coinage.

The more genuine Populist programs were the other four points of the finance plank. In 1891, with a population of 64,361,000, the United States had $1,497,441,000 in currency circulating outside the Treasury, or $23 plus per capita. In 1965, with a population of 194,572,000 and $39,720,000,000 circulating currency, the per-capita circulation was $204 plus. In 1865, with a population of 35,701,000, the per-capita circulation had been just over $30 in a total circulation of $1,083,-541,000. In 1866, the total circulation had dropped to $939,-678,000, with an increase of population to 36,538,000, or $26 per capita, and the ratio continued to drop through the 1870's. With a slight rise, the per-capita circulating currency held at $22 or so in the 1880's. In the Populist theory of money, an increase from $22 to $50 circulating per capita would double prices. For farmers, this would mean that loans could be paid instead of continuing to increase because of inabilities to meet even interest payments. The probable effect of doubled prices on wage laborers indicates that profession of solidarity with all labor was not thought through by the Populists. However, the average hourly wage for the manufacturing industries in 1892 was 20 cents. The gross national product for the period 1889–1893 is estimated at $13.1 billions. With a doubled circulating currency, wages could increase, whereas with only $22 per capita in circulation, there wasn't the money available, or so it might appear to one reasoning according to the quantity theory of money.

Points 3 and 4 had appeared in some form in the various platforms since the St. Louis platform of 1889. During the period 1866–1893, the federal budget showed a surplus in every single year. This surplus resulted from customs, excise taxes on alcohol and tobacco, stamp taxes, and manufacturers' taxes. Until 1871, there had been some revenue from estate and gift taxes. The manufacturers' taxes, always small, had dropped to $2,000 by 1892. The income tax passed in 1861, initially 3 percent on income over $800 and twice increased, was allowed to expire in 1870. Taxes during this period were regressive. A look at the tables of federal expenditures shows that the surplus did indeed benefit the bondholders. The interest on the public debt was the highest category of federal expenditure in 1867–1872, 1877, and 1878. In 1873–1876 and 1879–1882, interest cost more than either the combined defense budget or veterans' compensation and pensions. From 1883 to 1888, it was greater than the combined defense budget. Interest cost more than the Navy Department in 1889–1891. Only in 1892 did interest drop below the other categories of federal spending. The plea for economy and limitation on revenue, looked at in the context of the federal surplus and categories of expenditures, did not contradict the appeal for an expansion of governmental power made in paragraph 9 of the preamble.

The demand for a postal savings system, point 5, in effect a call for government-owned and government-operated banks to take the place of commercial banks for deposits, was a new proposal with the St. Louis platform of 1892. It reflects the experience of the bank panics of 1873, 1888, and 1890, when banks failed or refused to convert deposits into currency. Due to the operations of the market in securities, bankers' balances were concentrated in a few New York banks. When stock prices dropped so low that the market issued calls on the stocks bought on security collateral, this concentration of balances in New York banks affected banks throughout the country. The Populists, ignoring or discounting the operations of capital in their labor theory of value, wanted a safe depository for their money. They did not want their savings subjected to the manipulations of bankers.

Under the National Bank Act of 1863, no distinction was made between savings and demand deposits. The proposal for a postal savings bank was an attempt to put such a distinction into operation.

The idea of savings banks is as old as the early seventeenth century. In the eighteenth century, savings banks developed from municipal pawnshops in several European countries. Early in the nineteenth century, proposals for a post office savings system were introduced into the British parliament, and they were discussed at various times until William E. Gladstone and Sir Rowland Hill pushed through a bill in 1861. The system in Britain provided a means for the poor to save money at small interest with no risk. It was this system that the Populists, no doubt, used as a model for their proposal.

In the St. Louis version of the platform, the plank on land preceded the plank on transportation, and the proposal for nationalization of telegraph and telephone appeared as point "a" under the proposal for nationalization of railroads. Because railroads had been given enormous tracts of western land as incentives for building roads, the land and transportation planks were closely connected. The change in the Omaha platform indicates that the Populists felt transportation and communication to be somewhat more important in July than they had in February of 1892. The statement on land had appeared in the St. Louis demands of December 1889 in both the Southern and Northern Alliance statements, as well as in the Ocala demands of December 1890 and the Cincinnati platform of May 1891. The statement on transportation and communication, however, after appearing in the statements of 1889, was modified to a call for rigid federal supervision, which failing, they should be nationalized.

The railroads had long been the target for the grievances of the western farmers. They attributed the difference between the price grain brought on the New York market and the price they had sold it for—frequently 10 percent or less of the New York price—to the high cost of transportation. Freight charges were wildly inconsistent. They differed between states, between long hauls and short hauls, and between products, and there was no effective competition between roads to keep prices down. Just about every form of collusion imaginable was charged to the railroads and the elevator operators, the railroads and the grain merchants, the railroads and the politicians. Their influence was strongly felt in the governments of all the western states.

During the 1870's, attempts to regulate the railroad did not pass through Congress, but many states passed "Granger laws" regulating the roads. Although these state laws received Supreme Court approval in *Munn* v. *Illinois* (1877), they were overruled in the *Wabash Case* (1886). In February 1887, the Interstate Commerce Act created the commission. The Interstate Commerce Commission was supposed to see to it that rates were reasonable and just, that pooling operations, drawbacks, and rebates were stopped, and that short and long hauls were priced at the same rate. Although authorized to investigate railroads through summoning witness and company records, the commission's rulings did not have the force of a court order. Equity proceedings could be brought in federal courts by the commission, but the difficulties of interpreting and enforcing the law made the commission practically useless. With this experience, Populists in 1892 would have believed regulation impossible. The only solution was public ownership of the railroads.

The vast public domain, as was seen in earlier discussions of the Northwest Ordinance and Morrill Act, became involved in many of the political debates throughout the nineteenth century. The necessity of treating it as a capital resource immediately after the Revolution was perpetuated by the decision expressed in the Ohio Enabling Act (1802) to retain federal title instead of turning over the public land to the states upon admission to the Union. The eastern states continued to look upon the public land as a source of revenue and favored policies that put the land into the hands of speculators. Although after 1850 these states became willing to support the homestead principle and grants for state improvements in exchange for western support for high tariffs, favorable immigration laws, a national banking system, and ship subsidies, the land policy continued to favor speculators over actual settlement by farmers. In 1892, vast areas of the West were held by nonresidents—"alien ownership." The first Pacific Railway Act (1862) had granted ten alternate sections per mile of public domain on both sides of the road, and this was doubled by the second act (1864). Sales of the 44 million acres granted the Northern Pacific, for example, resulted in $136 million by 1917. By calling for reclaiming the land not held by resident owners and not needed for the roads, the Populists were demanding a basic reconstruction of public-land policy. The homestead-land policy had been contradicted by other legislation, such as the Morrill Act. Roughly six times more land had been acquired by purchase than had been acquired free during the first forty years after the Homestead Act. The Populist expression on land follows from their labor theory of value. Land belongs to those who actually work it.

The ten points listed under "expression of sentiments" represent an attempt to broaden the appeal of the party. All except plutocrats, it was hoped, could agree upon points directly related to questions of national financial policy; but all who could agree on financial questions could not agree upon other reform issues. This device of "resolving" sentiments of the convention was first used by the Populists at the Cincinnati meeting of May 1891. It was at this meeting that they first considered themselves a "political party." Resolutions political conventions adopt after the platform has been passed are something like toasts, designed to make everyone feel good. The resolutions of the Omaha convention are something more than toasts, but something less than positions the party committed itself to hold at all costs.

The sentiments of the Omaha platform fall into four categories. Government operations are dealt with in points 1, 7, and 8; government finance in points 2 and 9; benefits for Civil War veterans in point 3; and the conditions of wage laborers in points 4, 5, 6, and 10. The resolutions of the Cincinnati and St. Louis conventions had not been so extensive. The Cincinnati meeting had called for universal suffrage, payments to Union veterans that would raise their compensation to a par with gold, eight-hour workday legislation, and swift settlement of the legal complications involved in Oklahoma homesteading, and had condemned the labor policy of the directors of the Columbian Exposition. The St. Louis platform had merely urged female suffrage and increased veterans' benefits. Fully committed by the Omaha convention to a fight for the presidency, the Populists were throwing the net over all the "industrial classes."

The appeal to wage labor was stronger than in any previous official statement. The period since the Civil War had been punctuated by strikes, strikebreaking, the organization of unions, and the infiltration of unions by Pinkerton men (the original Finks), agitation for an eight-hour day, and attempted boycotts. Although resolution 4 might appear pure xenophobia, when looked at in the context where contract labor and recent immigrants were used as strikebreakers, it changes color. Contract labor had been permitted to enter the United States for a period of twelve months, by a ruling of the Office of Commissioner of Immigration in 1865. By the 1880's, the function of such labor was largely strikebreaking. In its edition of July 20, 1884, *John Swinton's Paper* quoted an agency in Castle Garden, New York, as saying it had imported 14,000 Italians on contract, of which only 6,000 returned to Italy. Presumably the rest became part of the pool of strikebreakers. Although an anti-contract labor law was passed in February 1885, it excluded skilled labor and was therefore not nearly effective enough. The ineffectiveness of legislation had also been illustrated by the eight-hour-day law for federal employees and workers on government contract jobs. Lacking a penalty clause, called for by resolution 5, employers with government contracts could easily evade the law. The activities of the Pinkerton Detective Agency were truly sinister during this period. Beginning with the infiltration of the Molly Maguires in the Pennsylvania hard-coal fields during the 1870's, by the middle of the 1880's, the agency was circulating secret advertisements for detectives to infiltrate and discover union and strike plans. Its abolition, called for in resolution 8, seemed clear necessity. By ending their resolutions with a call for all to join the Knights of Labor boycott, the Populists deliberately left an impression of their solidarity with wage labor.

In their resolutions concerning government operation and finance, the Populists included a number of proposals that reformers had been advocating for the last quarter century. These were proposals toward more popular democracy to counteract the manipulations of the party bosses. The Australian ballot system, first introduced in South Australia in 1858, eliminated opportunities for ballot-box stuffing and the intimidation of voters that the earlier system of ballots distributed by political parties had facilitated. Under this system, the nomination of candidates was regulated by law. Only ballots furnished by the state could be used, and these were to be distributed by its sworn representatives. Furthermore, ballots had to be marked in secret. Both initiative and referendum had long been favorite proposals of reform organizations. Initiative had been adopted in the first constitution of Georgia in 1777 for constitutional changes, but for regular legislation neither procedure was adopted until South Dakota provided for both in 1898. Direct elections were also favorite reformers' plans. The Populists' Cincinnati convention had made direct elections of President, Vice-President, and senators part of the actual platform. Limitation of executive offices to one term in the Omaha platform was a more conservative formulation of the proposals for more direct democracy.

In financial proposals, the Populists also followed the common reform sentiments. There had been many proposals for a graduated income tax since the Civil War income tax had been allowed to lapse. The combination of an income tax with the reduction of taxation on domestic industries, called for in resolution 2, however, is strange, because in 1892 and for many years before there had been no manufacturers' taxes to speak of. The opposition to federal subsidies, in resolution 9, helps to explain this paradox. Those who opposed subsidies

were the small-business and professional classes who had supported reform, especially civil service reform, since the Civil
War. In the resolutions on government elections and finance,
the Populists were reaching for support from groups who
might not support their platform proposals but who would
sympathize with their resolutions. These resolutions had a
more conservative tone than similar statements made in the
past. The resolution on veterans' pensions, number 3, only
called for "fair and liberal pensions," not "the issue of legal
tender and treasury notes in sufficient amount to make the
pay of the soldiers equal to par with coin," as the Cincinnati
platform had demanded. The Populists were not entering the
Presidential race of 1892 simply to protest; they wanted to win
and were tailoring their statements accordingly.

The Populists lost big enough for their proposals to be absorbed by the major parties. Writing in 1931, John Hicks observed that "to list these [Populist] demands is to cite the chief
political innovations made in the United States during recent
times." Hicks referred to their secondary proposals for the
most part, the "expression of sentiments," more than the actual
planks of the platform. Since 1931, with reform of the currency
and various agricultural acts during the New Deal, most of the
rest of the Populist platform has become part of the machinery
of federal government.

By absorbing proposals, the major parties managed to kill
the spirit that informed them. The spirit of the Populist Party
demanded an end to government by political party manipulations. The Populists saw that the power struggle between two
established parties prevented effective expression of the popular will. The two political parties in the United States act
toward third parties like the British Establishment is said to
act toward expressions of discontent among the working class:

the bright ones are absorbed into the Establishment. By adopting proposals of third parties, the major parties see to it that there will be no effective change in the profitable struggle for power. Perhaps one of the best recent examples of this was John Kennedy's reaction to the civil rights march on Washington in the summer of 1963. The marchers were provided with buses to take them from the stations to the grounds around the Washington Monument. The protest was changed into a picnic. The liberal, by absorbing the letter of protest, has managed to develop a conservative policy that seems impossible to change.

XI

Foreign Policy by Emotional Management

Woodrow Wilson

ADDRESS TO CONGRESS

January 8, 1918

(On War Aims and Peace Terms)

Gentlemen of the Congress:

(1) Once more, as repeatedly before, the spokesmen of the Central Empires have indicated their desire to discuss the objects of the war and the possible basis of a general peace. Parleys have been in progress at Brest-Litovsk between Russian representatives and representatives of the Central Powers, to which the attention of all the belligerents has been invited for the purpose of ascertaining whether it may be possible to extend these parleys into a general conference with regard to terms of peace and settlement. The Russian representatives presented not only a perfectly definite statement of the principles upon which they would be willing to conclude peace, but also an equally definite program for the concrete application of those principles. The representatives of the Central Powers, on their part, presented an outline of settlement which, if much less definite, seemed susceptible of liberal interpretation

until their specific program of practical terms was added. That program proposed no concessions at all, either to the sovereignty of Russia or to the preferences of the population with whose fortunes it dealt, but meant, in a word, that the Central Empires were to keep every foot of territory their armed forces had occupied—every province, every city, every point of vantage—as a permanent addition to their territories and their power. It is a reasonable conjecture that the general principles of settlement which they at first suggested originated with the more liberal statesmen of Germany and Austria, the men who have begun to feel the force of their own peoples' thought and purpose, while the concrete terms of actual settlement came from the military leaders who have no thought but to keep what they have got. The negotiations have been broken off. The Russian representatives were sincere and in earnest. They cannot entertain such proposals of conquest and domination.

(2) The whole incident is full of significance. It is also full of perplexity. With whom are the Russian representatives dealing? For whom are the representatives of the Central Empires speaking? Are they speaking for the majorities of their respective Parliaments or for the minority parties, that military and imperialistic minority which has so far dominated their whole policy and controlled the affairs of Turkey and of the Balkan States which have felt obliged to become their associates in this war? The Russian representatives have insisted, very justly, very wisely, and in the true spirit of modern democracy, that the conferences they have been holding with the Teutonic and Turkish statesmen should be held with open, not closed, doors, and all the world has been audience, as was desired. To whom have we been listening, then? To those who speak the spirit and intention of the resolutions of the German Reichstag of

the ninth of July last, the spirit and intention of the liberal leaders and parties of Germany, or to those who resist and defy that spirit and intention and insist upon conquest and subjugation? Or are we listening, in fact, to both, unreconciled and in open and hopeless contradiction? These are very serious and pregnant questions. Upon the answer to them depends the peace of the world.

(3) But whatever the results of the parleys at Brest-Litovsk, whatever the confusions of counsel and of purpose in the utterances of the spokesmen of the Central Empires, they have again attempted to acquaint the world with their objects in the war and have again challenged their adversaries to say what their objects are and what sort of settlement they would deem just and satisfactory. There is no good reason why that challenge should not be responded to, and responded to with the utmost candor. We did not wait for it. Not once, but again and again, we have laid our whole thought and purpose before the world, not in general terms only, but each time with sufficient definition to make it clear what sort of definite terms of settlement must necessarily spring out of them. Within the last week Mr. Lloyd George has spoken with admirable candor and in admirable spirit for the people and Government of Great Britain. There is no confusion of counsel among the adversaries of the Central Powers, no uncertainty of principle, no vagueness of detail. The only secrecy of counsel, the only lack of fearless frankness, the only failure to make definite statement of the objects of the war, lie with Germany and her allies. The issues of life and death hang upon these definitions. No statesman who has the least conception of his responsibility ought for a moment to permit himself to continue this tragical and appalling outpouring of blood and treasure unless he is

sure beyond a peradventure that the objects of the vital sacrifice are part and parcel of the very life of society and that the
people for whom he speaks think them right and imperative
as he does.

(4) There is, moreover, a voice calling for these definitions of
principle and of purpose which is, it seems to me, more thrill-
ing and more compelling than any of the many moving voices
with which the troubled air of the world is filled. It is the voice
of the Russian people. They are prostrate and all but helpless,
it would seem, before the grim power of Germany, which has
hitherto known no relenting and no pity. Their power apparently is shattered. And yet their soul is not subservient. They
will not yield either in principle or in action. Their conception of what is right, of what is humane and honorable for
them to accept, has been stated with a frankness, a largeness
of view, a generosity of spirit, and a universal human sympathy which must challenge the admiration of every friend of
mankind; and they have refused to compound their ideals or
desert others that they themselves may be safe. They call to
us to say what it is that we desire, in what, if in anything, our
purpose and our spirit differ from theirs; and I believe that
the people of the United States would wish me to respond with
utter simplicity and frankness. Whether their present leaders
believe it or not, it is our heartfelt desire and hope that some
way may be opened whereby we may be privileged to assist
the people of Russia to attain their utmost hope of liberty and
ordered peace.

(5) It will be our wish and purpose that the processes of peace,
when they are begun, shall be absolutely open, and that they
shall involve and permit henceforth no secret understandings

of any kind. The day of conquest and aggrandizement is gone by; so is also the day of secret covenants entered into in the interest of particular governments and likely at some unlooked-for moment to upset the peace of the world. It is this happy fact, now clear to the view of every public man whose thoughts do not still linger in an age that is dead and gone, which makes it possible for every nation whose purposes are consistent with justice and the peace of the world to avow now or at any other time the objects it has in view.

(6) We entered this war because violations of right had occurred which touched us to the quick and made the life of our own people impossible unless they were corrected and the world secured once for all against their recurrence. What we demand in this war, therefore, is nothing peculiar to ourselves. It is that the world be made fit and safe to live in; and particularly that it be made safe for every peace-loving nation which, like our own, wishes to live its own life, determine its own institutions, be assured of justice and fair dealings by the other peoples of the world, as against force and selfish aggression. All the peoples of the world are in effect partners in this interest, and for our own part we see very clearly that unless justice be done to others it will not be done to us.

(7) The program of the world's peace, therefore, is our program, and that program, the only possible program, as we see it, is this:

I.—Open covenants of peace, openly arrived at, after which there shall be no private international understandings of any kind, but diplomacy shall proceed always frankly and in the public view.

II.—Absolute freedom of navigation upon the seas, outside territorial waters, alike in peace and in war, except as the seas may be closed in whole or in part by international action for the enforcement of international covenants.

III.—The removal, so far as possible, of all economic barriers and the establishment of an equality of trade conditions among all the nations consenting to the peace and associating themselves for its maintenance.

IV.—Adequate guarantees given and taken that national armaments will be reduced to the lowest point consistent with domestic safety.

V.—Free, open-minded, and absolutely impartial adjustment of all colonial claims, based upon a strict observance of the principle that in determining all such questions of sovereignty the interests of the population concerned must have equal weight with the equitable claims of the Government whose title is to be determined.

VI.—The evacuation of all Russian territory and such a settlement of all questions affecting Russia as will secure the best and freest cooperation of the other nations of the world in obtaining for her an unhampered and unembarrassed opportunity for the independent determination of her own political development and national policy, and assure her of a sincere welcome into the society of free nations under institutions of her own choosing; and, more than a welcome, assistance also of every kind that she may need and may herself desire. The treatment accorded Russia by her sister nations in the months to come will be the acid test of their good-will, of their comprehension of her needs as distinguished from their own interests, and of their intelligent and unselfish sympathy.

VII.—Belgium, the whole world will agree, must be evacuated and restored, without any attempt to limit the sovereignty which she enjoys in common with all other free nations. No other single act will serve as this will serve to restore confidence among the nations in the laws which they have themselves set and determined for the government of their relations with one another. Without this healing act the whole structure and validity of international law is forever impaired.

VIII.—All French territory should be freed and the invaded portions restored, and the wrong done to France by Prussia in 1871 in the matter of Alsace-Lorraine, which has unsettled the peace of the world for nearly fifty years, should be righted, in order that peace may once more be made secure in the interest of all.

IX.—A readjustment of the frontiers of Italy should be effected along clearly recognizable lines of nationality.

X.—The peoples of Austria-Hungary, whose place among the nations we wish to see safeguarded and assured, should be accorded the freest opportunity of autonomous development.

XI.—Rumania, Serbia, and Montenegro should be evacuated; occupied territories restored; Serbia accorded free and secure access to the sea; and the relations of the several Balkan States to one another determined by friendly counsel along historically established lines of allegiance and nationality; and international guarantees of the political and economic independence and territorial integrity of the several Balkan States should be entered into.

XII.—The Turkish portions of the present Ottoman Empire should be assured a secure sovereignty, but the other nationalities which are now under Turkish rule should be assured an undoubted security of life and an absolutely unmolested opportunity of autonomous development, and the

Dardanelles should be permanently opened as a free passage to the ships and commerce of all nations under international guarantees.

XIII.—An independent Polish State should be erected which should include the territories inhabited by indisputably Polish populations, which should be assured a free and secure access to the sea, and whose political and economic independence and territorial integrity should be guaranteed by international covenant.

XIV.—A general association of nations must be formed under specific covenants for the purpose of affording mutual guarantees of political independence and territorial integrity to great and small states alike.

(8) In regard to these essential rectifications of wrong and assertions of right, we feel ourselves to be intimate partners of all the governments and peoples associated together against the imperialists. We cannot be separated in interest or divided in purpose. We stand together until the end.

(9) For such arrangements and covenants we are willing to fight and to continue to fight until they are achieved; but only because we wish the right to prevail and desire a just and stable peace, such as can be secured only by removing the chief provocations to war, which this program does remove. We have no jealousy of German greatness, and there is nothing in this program that impairs it. We grudge her no achievement or distinction of learning or of pacific enterprise such as have made her record very bright and very enviable. We do not wish to injure her or to block in any way her legitimate influence or power. We do not wish to fight her either with arms or with hostile arrangements of trade, if she is willing to associate herself with us and the

other peace-loving nations of the world in covenants of justice and law and fair dealing. We wish her only to accept a place of equality among the peoples of the world—the new world in which we now live—instead of a place of mastery.

(10) Neither do we presume to suggest to her any alteration or modification of her institutions. But it is necessary, we must frankly say, and necessary as a preliminary to any intelligent dealings with her on our part, that we should know whom her spokesmen speak for when they speak to us, whether for the Reichstag majority or for the military party and the men whose creed is imperial domination.

(11) We have spoken, now, surely, in terms too concrete to admit of any further doubt or question. An evident principle runs through the whole program I have outlined. It is the principle of justice to all peoples and nationalities, and their right to live on equal terms of liberty and safety with one another, whether they be strong or weak. Unless this principle be made its foundation, no part of the structure of international justice can stand. The people of the United States could act upon no other principle, and to the vindication of this principle they are ready to devote their lives, their honor, and everything that they possess. The moral climax of this, the culminating and final war for human liberty, has come, and they are ready to put their own strength, their own highest purpose, their own integrity and devotion to the test.

Foreign Policy by
Emotional Management

COMMENTARY

THE first historians of the American Revolution set out the
terms for the debate on American foreign policy. Diplomacy,
it would seem, must be a function of the nation's view of
itself. Expansionist powers, such as Athens and Rome in the
ancient world, or Great Britain and the United States in
recent times, regard their "civilizations" as superior. As such,
it is incumbent upon them to extend the "blessings" either
through military means, as did Rome and Nazi Germany,
through commercial activity, as did Athens, or through some
combination of the two, as did the British in the nineteenth
century and the United States following World War II.
Contractionist nations, while they may feel just as superior as
the great powers, seek the blessings for their own people, as

have the Swiss and the Scandinavian countries in this century. David Ramsay, Mercy Otis Warren, and John Marshall, writing around 1800, saw the revolutionary origins of the United States determining its proper foreign policy.

For the moderate Federalist Ramsay, the progress of opinion from the Stamp Act Congress of 1767 to the Constitution of 1787 was the working out of a model government that could serve as a text for the instruction of the world. Mrs. Warren, the extreme republican, saw the process of revolution, directed by the active will of God, as the American contribution to world history. She found evidence for this view in the European revolutions and thought that the United States ought to be actively participating in the transformation of the human condition. Independence for the benefit of the American community resulted from the war according to the extreme Federalist, or nationalistic, interpretation of the Chief Justice. Proper foreign policy, in his view, should further the enlightened self-interest of the nation.

During most of the nineteenth century, American foreign policy followed Ramsay's line by avoiding, in Thomas Jefferson's phrase, "entangling Alliances." In the Mexican and Spanish-American wars, Marshall's vision came to the fore, as it may be argued it did in the northern prosecution of the Civil War. Only with Woodrow Wilson's intervention into European affairs did American foreign policy take a direction toward Mrs. Warren's extreme republican view of the meaning of the Revolution.

Wilson wanted the United States to be a mediator, from the beginning of World War I. His first public appeal, August 19, 1914, was for Americans to be "impartial in thought as well as in action." During the controversy with the British over the shipping rights of neutrals, he wrote to his strongly pro-British ambassador, Walter Hines Page, in a letter dated October 28, 1914, that American neutrality was "in the interest of all the belligerents no less than in our own interest. I mean that if we are to remain neutral and to afford Europe the legitimate assistance possible in such circumstances, the course we have been pursuing is the absolutely necessary course." Early in 1915, Wilson sent his private adviser, Edward M. House, to Europe with an "informal commission." In his letter to House, January 29, 1915, Wilson stated: "Our single object is to be serviceable, if we may, in bringing about the preliminary willingness to parley which must be the first step towards discussing and determining the conditions of peace." "The allies on both sides," the letter concluded, "have seemed to turn to the United States as to a sort of court of opinion in this great struggle, but we have no wish to be judges; we desire only to play the part of disinterested friends who have nothing at stake except their interest in the peace of the world." Throughout the late winter and early spring, House visited London, Paris, and Berlin, but Wilson's view of the importance of American opinion was premature.

After the crises over the German sinking of the "Lusitania" (May–July) and the "Arabic" (August–October) in 1915, Wilson again attempted to initiate a negotiated peace. House spent the months of January and February 1916 in Europe attempting to formulate the peace terms desired by the opposing sides. His discussions with the German, French, and British statesmen resulted in the "House Memorandum" to Sir Edward Grey, the British Foreign Minister. On Wilson's behalf, House promised, in the memorandum dated February 22, 1916, that should England and France agree to mediation by the United States, but Germany refuse, America would probably enter the war on the side of the Entente. The conditions that the United States was willing to negotiate were the withdrawal of the Central Powers from Belgium and Serbia, the return of Alsace-Lorraine to France, the cession of Constantinople to Russia, the acquisition of the Italian-speaking parts of Austria by Italy, the independence of Poland, and the expansion of German colonial areas and overseas markets in exchange for the reduction of German naval construction. Wilson endorsed the memorandum on March 6, but the Entente, hoping for victory in the 1916 offensive, did not follow up the proposal.

After the indecisive summer of 1916 on the western front, the German ambassador to the United States inquired early in September if the United States would be willing to provide its good offices should Germany guarantee Belgium's restoration. Put off until the "He kept us out of war" presidential campaign, Wilson's efforts toward peace were renewed after the election, and by November 25 he had drafted a proposal for a "conference of representatives of the belligerent governments and of the governments not now engaged in the war whose interests may be thought to be most directly involved. . . ." In this draft, Wilson asked

> for a concrete definition of the guarantees which the belligerents on the one side and the other deem it their duty to demand as a practical satisfaction of the objects they are aiming at in this contest of force, in addition to the very great and substantial guarantee which will, I feel perfectly confident, be supplied by a league of nations formed to unite their force in active cooperation for the preservation of the world's peace when this war is over.

The publication of this plan was delayed by the hostile reaction to all peace feelers in England and France; and before

Wilson thought it the right moment to publish his plan, the German government sent a note to the United States, December 12, requesting that she inform the Entente governments that the Central Powers were prepared to negotiate peace.

Because no specific terms were mentioned in the German note, Wilson addressed a note to all belligerent powers, on December 18, requesting a statement of their war aims. The Central Powers replied on December 26 with similar notes that evaded any statement of war aims by proposing, in the words of the German note, "the speedy assembly, on neutral ground, of delegates of the warring States." The Entente governments, in a joint note dated December 29, rejected the German proposal because it contained no terms for negotiation. On January 10, 1917, they replied to Wilson's request for war aims with a specification of terms that could be demanded only by victorious powers, a fact which they recognized by concluding the message with the pledge that "the Allies are determined, individually and collectively, to act with all their power and to consent to all sacrifices to bring to a victorious close a conflict upon which they are convinced not only their own safety and prosperity depends but also the future of civilization itself." To this, Wilson's reply was his "peace without victory" speech to the Senate on January 22.

A rhetorical appeal to the "peoples" over their governments, the text of the speech was sent to the American ambassadors in Europe on January 15. In summarizing his peace proposals, Wilson made his diplomatic position clear:

> I am proposing, as it were, that the nations should with one accord adopt the doctrine of President Monroe as the doctrine of

the world: that no nation should seek to extend its polity over any other nation or people, but that every people should be left free to determine its own polity, its own way of development, unhindered, unthreatened, unafraid, the little along with the great and powerful.

I am proposing that all nations henceforth avoid entangling alliance which would draw them into competitions of power, catch them in a net of intrigue and selfish rivalry, and disturb their own affairs with influences intruded from without. There is no entangling alliance in a concert of power. When all unite to act in the same sense and with the same purpose, all act in the common interest and are free to live their own lives under a common protection.

I am proposing government by the consent of the governed; that freedom of the seas which in international conference after conference representatives of the United States have urged with the eloquence of those who are the convinced disciples of liberty; and that moderation of armaments which makes of armies and navies a power for order merely, not an instrument of aggression or of selfish violence.

These are American principles, American policies. We could stand for no others. And they are also the principles and policies of forward looking men and women everywhere, of every modern nation, of every enlightened community. They are the principles of mankind and must prevail.

With Germany's resumption of unrestricted submarine warfare on February 1, however, Wilson's attempts to be a mediator halted. On February 3, Wilson announced the break in diplomatic relations with Germany. He was slow to ask for a declaration of war and waited for some overt German act. Toward the end of February, the British intercepted the Zimmerman telegram, and during February and March several American ships were sunk. With the establish-

ment of a provisional government in Russia and the abdica-
tion of the Tzar in mid-March, the war seemed to be entering
a new phase of democratic against autocratic powers. Wilson's
cabinet voted unanimously for war on March 20, and, on
March 21, Wilson issued a call for a special session of Congress
to meet on April 2. In his war message of that day, he drew
a firm distinction between the German people and government. The United States had "no quarrel with the German
people." The war was to be against "Prussian autocracy."
Much like his speech of January 22, the war message was
a rhetorical appeal to the peoples distinct from their governments. The United States was "to fight . . . for the ultimate
peace of the world and for the liberation of its peoples—the
German people included—for the rights of nations great and
small and the privilege of men everywhere to choose their
way of life and of obedience." Wilson had changed his role
of world mediator for that of world peacemaker.

Viewing the United States as fighting "for the ultimate
peace of the world," and believing that the Entente, through
its interlocking secret treaties, aimed first of all at territorial
expansion, Wilson refused to allow the United States to
become formally allied with the group, insisting that she
be known as an "Associated Power" in what then was called
the "Allied and Associated Powers." In his role of world
peacemaker, Wilson moved cautiously. His next opportunity
came with the publication of Pope Benedict's peace proposal on August 1, 1917. Essentially, the Pope called for
a return to a territorial status quo ante and the establishment
of machinery for effective arbitration. This would mean
German retention of Alsace-Lorraine and Austrian retention
of territory that Italy had entered the war to obtain. With
Wilson's previous statements on territorial war-gains well

known, the Entente governments feared that he would use the occasion to repudiate the secret treaties. He used the opportunity, after having submitted drafts and received approval of the reply from the European Allies, to restate his distinction between the German people and government. This distinction served as a clever device for indicating to the Germans that a change in their government was prerequisite for peace. France and England were delighted with Wilson's insistence on the distinction, because a weakened German government would facilitate the achievement of their own war aims.

Almost immediately after the reply to the Pope, Wilson set in motion the machinery that resulted in "the Inquiry," a group of professors and social-planners that formulated positions for the peace conference. On September 2, he wrote to House suggesting that such a group be formed and offered to pay the bills out of funds in the executive office. House at once began to get recommendations for men who might serve. By December 22, the Inquiry had formulated a memorandum on specific peace terms. Revised and lengthened, it was submitted to Wilson on January 2, 1918 as "A Suggested Statement of Peace Terms."

Events during the fall of 1917 were forcing Wilson to speed up his efforts for peace, if he did not want to lose the position of peacemaker to the Russians. On November 6, the Soviets overthrew the Kerensky government and the next day issued their peace decree. Realizing that peace could not be decreed, Trotsky, as commissioner for foreign affairs, addressed a formal note to all belligerents on November 20 asking for a conference to make a "democratic peace on the basis of no annexations or indemnities and self-determination of nations." Getting no response from the Allied governments, *Izvestia*, in an effort to force a reply, began publishing the Entente secret treaties on November 23. Five days later, the Allied Military Missions in Russia issued a formal protest to the Russian Commander-in-Chief. But on the twenty-eighth, the Soviets announced an armistice with the Central Powers, to be postponed until December 2, however, to allow the Allied governments time to agree. From November 29 to December 3, an Interallied Conference met at Paris without reaching an agreement. In Wilson's message to Congress recommending war with Austria-Hungary, on December 4, he attempted to counteract the Soviet formula—"no annexations or indemnities" —with the observation that "just because this crude formula expresses the instinctive judgment as to right of plain men everywhere it has been made diligent use of by the masters of German intrigue to lead the people of Russia astray. . . ." The next day an armistice was concluded between Russia and the Central Powers at Brest-Litovsk.

In Washington, there was a great deal of confusion about what attitude to take toward events in Russia as well as toward the Interallied Conference. House, at the conference, cabled Wilson, November 30, for his approval on a resolution specifying that the "Allies and the United States . . . are not waging war for the purpose of aggression or indemnity." Wilson replied, December 1, with approval and stressed that the conference must discuss war aims in a spirit compatible with his "peace without victory" speech of January 1917. Unable to obtain agreement on this point, House and his delegation landed in New York, December 15, and dispatched their pessimistic reports to Wilson. Having determined that the French and British meant to ignore the existence of the Soviet government, Secretary of State Lansing wired American diplomats on the fifteenth to have no official relations with Soviet officials.

Meeting with House on the eighteenth, Wilson decided to issue a separate American statement of war aims, since it was impossible for the Allies to agree.

Events in Russia continued to complicate Wilson's role as peacemaker. The Brest-Litovsk peace conference opened on December 22, and on the twenty-fifth, the Central Powers accepted the formula of no annexations or indemnities, if the Allies could be persuaded to accept it within ten days. Trotsky addressed a letter to "the peoples and governments of the Allied countries" on the thirty-first. He called for "peace on the basis of an entire and complete recognition of the principle of self-determination for all peoples and in all states. . . ." The implications of this he made clear by inquiring if the Allies were "willing on their part to give the right of self-determination to the peoples of Ireland, Egypt, India, Madagascar, Indo-China, etc. . . ." And he charged that "up to now the Allied Governments have decidedly not manifested in any way their readiness to enter upon a really democratic peace. . . ." In Lansing's transmittal of this letter to Wilson, on January 2, 1918, he characterized it as a program for "international anarchy." "Any sort of reply," he felt, "would be contrary to the dignity of the United States. . . ."

Wilson did not agree. The next afternoon, in conversation with Sir Cecil Spring Rice, retiring British ambassador, Wilson, according to Spring Rice's report, spoke of the urgency of counteracting the Soviet moves. They had adopted the policy he had initiated when he

had made an appeal to the German people behind the back of the German Government. . . . They had issued an appeal to all the nations of the world, to the peoples and not to the governments. He was without information at present, or at least without certain information, as to what reception had been given to this appeal. But there was evidence at hand that certainly in Italy and probably also in England and France, the appeal had not been without its effect. In the United States active agitation was proceeding. It was too early yet to say with positive certainty how successful this agitation had been. But it was evident that if the appeal of the Bolsheviki was allowed to remain unanswered, if nothing were done to counteract it, the effect would be great and would increase.

In addition, Spring Rice reported, Wilson stated that it was necessary to counteract the impression among both the German and the American people that the "Allies now fighting in Europe would find it extremely difficult to agree on any definite programme which did not look on the face of it as if its object, and its main object, was aggression and conquest."

Wilson and House worked on the speech, to be delivered to Congress on the eighth, late into the evening of January 4 and again the next morning, when the final outline was decided upon. Late in the afternoon of the fifth, Lloyd George's speech on war aims was printed in the Washington papers. This address to the British Trade Union Congress was the result of labor's insistence upon a statement for its continued cooperation. Explaining the lack of advanced consultation, Foreign Secretary Balfour telegraphed House that the speech had been written to be consistent with Wilson's pronouncements on the subject. After reading the speech, House reports in his diary, Wilson was depressed because Lloyd George's points were almost the same as the ones he intended to make. House, however, assured him that his speech would overshadow Lloyd George's, "and that he, the President, would once more become the spokesman for the Entente, and, indeed the spokesman for the liberals of the world." The next day,

January 6, Wilson and House again worked on the speech in the light of Wilson's insistence, according to House, "that nothing be put in the message of an argumentative nature. . . ." On the seventh, the speech was read to Secretary of State Lansing, who suggested some verbal changes. The next day at noon, Tuesday, January 8, Wilson delivered his Fourteen Points Address to an unprepared Congress. In order to prevent newspaper speculation about what he might say, he had not given advanced notice that he was about to state the war aims of the United States.

Wilson's problem, in addressing Congress, was how to reassert his role effectively as the world's leading peacemaker, a role being challenged on all sides. He had to counteract the Soviet initiative of the last two months, an initiative he had publicly recognized in his speech calling for war on Austria-Hungary. The problem of replying to Trotsky's letter of December 31 was especially acute. Whatever the Central Powers were trying to do at Brest-Litovsk behind the scenes, they had called the bluff of the Western Allies by agreeing to the Soviet formula for peace, providing it could be made general. Because the Interallied Conference had been unable to agree on war aims, Wilson had meant to force agreement by proposing, in effect, separate American peace terms. Lloyd George's apparent acceptance of Wilson's terms on the fifth, however, seemed to put the United States fourth in the race toward peace, behind the Soviets, the Central Powers, and England.

Wilson's major concern, therefore, in speaking to Congress on January 8, 1918, was his image. In the language of rhetorical analysis, how was he to restore his "ethical appeal"? The problem was complicated by Wilson's view of the position of an American president. On the afternoon of January 3, Wilson had told Spring Rice, by way of a preface to the remarks on the Russian situation, that

> the problem which an American President had to face was in the main a psychological one. He had to gauge public opinion. He had to take the course which commended itself to the great majority of the American people whose interpreter he was bound to be. No action could be taken or at least usefully taken unless it received the support of the great majority. It was not so much a question of what was the right thing to do from the abstract viewpoint as what was the possible thing to do, from the point of view of the popular condition of mind. It was his duty to divine the moment when the country required action and to take that action which the great majority demanded.

Such an attitude perhaps accounts for the vagueness and lack of argument in the speech. Wilson was twisting his statements to present them in a way he thought the audience wanted to hear.

The opening paragraph presents the immediate occasion for the speech. Wilson, having better sources of information than had his audience—Congress, the American public, and the European public, in that order—purports to give the background of events. Instead of stating that a reply to Trotsky's letter of December 31 was necessary, Wilson opened by stating that the Central Powers wished to discuss war aims and peace terms. This was in no sense true. What had happened at Brest-Litovsk was that the Central Powers had agreed to give the Soviets a grace period, until January 4, in which to get the Western Allies to agree to the formula of no annexations and no indemnities, which had been accepted as a basis for peace on December 25. In further discussions about the details be-

fore the beginning of the recess on December 28, the Central
Powers had made it clear to the Soviet delegates that they understood by "no annexations" no forcible annexations. By this
they meant that the Polish and Baltic states, which had been
created under military occupation of these parts of the Russian Empire, were not a subject for negotiation with the Soviets. This interpretation perhaps accounts for the urgency
of Trotsky's letter. The Central Powers, especially Germany,
were determined to dictate terms favorable to themselves, and,
on January 5, they wired the Soviets that since the Western
Allies had not replied to the agreement of December 25, it was
no longer binding. The conference resumed on January 9. Wilson's statement that "negotiations have been broken off" was
false. Trotsky did break off negotiations on February 10 after
the Central Powers signed a treaty with the Ukraine on February 9, but on January 8 the delegates at Brest-Litovsk were
preparing to resume discussions the next day. In this opening
paragraph, Wilson was making a covert appeal to the Soviets.
By describing their representatives as "sincere" and "earnest"
men who had refused to "entertain . . . proposals of conquest
and domination," he distorted his report for propaganda purposes.

This distorted description formed the basis for the series of
rhetorical questions in paragraph 2. These questions are
framed in such a way as to flatter a Russian audience while
presenting the Soviets as naive to the American and Western
European audiences. His familiar disjunction between people
and government forms the basis for the seemingly ingenuous
questions about the representative character of German statements. By citing the Reichstag resolution of July 19, 1917
(not "ninth of July" as he mistakenly dates it), which had
called for a peace of "mutual understanding and lasting recon-

ciliation" without "forced acquisitions of territory and political, economic, and financial violations," together with references to those who "insist upon conquest and subjugation," Wilson attempted to indicate confusion within the Central Powers. The rhetorical questions stand for arguments as he abruptly turns, in paragraph 3, to assert the solidarity of the West.

The assertions of unity preface a statement of Western peace terms. As in the opening sentence of the speech, so in the first sentence of paragraph 3, Wilson distorts the case. Trotsky had challenged the West to state its peace terms. The only way that Wilson could ignore the Soviets and still counteract what he considered the propaganda value of Trotsky's letter was to treat Trotsky as some sort of mouthpiece for the Central Powers. Although there may be some justification for distortion given the circumstances of revolution and confusion in Russia, there can be no explanation except a deliberate attempt to fool his audience for the remainder of the paragraph. Wilson seems to be speaking for both the entire Western bloc and himself when he asserts, "We did not wait for it" (i.e., the challenge to state peace terms). While Wilson perhaps would have seemed only too ready with statements to an astute contemporary observer, the Entente was notoriously reluctant to expose its true peace aims, which were embodied in a number of secret treaties. The only evidence Wilson could possibly have for his assertion of Western unity was Lloyd George's speech of January 5. This speech, Wilson knew perfectly well from Foreign Secretary Balfour's telegraph of the fifth to House, was Lloyd George's expedient means to gain the cooperation of the trade unions. Assertions that "confusion" and "secrecy" were all on the side of the Central Powers are pure falsehoods designed to make a naive audience think that the

Western allies must have had the better case because they knew what they were doing. In the rhetorical wind of "appalling outpouring of blood and treasure," in the last sentence of the paragraph, Wilson shifts into unadulterated statement of emotion designed to prevent the audience from exercising critical thought.

Paragraph 4 continues the pure emotionalism with an attempt to turn Trotsky's letter back upon the Soviets. The gross flattery of the Russian people, carefully distinguished from the "present leaders" in the last sentence of the paragraph, is painfully obvious in its hypocrisy. The picture of the Russian people "prostrate and all but helpless," "yet their soul is not subservient" "before the grim power of Germany" is constructed in nauseatingly prefabricated prose. Wilson's protestation that he is responding to the call of the Russian people, by which he means Trotsky's letter, with "utter simplicity and frankness" is in the language of complete deviousness.

The deviousness is, if anything, increased by paragraph 5. Wilson states as fact what any reader of newspapers and certainly anyone having to do with the legislative or executive branches of any government knew was completely otherwise. The day of secret covenants, conquest, and aggrandizement most emphatically was not gone by. To state it as fact can only be an attempt to force the audience to believe it simply on the authority of the speaker's person. Such statements of Wilson's are not at all like the opening statements of the Declaration of Independence, for example. The statements there about human equality and self-government are valid because they are necessary within the philosophical system employed. They do not depend for their validity upon empirical evidence. The problem, should the empirical evidence contradict them, is to change the evidence, which is exactly what a revolution does. Wilson, on the other hand, is making statements about what exists in the world. Such statements are neither valid nor invalid logically, they are either true or false depending upon their agreement with the empirical evidence. Because Wilson's assertions about conquest, aggrandizement, and secret treaties do not agree with the evidence, they are simply false and therefore can only be considered a trick to force his audience to believe what he wants it to believe on the simple authority of his presence.

This authority is reinforced by the specious high-mindedness of paragraph 6. Taking his tone from British Liberal justifications of the first year of the war, such as H. G. Wells's series of newspaper articles on the "war to end war," Wilson gives as reason for believing in American pronouncements the sanctity of her motives for entering the war. The unselfishness of America is used to justify the correctness of the demands for peace that Wilson will make on behalf of the United States.

Presumably, this unselfishness is the justification for identifying the Fourteen Points as the "only possible program," when introducing them in paragraph 7. These points repeat most of Lloyd George's discussion of the fifth, but, by numbering them, Wilson gives a semblance of logical reasoning. The points are of three kinds. The first four repeat the "idealistic" grounds for peace Wilson pronounced in his "peace without victory" speech of January 22, 1917. Points V through XIII deal with the territorial questions of the war. And Point XIV calls for an "association of nations," something that had been discussed on both sides of the Atlantic for years.

Examined, the four idealistic points turn out to be eyewash. Within two months, Wilson contradicted Point I. On March 12, 1918, he instructed Secretary of State Lansing to oppose

Borah's resolution requiring that the Senate consider all treaties in open executive sessions. He wrote:

> I take it for granted that you feel as I do that this is no time to act as the resolution prescribes, and certainly when I pronounced for open diplomacy, I meant not that there should be no private discussions of delicate matters, but that no secret agreements of any sort should be entered into and that all international relations, when fixed, should be open, above-board, and explicit.

Whatever Wilson may have thought he meant, the words of Point I are quite otherwise. The language is clear, unambiguous, and straightforward. If he meant something other than that "diplomacy shall proceed always frankly and in the public view," we can only conclude that he was either attempting to cover up what he meant or that he regarded all language as logically meaningless, a mere device for affecting the emotions of the listeners.

Points II and III apparently demand free trade. The qualifications, however, vitiate any meaning. By allowing that "the seas may be closed in whole or in part by international action for the enforcement of international covenants," Wilson contradicts "absolute freedom of navigation." The insertion "so far as possible" in Point III allows all sorts of "economic barriers," because it is never "possible" to remove them. These statements are really disingenuous, as is Point IV. To reduce armaments "to the lowest point consistent with domestic safety" is completely ambiguous and allows any interpretation from self-interest, for a nation in arms may be considered necessary for domestic safety under the formula. Far more straightforward was Lloyd George's statement on the fifth: "Owing to the diversion of human effort to warlike pursuits, there must follow a world shortage of raw materials which will increase the longer the war lasts, and it is inevitable that those countries which have control of the raw materials will desire to help themselves and their friends first." Wilson's idealism, it seems, was a mere attempt to appear high-minded.

The points on territorial questions are only a little less ambiguous than the idealistic points. Lloyd George had stated on the fifth that "the general principle of national self-determination is therefore as applicable in their cases [i.e., the colonial questions] as in those of occupied European territories." Reacting to the application of self-determination in Trotsky's letter, Wilson carefully avoided the phrase "national self-determination" and chose instead to speak of "populations" and "nationality." On the colonial question, his formulation —"the interests of the population concerned must have equal weight with the equitable claims of the Government whose title is to be determined"—is hopelessly inadequate as a basis for discussion, even though he stressed its importance through the use of *must* as opposed to the use of *should* in connection with some of the other territorial questions.

"Nationality" and "peoples" instead of self-determination, in the points dealing with Italy, Austria-Hungary, the Balkans, and the Ottoman Empire, completely confused the issue. "Recognizable lines of nationality" as a basis for the Italian frontiers or "historically established lines of allegiance and nationality" for the Balkans are both meaningless phrases. A look at a language map of Europe for this period shows an extremely complicated pattern of pockets within larger linguistic areas. The use of "autonomous development" in connection with the Ottoman Empire and Austria-Hungary could either mean absolutely nothing would be done for the minority peoples or that they would be given statehood.

In dealing with the question of Russian territory, Wilson

attempted to continue his flattery of the Russian people. The involved syntax of the first statement under Point VI, however, not only is difficult to understand but also reveals his uncertainty as well. The second statement about Russia's needs has a peculiar ring in view of the fact that the United States as well as the rest of the Western Allies were refusing to have anything to do with the Soviet government. Point XIII calling for an independent Polish state, already established by Germany, contradicts the demand for the evacuation of all Russian territory in point VI. This demand can hardly be considered "sympathy" for Russia when the Soviet delegates were getting ready at Brest-Litovsk to resist German demands that all non-Russian speaking areas of western Russia be given statehood. In fact, if by "Russia" Wilson meant the areas speaking Russian, then the Central Powers could hardly be said to have entered the country.

The only unequivocal points of the entire fourteen are VII and VIII. The demand that Belgium be "evacuated and restored" and that the occupied territory of France be freed and restored clearly implies restoration at the expense of the Central Powers. The position on Alsace-Lorraine, however, is not clear. Return of territory is not the only way that "wrong" may be "righted."

Point XIV, the one generally associated with Wilson and generally thought to be the most important of all, is, like the others, too ambiguous to serve as a basis for real discussion. Almost anything can be read into "a general association of nations." No mention of means for enforcing "mutual guarantees" is even mentioned, nor how they are to come about.

Wilson turned from the Fourteen Points to address the German people in paragraphs 8, 9, and 10. Here the language becomes much clearer. There could be no doubt that Wilson ruled out any chance of a separate American peace. Professed solidarity with the Entente, in paragraph 8, made flattery of the German people in paragraph 9 more effective in order to dissociate them from the German government in paragraph 10. Unlike the ambiguities in most of the Fourteen Points, which could mean whatever the interpreter wanted them to mean, the ambiguities in paragraphs 9 and 10 are calculated to show Germans that a "democratic" government is prerequisite for peace, without actually making it an open demand.

In summing up the effect of what he has said, in paragraph 11, Wilson continues pronouncing without bothering to argue. It is simply not the case that the "terms [are] too concrete to admit of any further doubt or question." Nor can "the principle of justice to all peoples and nationalities," whatever it may mean, run "through the whole program." Surely the first prerequisite for applying a principle is that it must be unambiguous and consistent. Wilson is neither consistent nor clear. Rather, his principle seems to be to put statements in such a way that they can be understood by any listener to his own advantage. To those in Austria-Hungary wishing to preserve the dual monarchy, Point X might not seem to ask for its destruction. But to minority groups "autonomous development" would mean statehood. And so on, with the rest of the Fourteen Points. After trying for universal agreement in this way, Wilson tells his audience that they have been agreeing to "justice" and that "the moral climax of this, the culminating and final war for human liberty" will be international justice. The last two sentences flatter the moral character of the American audience in a last attempt to use language, not as a means for statement, but as a device for emotional management.

Attempts at emotional management define demagogic rhetoric. Of course, any attempt at persuasion involves getting the audience's sympathy with the argument. What distinguishes ethical from demagogic rhetoric is argument. An argument presents logical and empirical evidence for the conviction it seeks. Wilson, in the Address to Congress, January 8, 1918, "On War Aims and Peace Terms," presented no argument. The only reason given for the audience to believe what he said was that he said it. He attempted to present himself as the morally superior man, the man concerned with justice. The ambiguities, allowing the audience to read into the pronouncements what it already believed, show that he pictured his audience as people whose opinions depend upon their emotions, rather than their reason. By playing upon these emotions, Wilson elevates himself into the role of perpetual peacemaker. This speech was a major statement. Perhaps it is not too much to assert that such an attempt at trickery was one of the chief reasons for the defeat of the League of Nations in the Senate.

XII

Agrarian Ideal Applied to Urban Reality

AN ACT *

To relieve the existing national economic emergency by increasing agricultural purchasing power, to raise revenue for extraordinary expenses incurred by reason of such emergency, to provide emergency relief with respect to agricultural indebtedness, to provide for the orderly liquidation of joint-stock land banks, and for other purposes.

May 12, 1933.
[H.R. 3835.]
[Public, No. 10.]

Be it enacted by the Senate and House of Representatives of the United States of America in Congress assembled,

Agricultural
Adjustment Act.
Post, pp. 199, 354.

Title I—AGRICULTURAL ADJUSTMENT

AGRICULTURAL
ADJUSTMENT.

DECLARATION OF EMERGENCY

That the present acute economic emergency being in part the consequence of a severe and in-

Declaration of
emergency.

---

* Portions of the bill that are merely technical and do not add to the understanding of its presuppositions have been omitted.

creasing disparity between the prices of agricultural and other commodities, which disparity has
largely destroyed the purchasing power of farmers for industrial products, has broken down the
orderly exchange of commodities, and has seriously impaired the agricultural assets supporting
the national credit structure, it is hereby declared that these conditions in the basic industry
of agriculture have affected transactions in agricultural commodities with a national public interest, have burdened and obstructed the normal
currents of commerce in such commodities, and
render imperative the immediate enactment of
title I of this Act.

Declaration o
policy

Declaration of Policy
SEC. 2. It is hereby declared to be the policy
of Congress—

Balance between
production and
consumption to be
established, etc.

(1) To establish and maintain such balance between the production and consumption of agricultural commodities, and such marketing conditions therefor, as will reestablish prices to farmers
at a level that will give agricultural commodities
a purchasing power with respect to articles that
farmers buy, equivalent to the purchasing power

Base period,
except for tobacco.

of agricultural commodities in the base period.
The base period in the case of all agricultural
commodities except tobacco shall be the prewar
period, August 1909–July 1914. In the case of

For tobacco.

tobacco, the base period shall be the postwar period August 1919–July 1929.

(2) To approach such equality of purchasing power by gradual correction of the present inequalities therein at as rapid a rate as is deemed feasible in view of the current consumptive demand in domestic and foreign markets.

Correcting present inequalities.

(3) To protect the consumers' interest by readjusting farm production at such level as will not increase the percentage of the consumers' retail expenditures for agricultural commodities, or products derived therefrom, which is returned to the farmer, above the percentage which was returned to the farmer in the prewar period, August 1909–July 1914.

Protecting consumers' interest.

.   .   .

PART 2—COMMODITY BENEFITS

Commodity benefits.

General Powers

General powers.

SEC. 8. In order to effecuate[1] the declared policy, the Secretary of Agriculture shall have power—

Secretary of Agriculture.

(1) To provide for reduction in the acreage or reduction in the production for market, or both, of any basic agricultural commodity, through agreements with producers or by other voluntary methods, and to provide for rental or benefit payments in connection therewith or upon that part of the production of any basic agricultural commodity required for domestic consumption, in such amounts as the Secretary deems fair and reasonable, to be paid out of any moneys

To reduce production of basic agricultural commodities. *Post*, p. 676.

Rental or benefit payments.

[1] So in original.

Storage of non-perishable commodities on the farm, etc.

available for such payments. Under regulations of the Secretary of Agriculture requiring adequate facilities for the storage of any nonperishable agricultural commodity on the farm, inspection and measurement of any such com-

Protection, marketing, etc.

modity so stored, and the locking and sealing thereof, and such other regulations as may be prescribed by the Secretary of Agriculture for

Advances, deduction for inspection costs, etc.

the protection of such commodity and for the marketing thereof, a reasonable percentage of any benefit payment may be advanced on any such commodity so stored. In any such case, such deduction may be made from the amount of the benefit payment as the Secretary of Agriculture determines will reasonably compensate for the cost of inspection and sealing, but no deduction may be made for interest.

To enter into marketing agreements with respect to any agricultural commodity, etc.

(2) To enter into marketing agreements with processors, associations of producers, and others engaged in the handling, in the current of interstate or foreign commerce of any agricultural commodity or product thereof, after due notice

Not to be held as violating antitrust laws.

and opportunity for hearing to interested parties. The making of any such agreement shall not be held to be in violation of any of the antitrust laws of the United States, and any such agree-

Proviso.
Duration of agreement.
Loans to parties entering agreement; limitation.
Vol. 47, p. 6.

ment shall be deemed to be lawful: *Provided,* That no such agreement shall remain in force after the termination of this Act. For the purpose of carrying out any such agreement the parties thereto shall be eligible for loans from the Reconstruction Finance Corporation under section 5 of the Reconstruction Finance Corporation Act. Such loans shall not be in excess of such amounts as may be authorized by the agreements.

(3) To issue licenses permitting processors, associations of producers, and others to engage in the handling, in the current of interstate or foreign commerce, of any agricultural commodity or product thereof, or any competing commodity or product thereof. Such licenses shall be subject to such terms and conditions, not in conflict with existing Acts of Congress or regulations pursuant thereto, as may be necessary to eliminate unfair practices or charges that prevent or tend to prevent the effectuation of the declared policy and the restoration of normal economic conditions in the marketing of such commodities or products and the financing thereof. The Secretary of Agriculture may suspend or revoke any such license, after due notice and opportunity for hearing, for violations of the terms or conditions thereof. Any order of the Secretary suspending or revoking any such license shall be final if in accordance with law. Any such person engaged in such handling without a license as required by the Secretary under this section shall be subject to a fine of not more than $1,000 for each day during which the violation continues.

To issue licenses, permitting handling of any agricultural commodity or competing product thereof. Terms of issue.

Licenses may be suspended or revoked.

Secretary's order final.

Penalty for violation.

(4) To require any licensee under this section to furnish such reports as to quantities of agricultural commodities or products thereof bought and sold and the prices thereof, and as to trade

To require licensee to furnish reports and to keep system of accounts.

practices and charges, and to keep such systems of accounts, as may be necessary for the purpose of part 2 of this title.

Removal, on which warehouse receipt is outstanding, unlawful. (5) No person engaged in the storage in a public warehouse of any basic agricultural commodity in the current of interstate or foreign commerce, shall deliver any such commodity upon which a warehouse receipt has been issued and is Punishment for. outstanding, without prior surrender and cancellation of such warehouse receipt. Any person violating any of the provisions of this subsection shall, upon conviction, be punished by a fine of not more than $5,000, or by imprisonment for Revocation of license for violation. not more than two years, or both. The Secretary of Agriculture may revoke any license issued under subsection (3) of this section, if he finds, after *Post*, p. 672. due notice and opportunity for hearing, that the licensee has violated the provisions of this subsection.

Processing tax.

PROCESSING TAX

Levy of, to meet economic emergencies.
Post, p. 676.
Rental, etc., payments. SEC. 9. (a) To obtain revenue for extraordinary expenses incurred by reason of the national economic emergency, there shall be levied processing taxes as hereinafter provided. When the Secretary of Agriculture determines that rental or benefit payments are to be made with respect to any basic agricultural commodity, he shall proclaim such determination, and a processing Effective date of tax. tax shall be in effect with respect to such commodity from the beginning of the marketing year

therefor next following the date of such procla-
mation. The processing tax shall be levied, as- Levy, assessment, etc.
sessed, and collected upon the first domestic
processing of the commodity, whether of domestic production or imported, and shall be
paid by the processor. The rate of tax shall con- Rate.
form to the requirements of subsection (b). Such
rate shall be determined by the Secretary of Agriculture as of the date the tax first takes effect,
and the rate so determined shall, at such inter-
vals as the Secretary finds necessary to effectuate
the declared policy, be adjusted by him to conform to such requirements. The processing tax
shall terminate at the end of the marketing year Termination.
current at the time the Secretary proclaims that
rental or benefit payments are to be discontinued
with respect to such commodity. The marketing
year for each commodity shall be ascertained and
prescribed by regulations of the Secretary of Ag-
riculture: *Provided,* That upon any article upon *Proviso.* Manufacturers'
which a manufacturers' sales tax is levied under sales tax computed.
the authority of the Revenue Act of 1932 and Vol. 47, p. 259.
which manufacturers' sales tax is computed on
the basis of weight, such manufacturers' sales tax
shall be computed on the basis of the weight of
said finished article less the weight of the proc-
essed cotton contained therein on which a processing tax has been paid.

(b) The processing tax shall be at such rate as Rate to equal difference between
equals the difference between the current aver- current farm price and fair exchange
age farm price for the commodity and the fair value.
exchange value of the commodity; except that if Factors to be considered. *Post,* p. 671.

the Secretary has reason to believe that the tax at such rate will cause such reduction in the quantity of the commodity or products thereof domestically consumed as to result in the accumulation of surplus stocks of the commodity or products thereof or in the depression of the farm price of the commodity, then he shall cause an appropriate investigation to be made and afford due notice and opportunity for hearing to interested parties. If thereupon the Secretary finds that such result will occur, then the processing tax shall be at such rate as will prevent such accumulation of surplus stocks and depression of the farm price of the commodity. In computing the current average farm price in the case of wheat, premiums paid producers for protein content shall not be taken into account.

To prevent accumulation of surplus and depression of farm price.

Protein content of wheat.

(c) For the purposes of part 2 of this title, the fair exchange value of a commodity shall be the price therefor that will give the commodity the same purchasing power, with respect to articles farmers buy, as such commodity had during the base period specified in section 2; and the current average farm price and the fair exchange value shall be ascertained by the Secretary of Agriculture from available statistics of the Department of Agriculture.

Fair exchange value defined.

How ascertained.

(d) As used in part 2 of this title—

(1) In case of wheat, rice, and corn, the term "processing" means the milling or other processing (except cleaning and drying) of wheat, rice, or corn for market, including custom milling for

"Processing" defined.
Post, pp. 528, 670.

toll as well as commercial milling, but shall not include the grinding or cracking thereof not in the form of flour for feed purposes only.

(2) In case of cotton, the term "processing" means the spinning, manufacturing, or other processing (except ginning) of cotton; and the term "cotton" shall not include cotton linters.

(3) In case of tobacco, the term "processing" means the manufacturing or other processing (except drying or converting into insecticides and fertilizers) of tobacco.

(4) In case of hogs, the term "processing" means the slaughter of hogs for market.

Post, p. 1242.

(5) In the case of any other commodity, the term "processing" means any manufacturing or other processing involving a change in the form of the commodity or its preparation for market, as defined by regulations of the Secretary of Agriculture; and in prescribing such regulations the Secretary shall give due weight to the customs of the industry.

Post, pp. 528, 675, 1242.

(e) When any processing tax, or increase or decrease therein, takes effect in respect of a commodity the Secretary of Agriculture, in order to prevent pyramiding of the processing tax and profiteering in the sale of the products derived from the commodity, shall make public such information as he deems necessary regarding (1) the relationship between the processing tax and the price paid to producers of the commodity, (2) the effect of the processing tax upon prices to consumers of products of the commodity, (3) the

Pyramiding tax, profiteering, etc. Measures to prevent.

Information to be published.

relationship, in previous periods, between prices paid to the producers of the commodity and prices to consumers of the products thereof, and

Post, p. 675.

(4) the situation in foreign countries relating to prices paid to producers of the commodity and prices to consumers of the products thereof.

. . .

COMMODITIES

"Basic agricultural commodity."
Products included.
Post, pp. 528, 670, 1184.
Authority to exclude any commodity.

SEC. 11. As used in this title, the term "basic agricultural commodity" means wheat, cotton, field corn, hogs, rice, tobacco, and milk and its products, and any regional or market classification, type, or grade thereof; but the Secretary of Agriculture shall exclude from the operation of the provisions of this title, during any period, any such commodity or classification, type, or grade thereof if he finds, upon investigation at any time and after due notice and opportunity for hearing to interested parties, that the conditions of production, marketing, and consumption are such that during such period this title can not be effectively administered to the end of effectuating the declared policy with respect to such commodity or classification, type, or grade thereof.

. . .

Agrarian Ideal Applied
to Urban Reality

COMMENTARY

ATTEMPTING to bequeath the wisdom of the Revolutionary generation, David Ramsay, one of the first historians of the new United States, codified it into three maxims. The first and third had to do with the moral concerns that ought to inform public policy, while the second argued that "from the great excess of the number of independent farmers in these states, over and above all other classes of inhabitants, the long continuance of your liberties may be reasonably presumed." The agrarian ideal was assumed by the Federalist Ramsay quite as much as by the Republican Jefferson. Common to almost all the men who argued out the Constitution of 1787, this assumption held that land is the ultimate basis of all wealth. Ownership of land is a natural right, given to men in exchange for their labor on the land. Through ownership, men gain independence, while they become virtuous and happy through contact with nature. The new United States, so ran the Revolutionary generation's consensus, uniquely embodied the agrarian ideal. Therefore, it was the government's business to protect the independent farmer.

The agrarian myth has an old and aristocratic history. From the Athenians, who preferred to live on their lands outside the walls of Athens, to the Roman readers of Horace, through the medieval knights on their manors, to the French philosophers of the Enlightenment, the free man has been pictured standing on his own ground. The fact that any real farmer with the leisure to become involved in public affairs must necessarily be supported by a large force of cheap labor usually has been ignored by the extollers of the agrarian ideal. One man's freedom in any actual agrarian environment is paid for by the slavery of many men.

One's ability to trick oneself, however, is infinite. Throughout the history of the United States, there has been no lack of public men eager to preach the virtues of the agrarian life, even when these men themselves experienced the grubby existence of farm laborers in their youth. Perhaps today the glow is finally fading; yet one still hears of prosperous men retiring to the country and of hippies desiring to set up country communities of love. Until less than a decade ago, it was commonplace for national political figures to find some place in their major speeches for some form of Ramsay's second maxim.

It has been a long time since the factual aspect of the maxim was in any sense true. Although the national census did not show urban exceeding rural population until 1920, by that date there were almost as many white-collar workers (10,529,000) as farmers (11,390,000), while blue-collar workers outnumbered farmers almost two to one (20,287,000 blue-collar workers). As early as 1900, the first occupational census, blue-collar workers outnumbered farmers by over 2 million (13,027,000 to 10,888,000). By 1930, there were 4 million more white-collar workers than farmers, and the trend has, of course, accelerated. The United States has not had a preponderantly agricultural population in this century, nor has agriculture led production. As long ago as 1884, manufacturing first exceeded agriculture in the gross national product.

In the way that myths control action, however, substantial government aid to farmers was not given until long after the country was predominately industrial, despite the fact that there were two sustained agricultural depressions during the nineteenth century. After a period during which agricultural wholesale prices exceeded the 1910–1914 index, from 1813 to 1818, there was a long decline when they were below the index, until 1863. Again, after 1874, prices fell below the index until the end of the century. During the twentieth century, wholesale agricultural prices exceeded the 1926 index from 1917 to 1920, in 1924 and 1925, and again in 1928 and 1929. From then until 1942, they were well below 100.0, reaching a low of 48.2 in 1932. Throughout the nineteenth century, wholesale farm prices were well below the combined price for all commodities. In this century, up until 1940, farm prices during the better years slightly exceeded the combined prices, and during the second half of the 1920's, they were definitely ahead of nonfarm prices.

From the statistics, it would appear that farmers were worse off during the nineteenth century, when no government aid was extended to them, than they have been in this century with increasing government assistance. Although the national government began to take a direct interest in agriculture through the establishment of a Department of Agriculture in 1862, and provided federal subsidies for state experimental stations through the Hatch Act of 1887, not until the Farm Loan and the Warehouse Acts of 1916 were individual farmers directly assisted. The Loan Act set up a federal Farm Loan Board to supervise Farm Loan Banks in each of the twelve Federal Reserve districts. Cooperative farm loan associations were members of the banks, and individuals in the associations could get mortgages on their farms at lower rates than at commercial banks. The Warehouse Act provided a means for assisting crop financing through its authorization of storage-receipts, from licensed and bonded warehouses, as negotiable paper. In 1923, the Intermediate Credit Act extended short-term agricultural credit through intermediate credit banks in the Federal Reserve districts, again using farmers' cooperative associations as agents. The year before, the Cooperative Marketing Act (1922) had exempted these associations from the antitrust laws.

Because credit did not solve the problem of a market for farm products that had fallen from a wholesale index of 150.7 in 1920 to 88.4 in 1921, Senator McNary of Oregon and Representative Haugen of Iowa, simultaneously in both houses of Congress (January 16, 1924), introduced a bill that would provide for control of surplus and support for prices. Defeated by the House in June 1924, it was reintroduced into Congress but defeated in both houses in the late spring of 1926. Early in the following year, it was taken up again and passed. Coolidge vetoed it, however, on February 25, 1927, with the argument that the bill would fix prices and benefit special interests. Passed again in the spring of 1928, Coolidge again vetoed it, adding to his previous argument that the equalization fee scheme, whereby the producers of agricultural commodities would make up the difference between the price the government had paid for the surplus and the price it would receive when the goods were sold on the world market, was an improper tax, that the bill encouraged overproduction, and that it would antagonize foreign markets. Ironically, during 1927 and 1928, the wholesale price index for farm products was higher than for all commodities beside farm products, 99.4 versus 94.0 in 1927, and 105.9 versus 92.9 in 1928.

The next year, Hoover's first in office, a special session of Congress was called to deal with farm relief, although the index for nonfarm commodities was falling faster than for farm products, reaching a figure of 91.6 for the year versus 104.9 for farm products. Hoover successfully blocked the plan favored by the farm organizations to pay a bounty on exported goods out of tariff duties. Instead, the administration's Agricultural Marketing Act was passed (June 15, 1929), which established a federal Farm Board to administer a revolving loan fund available to agricultural cooperatives. The board set up stabilization corporations for cotton, grain, and wool, but their efforts to stabilize prices by buying commodities on the open market failed because farmers did not reduce acreages. Agricultural prices fell to 88.3 in 1930 and to 64.8 the following year, dropping for the first time since 1924 to a figure below the index for other commodities, which stood at 75.0 for 1931. The trend continued and agricultural prices hit a low of 48.2 for 1932, while nonfarm prices fell to only 70.2. In 1931, the purchasing program was abandoned and the board went out of existence in 1933.

Elected on a platform that called for the "enactment of every constitutional measure that will aid the farmer to receive for basic farm commodities prices in excess of the cost of production," the Roosevelt administration sent its agricultural bill to Congress on March 16, 1933, immediately after the Senate had passed the administration's Economy Act (March 15), which had followed upon the Emergency Banking Relief Act's introduction, passage, and signing on March 9, the day Roosevelt had convened Congress into special session. Neither the cutting of federal spending by $500 million, nor the support of the existing banking system through federal aid were any less economically conservative than Hoover's plans; rather more so. The speed with which Roosevelt had moved, however, restored confidence in the federal government at a time when revolution was a seriously considered solution. Violence in farming areas had already become a common way to prevent foreclosures during the winter of 1932–1933. After easy success with the banking bill, Secretary of Agriculture Henry Wallace was able to persuade Roosevelt to hold Congress in session until a farm bill was passed. The bill Wallace proposed was an omnibus bill bringing together the different alternatives proposed in recent years. Titles II (Emergency Farm Mortgage Act of 1933) and III (an amendment sponsored by Senator Elmer Thomas of Oklahoma authorizing the President to pursue an inflationary policy with the currency) do not show the agrarian myth as directly as does Title I.

The "Declaration of Emergency" prefacing Title I is an unusual device in a bill. Until March 16, the Roosevelt administration had responded to depression in orthodox fashion. Conservatives reacted to the agricultural bill with a predictable jerk. "The bill before the House is more bolshevistic than any law or regulation existing in Soviet Russia," was the evaluation of Representative Fred Britten of Illinois, for example. As the first of a number of "planned economy" measures, Agricultural Adjustment, perhaps, needed some internal argument to support it. However, this constricted verbiage makes comprehension too difficult for most people, as well as congressmen, to bother with, and is the first of several indications that the bill was hastily drafted.

Underlying the declaration is a causal analysis of the Depression. Although, as has already been pointed out, agricultural prices were running ahead of other commodities from 1924 through 1931, here it is assumed that a major cause of industrial falloff has been the inability of the farmers to buy because they have not been receiving adequate prices for their produce. Low prices have, in turn, prevented them from making mortgage payments, a situation that has severely affected the banks. This argument is too simple to account for the facts. Although it was true that farmers lacked cash, low prices did not account for the lack. Such an argument can only be advanced by men believing that agriculture is the source of all wealth, the floor of the economic pyramid. If this were so, it would follow that the farmers' inability to buy would have to be the result of inadequate prices. A more interlocking view of economic causation would have suggested that low industrial prices could just as easily account for the farmers' lack of sales. The agrarian myth, however, prevented the drafters of the bill from seeing the economy in a complex way. It was for Congress to "declare" the cause of the depression, and for Agricultural Adjustment to rectify it.

Unless agriculture is assumed to be the basic activity in a total economy, the "policy" declared in Section 2 is inconceivable. Here the bill commits the government to parity: a constant balance between the farmer's costs and returns. Only by assuming that farmers are the guardians of liberty, who must in turn be protected, can such a policy be considered equitable. If the farmer is not unique, it is an obvious imposition upon the rest of the population for government to work for agricultural parity without guaranteeing a constant balance between production costs and prices for the industrialist, between wages and prices for laborers, between wholesale and retail prices for salesmen, etc. In Section 2, paragraph 3, "consumers' interest" appears to be considered. After the tortured wording is unraveled, however, it is clear that the farmers' interest comes first. Farm production is to be "readjusted" so that the farmer will receive the percentage of the consumers' retail expenditures that he received during the base period.

In choosing August 1909–July 1914 as a base period, the bill followed the standard set by G. F. Warren and Frank A. Pearson when they took the years 1910–1914 as a base for their recently completed comprehensive wholesale price indexes. The period had been one of relatively high agricultural prices as well as a period that men looked back on after World War I as a time of social stability. Tobacco prices, however, had been low, around 10 cents per pound, and the period 1919–1929 was picked for tobacco because the price had been around 20 cents per pound during that decade. On the surface it appears that the bill chooses a period of agricultural prosperity and commits the government to revive it.

The statistics, however, do not show that a return to the prices of the base period would be particularly good for agriculture. In terms of 1929 prices, the per-capita income in the period 1907–1911 was $608, with a price index of 57. In the next five-year period, income went up to $632 per capita, and the price index went up to 64. Comparing this with the early thirties, we see that the per-capita income in 1930 was $772, with a price index of 96. In 1931, income dropped to $721, and the index dropped to 85. The next year, income was down to $611, with a price index of 77. In 1933, income fell to $590, the lowest it had been since the 1902–1906 period; but prices fell to only 75, higher than they had been at any time in the twentieth century before the United States entered World War I. It would seem that in the early thirties, prices were too high for many people to buy much of anything.

Statistics on food consumption make the choice of the base period more ambiguous. Per-capita food consumption, based on a 1947–1949 index, was 89 in 1909, 88 in 1910 and 1911, 89 in 1912, and 87 in 1913 and 1914. In the 1920's, the index rose to 91 in 1923 and held that figure until 1931, except for 1924 and 1926, when it was 92. In 1931, the index fell one point, and in 1932 and 1933, it fell to 88. Comparison of the figures for apparent civilian per-capita consumption of foods shows some changes. To compare 1912 with 1932: meat consumption—1912, 145.9 lbs.; 1932, 131.1 lbs.; fruit—1912, 159.7 lbs.; 1932, 128.9 lbs.; canned vegetables—1912, 18.7 lbs.; 1932, 22.1 lbs.; milk—1912, 763 lbs.; 1932, 832 lbs.; eggs—1912, 312; 1932, 313. It would seem that the Farmers' Union demand that government assure the farmer's cost of production would have been more flexible than an attempt to return to the prewar ratio of farm prices to costs, if the assumption that the farmer was a special citizen was really to become the basis of government economic planning.

That demand, along with demands for inflation, had been rejected by the administration, which adopted instead the "domestic allotment" scheme proposed by Professor M. L. Wilson of Montana State College. Domestic allotment was assumed in the "Declaration of Policy," in Section 2, and the machinery was spelled out under Part 2. The haste with which the bill was drafted is again shown not only in the opacity of the language but also in the misspelling pointed out in the note to the first sentence of Section 8.

The plan assumes direct connection between supply and demand. Farm prices have fallen, so the reasoning goes, because farmers have produced too much. Section 8, paragraph 1 provides for reduction of supply by taking land out of production and by storage of surplus. Again, the argument is much too simple. Taking 1912 and 1932 as comparisons, the population residing in the United States in 1912 was 95,331,-000; by 1932, it had increased to 124,840,000. The production of basic agricultural commodities, identified in Section 11 as "wheat, cotton, field corn, hogs, rice, tobacco, and milk," did not increase proportionately. Although the price on all these commodities was substantially lower in 1932, production had not risen so dramatically as to account for it.

Although production of wheat, hogs, and rice had increased (wheat—730,011 bushels in 1912 and 756,307 bushels in 1932; hogs—55,500,000 slaughtered in 1912 and 71,425,000 slaughtered in 1932; rice—10,665,000 cwt. in 1912 and 18,729,000 cwt. in 1932), corn, cotton, and tobacco production had actually fallen since the base period (corn—2,947,842 bushels in 1912 and 2,930,352 bushels in 1932; cotton—13,703,000 bales in 1912 and 13,003,000 bales in 1932; tobacco—1,254,304,000 lbs. in 1922 and 1,018,011,000 lbs. in 1932). The milk produced by 19,517,000 cows in 1912 had sold for $1.59 per hundred pounds, while the milk produced by 24,896,000 cows in 1932 sold at $1.28 per hundred pounds. However, the retail price had increased from 6.9 cents per quart in 1912 to 8.9 cents in 1932. A simple causal relationship between supply and prices obviously did not exist.

The means the bill provided under Section 8 for reduction of production and supply to the market were limited, by constitutional considerations, to individual farmers or to groups engaged in interstate commerce. Government rental payment for land voluntarily withdrawn from production was part of Wilson's domestic allotment plan. The plan for storing commodities and advancing government money against eventual sale is a variation on the Warehouse Act of 1916 that would put cash into the farmer's hands instead of negotiable paper. With Congress' power to regulate foreign and interstate commerce, under Article I, Section 8 of the Constitution, the drafters of the bill believed that provisions for requiring processors of agricultural products to be licensed for interstate and foreign trade was legal, an opinion controverted by the Supreme Court in *United States* v. *Butler* (1936). Licensing of processors would make ready information on marketing possible, as provided in paragraph 4, and this in turn would make possible agreements to limit supply between the Secretary of Agriculture and the processors, as implied in paragraph 2. In order to limit supply it was, of course, necessary to exempt these agreements from the antitrust laws, for which a precedent had been set by the Cooperative Marketing Act of 1922. The provision for loans to processors from the Reconstruction Finance Corporation was the sugar that made the compulsory licensing palatable.

The "processing tax," Section 9, the other feature of the bill declared unconstitutional in *United States* v. *Butler,* was the means in Wilson's scheme for obtaining funds to make payments to individual farmers. Again, it is difficult to see the equity of this tax unless agriculture is assumed to be the basis of all wealth. The bill specifies that the processing tax shall equal the difference between the average price paid the farmer and the "fair exchange value of the commodity" (paragraph b). The fair exchange is then defined in paragraph c as the purchasing power during the base period 1909–1914. However, should this rate result in the further depression of farm prices or in the accumulation of a surplus, the bill directs the Secretary of Agriculture in b to adjust the rate to prevent it. Not only is such direction fuzzy, its vagueness indicates that the drafters of the bill had no basis for predicting the effects of the program. Although taxing the processor would almost surely raise the retail price of the commodity involved, it could have no direct effect upon the prices paid to farmers, except perhaps to lower them. In effect, the underemployed urban population was supposed to make up the farmers' prices.

In a sense they did. For the base period 1909–1914, unemployment had ranged from 5.2 percent in 1909, through 4.4 percent in 1913, to 8.0 percent in 1914. From a high of 24.9 percent in 1933, it fell to a low of 14.3 percent in 1937, only to hit 17.2 percent in 1939. During the depression period 1930–1939, the parity ratio for farmers fell from 83 in 1930 to 58 in 1932. In 1933, it climbed to 64 and hit 93 in 1937, only to fall to 77 by 1939. The index of wholesale prices for farm products as well as the index of consumer prices for food was definitely higher for the period 1933–1939 than for the period 1909–1914. In 1937, farmers received 93 percent of parity, with wholesale prices 11 points higher than they had been during the highest year of the base period, 1910, and consumer food prices at 52.1, almost 12 points higher than they had been during the highest year of the base period, 1914.

From the statistics, it would be difficult to show that Agricultural Adjustment had much to do with the recovery of farm income during the thirties. Production was decreased and prices did increase somewhat, but it was not until the middle of World War II that farm income exceeded parity; and after a decade at parity or above, farm income fell to 92 in 1953. The trend continued with a fall to 80 percent of parity in 1960, and in 1964, it was down to 75, where the parity ratio stood in 1934. Throughout this entire period, the policy and the means to implement it have remained substantially the same. Immediately after *United States* v. *Butler,* Congress passed the Soil Conservation and Domestic Allotment Acts and, early in 1938, the second Agricultural Adjustment Act.[1]

Nevertheless Agricultural Adjustment has continued to be thought of as one of the high points of the Roosevelt administration. In *The Coming of the New Deal,* volume two of *The Age of Roosevelt,* Arthur Schlesinger, Jr., felt that "probably never in American history had so much social and legal inventiveness gone into a single legislative measure." He admiringly quotes Henry Wallace to the effect that Agricultural Adjustment was "a contrivance as new in the field of social relations as the first gasoline engine was in the field of mechanics." In the field of mechanics, preconceived ideas are shattered against the necessity to make the machine run. Legislation can be drawn and government policy can be put into effect, alas, without bumping into the facts. Analysis of this first piece of legislation in the "field of social relations" indicates why the United States has failed to enact viable social legislation. Marx is often quoted to the effect that the problem of philosophy is not to understand the world but to change it. American experience of the last thirty-five years shows that the world cannot be changed unless it is understood.

NOTE

[1] In his nationally syndicated column for June 6, 1968, Marquis Childs argued that the soil bank program was responsible for creating poverty in the 1960's. One of the striking examples is the second congressional district in Mississippi, where plantation owners representing three-tenths of 1 percent of the population collect as much as $23,563,554 in a single year, while 59.1 percent of the population live below the official poverty line. The fact that the second district is represented in Congress by Jamie L. Whitten, chairman of the Agriculture Subcommittee on Appropriations, suggests that there does in fact exist a conspiracy of the rich against the poor.

XIII

Self-interest Masked by Idealistic Pronouncement

Harry S. Truman

INAUGURAL ADDRESS

January 20, 1949

(1) Mr. Vice President, Mr. Chief Justice, and fellow citizens, I accept with humility the honor which the American people have conferred upon me. I accept it with a deep resolve to do all that I can for the welfare of this Nation and for the peace of the world.

(2) In performing the duties of my office, I need the help and prayers of every one of you. I ask for your encouragement and your support. The tasks we face are difficult, and we can accomplish them only if we work together.

(3) Each period of our national history has had its special challenges. Those that confront us now are as momentous as any in the past. Today marks the beginning not only of a new administration, but of a period that will be eventful, perhaps decisive, for us and for the world.

(4) It may be our lot to experience, and in large measure to

bring about, a major turning point in the long history of the human race. The first half of this century has been marked by unprecedented and brutal attacks on the rights of man, and by the two most frightful wars in history. The supreme need of our time is for men to learn to live together in peace and harmony.

(5) The peoples of the earth face the future with grave uncertainty, composed almost equally of great hopes and great fears. In this time of doubt, they look to the United States as never before for good will, strength, and wise leadership.

(6) It is fitting, therefore, that we take this occasion to proclaim to the world the essential principles of the faith by which we live, and to declare our aims to all peoples.

(7) The American people stand firm in the faith which has inspired this Nation from the beginning. We believe that all men have a right to equal justice under law and equal opportunity to share in the common good. We believe that all men have the right to freedom of thought and expression. We believe that all men are created equal because they are created in the image of God.

(8) From this faith we will not be moved.

(9) The American people desire, and are determined to work for, a world in which all nations and all peoples are free to govern themselves as they see fit and to achieve a decent and satisfying life. Above all else, our people desire, and are determined to work for, peace on earth—a just and lasting peace—based on genuine agreement freely arrived at by equals.

(10) In the pursuit of these aims, the United States and other like-minded nations find themselves directly opposed by a

regime with contrary aims and a totally different concept of life.

(11) That regime adheres to a false philosophy which purports to offer freedom, security, and greater opportunity to mankind. Misled by this philosophy, many peoples have sacrificed their liberties only to learn to their sorrow that deceit and mockery, poverty and tyranny, are their reward.

(12) That false philosophy is communism.

(13) Communism is based on the belief that man is so weak and inadequate that he is unable to govern himself, and therefore requires the rule of strong masters.

(14) Democracy is based on the conviction that man has the moral and intellectual capacity, as well as the inalienable right, to govern himself with reason and justice.

(15) Communism subjects the individual to arrest without lawful cause, punishment without trial, and forced labor as the chattel of the state. It decrees what information he shall receive, what art he shall produce, what leaders he shall follow, and what thoughts he shall think.

(16) Democracy maintains that government is established for the benefit of the individual, and is charged with the responsibility of protecting the rights of the individual and his freedom in the exercise of his abilities.

(17) Communism maintains that social wrongs can be corrected only by violence.

(18) Democracy has proved that social justice can be achieved through peaceful change.

(19) Communism holds that the world is so deeply divided into opposing classes that war is inevitable.

(20) Democracy holds that free nations can settle differences justly and maintain lasting peace.

(21) These differences between communism and democracy do not concern the United States alone. People everywhere are coming to realize that what is involved is material well-being, human dignity, and the right to believe in and worship God.

(22) I state these differences, not to draw issues of belief as such, but because the actions resulting from the Communist philosophy are a threat to the efforts of free nations to bring about world recovery and lasting peace.

(23) Since the end of hostilities, the United States has invested its substance and its energy in a great constructive effort to restore peace, stability, and freedom to the world.

(24) We have sought no territory and we have imposed our will on none. We have asked for no privileges we would not extend to others.

(25) We have constantly and vigorously supported the United Nations and related agencies as a means of applying democratic principles to international relations. We have consistently advocated and relied upon peaceful settlement of disputes among nations.

(26) We have made every effort to secure agreement on effective international control of our most powerful weapon, and we have worked steadily for the limitation and control of all armaments.

(27) We have encouraged, by precept and example, the expansion of world trade on a sound and fair basis.

(28) Almost a year ago, in company with 16 free nations of Europe, we launched the greatest cooperative economic program in history. The purpose of that unprecedented effort is to invigorate and strengthen democracy in Europe, so that the free people of that continent can resume their rightful place in the forefront of civilization and can contribute once more to the security and welfare of the world.

(29) Our efforts have brought new hope to all mankind. We have beaten back despair and defeatism. We have saved a number of countries from losing their liberty. Hundreds of millions of people all over the world now agree with us, that we need not have war—that we can have peace.

(30) The initiative is ours.

(31) We are moving on with other nations to build an even stronger structure of international order and justice. We shall have as our partners countries which, no longer solely concerned with the problem of national survival, are now working to improve the standards of living of all their people. We are ready to undertake new projects to strengthen the free world.

(32) In the coming years, our program for peace and freedom will emphasize four major courses of action.

(33) First. We will continue to give unfaltering support to the United Nations and related agencies, and we will continue to search for ways to strengthen their authority and increase their effectiveness. We believe that the United Nations will be strengthened by the new nations which are being formed in lands now advancing toward self-government under democratic principles.

(34) Second. We will continue our programs for world economic recovery.

(35) This means, first of all, that we must keep our full weight behind the European recovery program. We are confident of the success of this major venture in world recovery. We believe that our partners in this effort will achieve the status of self-supporting nations once again.

(36) In addition, we must carry out our plans for reducing the barriers to world trade and increasing its volume. Economic recovery and peace itself depend on increased world trade.

(37) Third. We will strengthen freedom-loving nations against the dangers of aggression.

(38) We are now working out with a number of countries a joint agreement designed to strengthen the security of the North Atlantic area. Such an agreement would take the form of a collective defense arrangement within the terms of the United Nations Charter.

(39) We have already established such a defense pact for the Western Hemisphere by the treaty of Rio de Janeiro.

(40) The primary purpose of these agreements is to provide unmistakable proof of the joint determination of the free countries to resist armed attack from any quarter. Each country participating in these arrangements must contribute all it can to the common defense.

(41) If we can make it sufficiently clear, in advance, that any armed attack affecting our national security would be met with overwhelming force, the armed attack might never occur.

(42) I hope soon to send to the Senate a treaty respecting the North Atlantic security plan.

(43) In addition, we will provide military advice and equipment to free nations which will cooperate with us in the maintenance of peace and security.

(44) Fourth. We must embark on a bold new program for making the benefits of our scientific advances and industrial progress available for the improvement and growth of underdeveloped areas.

(45) More than half the people of the world are living in conditions approaching misery. Their food is inadequate. They are victims of disease. Their economic life is primitive and stagnant. Their poverty is a handicap and a threat both to them and to more prosperous areas.

(46) For the first time in history humanity possesses the knowledge and the skill to relieve the suffering of these people.

(47) The United States is preeminent among nations in the development of industrial and scientific techniques. The material resources which we can afford to use for the assistance of other peoples are limited. But our imponderable resources in technical knowledge are constantly growing and are inexhaustible.

(48) I believe that we should make available to peace-loving peoples the benefits of our store of technical knowledge in order to help them realize their aspirations for a better life. And, in cooperation with other nations, we should foster capital investment in areas needing development.

(49) Our aim should be to help the free peoples of the world, through their own efforts, to produce more food, more cloth-

ing, more materials for housing, and more mechanical power to lighten their burdens.

(50) We invite other countries to pool their technological resources in this undertaking. Their contributions will be warmly welcomed. This should be a cooperative enterprise in which all nations work together through the United Nations and its specialized agencies wherever practicable. It must be a world-wide effort for the achievement of peace, plenty, and freedom.

(51) With the cooperation of business, private capital, agriculture, and labor in this country, this program can greatly increase the industrial activity in other nations and can raise substantially their standards of living.

(52) Such new economic developments must be devised and controlled to benefit the peoples of the areas in which they are established. Guaranties to the investor must be balanced by guaranties in the interest of the people whose resources and whose labor go into these developments.

(53) The old imperialism—exploitation for foreign profit—has no place in our plans. What we envisage is a program of development based on the concepts of democratic fair dealing.

(54) All countries, including our own, will greatly benefit from a constructive program for the better use of the world's human and natural resources. Experience shows that our commerce with other countries expands as they progress industrially and economically.

(55) Greater production is the key to prosperity and peace. And the key to greater production is a wider and more vig-

orous application of modern scientific and technical knowledge.

(56) Only by helping the least fortunate of its members to help themselves can the human family achieve the decent, satisfying life that is the right of all people.

(57) Democracy alone can supply the vitalizing force to stir the peoples of the world into triumphant action, not only against their human oppressors, but also against their ancient enemies —hunger, misery, and despair.

(58) On the basis of these four major courses of action we hope to help create the conditions that will lead eventually to personal freedom and happiness for all mankind.

(59) If we are to be successful in carrying out these policies, it is clear that we must have continued prosperity in this country and we must keep ourselves strong.

(60) Slowly but surely we are weaving a world fabric of international security and growing prosperity.

(61) We are aided by all who wish to live in freedom from fear —even by those who live today in fear under their own governments.

(62) We are aided by all who want relief from the lies of propaganda—who desire truth and sincerity.

(63) We are aided by all who desire self-government and a voice in deciding their own affairs.

(64) We are aided by all who long for economic security—for the security and abundance that men in free societies can enjoy.

(65) We are aided by all who desire freedom of speech, freedom of religion, and freedom to live their own lives for useful ends.

(66) Our allies are the millions who hunger and thirst after righteousness.

(67) In due time, as our stability becomes manifest, as more and more nations come to know the benefits of democracy and to participate in growing abundance, I believe that those countries which now oppose us will abandon their delusions and join with the free nations of the world in a just settlement of international differences.

(68) Events have brought our American democracy to new influence and new responsibilities. They will test our courage, our devotion to duty, and our concept of liberty.

(69) But I say to all men, what we have achieved in liberty, we will surpass in greater liberty.

(70) Steadfast in our faith in the Almighty, we will advance toward a world where man's freedom is secure.

(71) To that end we will devote our strength, our resources, and our firmness of resolve. With God's help, the future of mankind will be assured in a world of justice, harmony, and peace.

Self-interest Masked with Idealistic Pronouncement

COMMENTARY

AMERICAN foreign policy has shown amazing consistency through the administrations of the last four presidents. Since the spring of 1945, it has been the policy of this country to support established governments against "Communism." For twenty years, this policy has been astonishingly successful. Although "peoples' democracies" were established in the countries of Eastern Europe occupied by the Soviet army at the close of World War II, the Chinese Communist armies forced the Kuomintang army off the mainland late in 1949, and a Communist-led insurrection forced the French out of Indochina in 1954, no other country, with the exception of the anomalous government of Cuba, has "gone Communist." Truly, we are in an era of the *pax americana*.

The doctrines of this *pax americana* were developed during the first Truman administration and received their classic expressions in his inaugural address. Twenty-two months before this speech, Truman had accepted the pacification role for the United States in his address to Congress, March 12, 1947, asking for appropriations to assist the Greek and Turkish governments. Here he explicitly picked up the baton dropped by the British. They had informed the United States that they could no longer afford to assist the Greek government in its attempt to put down an insurrection. Since there is no other government "to which democratic Greece can turn," Truman argued, "the United States must supply this assistance."

In this speech setting forth what has since been known as the Truman Doctrine, he also adumbrated the now discredited domino theory:

> It is necessary only to glance at a map to realize that the survival and integrity of the Greek nation are of grave importance in a much wider situation. If Greece should fall under the control of an armed minority, the effect upon its neighbor, Turkey, would be immediate and serious. Confusion and disorder might well spread throughout the entire Middle East.
>
> Moreover, the disappearance of Greece as an independent state would have a profound effect upon those countries in Europe whose peoples are struggling against great difficulties to maintain their freedoms and their independence while they repair the damages of war.

Commenting upon the speech in his *Memoirs,* Truman expressed an opinion that has become the common attitude: "This was, I believe, the turning point in America's foreign policy, which now declared that whenever aggression, direct or indirect, threatened the peace, the security of the United States was involved." Truman committed the country to a policy analogous to that attempted by the Congress of Vienna, which, after the Napoleonic wars, attempted to prevent revolutionary disturbances. Aid to countries threatened by "Communism" was established as unalterable policy in Truman's speech of March 12, 1947. In his inaugural address, he attempted to specify the threat and broadened the meaning of aid.

The 1948 presidential election was one very few people thought Truman could win. After Democratic rule since 1933, it was generally asserted by the press that the people wanted a change. At the Democratic Convention, several southern delegations walked out, protesting the civil rights plank. Not only was the normal Democratic voting strength weakened by the resulting southern States' Rights ticket, it was also believed that left-wing Democrats would be attracted by the Progressive Party's opposition to Truman's increasingly anti-Communist foreign policy. Truman's campaign, based on the twin objectives of continuation of the Roosevelt domestic policies under the title "Fair Deal" and increased involvement in world politics as the leading opponent of the Soviet Union, however, resulted in better than a 2 million vote plurality over Thomas E. Dewey, the Republican candidate, while the States' Rights and Progressive parties polled a little better than 1 million votes each. In power under his own right, Truman could feel that these twin objectives united the majority of Americans, especially the second objective, because only the Progressives had opposed anti-Communism. The Republican and States' Rights parties were, if anything, more anti-Communist than the Democrats.

A look at the paragraphing of the inaugural address shows

that Truman adopted the technique of asserting points in a large number of paragraphs. This kind of division does not allow for sustained argument. Rather than argument, the speech depends upon conviction. The speaker presents himself as one asserting the beliefs of his audience.

In the first two paragraphs, Truman opens with an assertion of humility and a request for consensus. In the use of phrases like "deep resolve" and "help and prayers," he attempts to indicate the seriousness with which he looks upon his office. Identifying his subject as national welfare and world peace, he attempts to heighten the emotions surrounding these topics through the use of the prepositions "for" and "of." His phrases, "for the welfare of this Nation" and "for the peace of the world," have a sonorous quality that "national welfare" and "world peace" lack. Although it may be idle to speculate why *nation* was capitalized and *world* was not, perhaps this expressed Truman's priorities.

The emotions of the audience continue to be played upon in the identification of the present as a critical period in world history, in paragraphs 3–5. The flat statement opening paragraph 3 is immediately heightened to assert the uniqueness of the present, which opens a new period in world history. The conditional qualifying the decisiveness of this period and the subjunctive opening paragraph 4 lend certainty to these statements rather than qualifying them, because they add a reassuring sense of sober thoughtfulness. This qualified tone disappears completely at the end of paragraph 5, when Truman flatly asserts American leadership of "the peoples of the earth" (again, notice the prepositional construction to give sonorousness to the phrasing).

The uniqueness of the United States in a unique situation asserted, Truman turns to a characterization of American principles and goals (paragraphs 6–9). His statement of these

is couched in unexceptional terms, save for the sanctimoniousness of the phrasing. This sanctimonious phrasing implies
that *faith* and *believe,* words occurring in almost every line,
are synonymous with virtue. Pure motives make pure actions.
The attempted drama of the one sentence of paragraph 8 asserts as much. Further, it implies that there is virtue in stub-
bornness. Faith prevents movement, and rightly so, no matter
what the facts may be. The virtue of Americans is assured
through the assertion of the selflessness of their desires, expressed in paragraph 9.

Having endowed his audience with the virtues, Truman
turns, in a three-paragraph development (10–12), to the identification of virtue's antagonist. Familiar with the sort of
language used to describe virtue's antagonist from World War
II, the audience's only surprise could be in the attribution of
underhanded methods to the enemy. The Western powers had
characterized the Nazis as openly pursuing tyrannical goals.
Truman carefully attempts drama by allowing his audience
to guess that "regime" means Soviet Union and that the
"false philosophy" is Communism. In 1969, the climax of paragraph 12 is hollow, but perhaps in 1949 it was chilling. By
masking its despotism with the terms of virtue, Truman implies, the Soviet Union is an even more sinister power than
was Germany.

Truman draws out the implication in a four-point comparison between "communism" and "democracy" (paragraphs
13–20). The comparisons are designed to appeal to an audience convinced that there is virtue in believing, as such. Having made up its mind, the audience does not want to be confused. In this list, Truman is opposing incomparable things.
Communism, if it means anything at all anymore, refers to a
system for organizing the means of production. Democracy
refers to a system of representative government. Comparing

an economic with a constitutional system is like comparing a tree with an automobile. Such a metaphor might be striking in poetry, but it can only confuse a discussion of practical policy, as does the poetic device of personifying "communism" and "democracy" in such phrases as "communism subjects" and "democracy maintains." The comparisons are really charges against "communism" in language so familiar to the audience that the word "fascism" can replace "communism" with no change in meaning. Truman asserts the implication of his charges in the two paragraphs (21–22) that complete this section of the speech. The universalization of the issue is again a familiar device from World War II rhetoric, as is the assertion that belief in God hangs in the balance.

The vices of the enemy give way to the virtues of the audience as Truman turns to a list of American activities in the four years since the end of the war (paragraphs 23–31). The picture is one of patience overcome with righteous indignation. America's activities in world politics are presented in the language of self-evident virtue. "Substance" and "energy" have been "invested." "No privileges" are asked except those that are given. The United States has "constantly and vigorously" worked for peace. "Every effort" has been made to limit arms. Both "precept and example" have encouraged world trade. With such pure activity, it must be the case that "our efforts have brought new hope to all mankind." The self-flattery brings the audience up to the pitch where it can accept the pronouncement of paragraph 30 that "the initiative is ours." Although Truman is careful to include unspecified "other nations" in the movement for "an even stronger structure of international order and justice," from the tone of the speech it is clear that the *pax americana* is at hand.

In the longest section of the inaugural, he presents the four-point program for putting the *pax americana* into effect (par-

agraphs 32–58). The first three points elaborate upon the list
of virtuous actions given in paragraphs 23–31. In paragraph
25 Truman asserted that the United Nations was a "means of
applying democratic principles to international relations."
"Democratic" principles having been identified with the
United States in the opposition between "communism" and
"democracy" (paragraphs 13–20), the first point concerning
the enlargement of the United Nations clearly indicates to
the audience that this is one way of furthering American interests.

Point two repeats paragraphs 27 and 28. The emphasis upon
world trade here, as a means for achieving peace, is clearly in
the interest of a trading nation like the United States. Except for the years 1888 and 1934–1940, the United States balance of trade had shown an excess of exports over imports
since 1874. In 1948 this excess had been over $3 billion, and in
1949 it grew to over $4 billion.

Truman spends more time discussing point three, military
alliances, than his first two points, which seems to contradict
his assertion in paragraph 26 that "we have worked steadily
for the limitation and control of all armaments." Although
he mentions alliances only with Western Europe and South
America, paragraph 43 extends the potential commitment to
a worldwide arena. The assumption upon which the system
of alliances is based is detailed in paragraph 41. Although no
specific enemy is mentioned, by "any armed attack" he can
only mean one from the Soviet Union. In his *Memoirs*, he
tells us that the conclusion he took home from the Potsdam
Conference was that "the Russians were planning world conquest." Although paragraph 37 seems to limit American military aid to "freedom-loving nations," the fact that a pact had
been concluded with the dictatorships of South America gave
the name "freedom-loving" to those nations that were willing

to cooperate with the United States in the resistance to "Communism."

Point four was intended to be the dramatic announcement of the inaugural. Its presentation is designed to appeal to each segment of the complex American audience. Truman begins by flattering his audience for its "scientific advances and industrial progress." To unreflective idealists, a vision of aiding the "underdeveloped" strikes a chord from the old revivalist hymn, "Onward Christian Soldiers." Immediately (paragraph 45) he turns to the "practical men" and gains their attention with the commonplace that poverty threatens the prosperous. National pride is again appealed to (paragraphs 46–47) by placing the United States in the "preeminent" position among industrial and scientifically developed nations. Missionary idealism and business sense are combined in paragraph 48 with the references "to help them realize their aspirations" and "foster capital investment." This balance between appeals to idealism and appeals to self-interest continues through the discussion of point four.

In this discussion, Truman rejects the "old imperialism—exploitation for foreign profit," while the entire presentation of point four explicates the new American imperialism—exportation of political and economic conformity. "Democracy" seems both cause and effect. In paragraph 57, Truman asserts that only "democracy" can stimulate action against oppression, "hunger, misery, and despair." But paragraph 45 implies that poverty prevents democracy. Actually, the economic system is the underlying causal factor in human affairs, in Truman's discussion. Implied in point four is the enforcement of the American economic system upon the rest of the world. Almost twenty years later, when our AID missions are notoriously the covers for our CIA operations, this implication has become all too clear. New American aid has become, to the rest of the world, old European colonialism writ large.

In paragraphs 59–66, Truman gives reasons for expecting success. After nodding toward domestic prosperity and military strength as the basis for the *pax americana* in paragraph 59, he builds up a sanctimonious picture of the United States dispensing comfort to "the millions who hunger and thirst after righteousness." The words from Matthew 5:6, "The Sermon on the Mount," bring to mind a picture popular in Sunday schools when I was a child: Jesus surrounded by little children holding out their arms. This image is completed by the prediction of ultimate success in paragraph 67. American truth and righteousness are so manifestly apparent that even our enemies will be won over. Their "delusions" cannot withstand our "truth."

The final evidence, presented in the concluding four paragraphs, is "our firmness of resolve." Truman's recourse to biblical phrasing, "but I say to all men," again indicates the source of his argument: conviction. Backed by the concluding acknowledgment of "God's help," he has worked both himself and his audience into a position from which they can only reply to any opposition with self-righteous indignation.

The consistency with which Truman's program has been put into effect during the last two decades shows his understanding of the emotions of the American people. Americans are moved by the peculiar masking of self-interest with idealistic pronouncement. In January 1949, the implications of the rhetoric were evident to few, if any, Americans. In the summer of 1969, they are becoming clear through our failures in our "wars" on poverty at home and on "Communism" abroad. A rhetoric that depends for its persuasive powers upon personal conviction rather than upon an analysis of the facts succeeds only with those whose self-interest is contained within the conviction. The beliefs of middle-class Americans are neither in the self-interest of the poor black men here nor in the self-interest of those in the rest of the world outside the circle of beliefs that make up the peculiar culture of the West.

Perhaps one of the most illuminating anecdotes concerning the beginnings of the cold war is Truman's account in his *Memoirs* of his second meeting with Molotov, April 23, 1945. The first meeting, the evening before, had been pleasant enough, but now, Truman recalled, he "went straight to the point." The point was the formation of a Polish government, which the British and Americans argued should contain representatives from the wartime Polish exile government in London. Regarding Poland within its sphere, just as Belgium was within the Western sphere, the Soviet Union was adamant. It seems clear now that the dispute revolved around different conceptions of international politics. Each side, consequently, regarded the other as obstructionist. After speaking bluntly to Molotov about the Soviet Union's failure to stick to the agreement on Poland that Britain and the United States thought had been reached at the Yalta Conference, Truman quotes his reaction:

> "I have never been talked to like that in my life," Molotov said. I told him, "Carry out your agreements and you won't get talked to like that.

The picture is that of two poorly educated, but proud, peasants sizing each other up for a fight.

Truman's inaugural address gave "our case" in the fight. No President since has had the insight or the courage to change the terms.

XIV

"Restored to the Docket"

BROWN et al. *v.* BOARD OF EDUCATION OF TOPEKA et al.

No. 1. Appeal from the United States District Court for the District of Kansas*

Argued December 9, 1952.—Reargued December 8, 1953.—
Decided May 17, 1954.

Mr. Chief Justice Warren delivered the opinion of the Court.

(1) These cases come to us from the States of Kansas, South Carolina, Virginia, and Delaware. They are premised on different facts and different local conditions, but a common legal question justifies their consideration together in this consolidated opinion.[1]

---

* Together with No. 2, *Briggs et al.* v. *Elliott et al.,* on appeal from the United States District Court for the Eastern District of South Carolina, argued December 9–10, 1952, reargued December 7–8, 1953; No. 4, *Davis et al. v. County School Board of Prince Edward County, Virginia, et al.,* on appeal from the United States District Court for the Eastern District of Virginia, argued December 10, 1952, reargued December 7–8, 1953; and No. 10, *Gebhart et al.* v. *Belton et al.,* on certiorari to the Supreme Court of Delaware, argued December 11, 1952, reargued December 9, 1953.

[1] In the Kansas case, *Brown* v. *Board of Education,* the plaintiffs are Negro children of elementary school age residing in Topeka. They brought this action in the United States District Court for the District

(2) In each of the cases, minors of the Negro race, through their legal representatives, seek the aid of the courts in obtaining admission to the public schools of their community on a nonsegregated basis. In each instance, they had been denied admission to schools attended by white children under laws requiring or permitting segregation according to race. This segregation

---

of Kansas to enjoin enforcement of a Kansas statute which permits, but does not require, cities of more than 15,000 population to maintain separate school facilities for Negro and white students. Kan. Gen. Stat. § 72–1724 (1949). Pursuant to that authority, the Topeka Board of Education elected to establish segregated elementary schools. Other public schools in the community, however, are operated on a nonsegregated basis. The three-judge District Court, convened under 28 U. S. C. §§ 2281 and 2284, found that segregation in public education has a detrimental effect upon Negro children, but denied relief on the ground that the Negro and white schools were substantially equal with respect to buildings, transportation, curricula, and educational qualifications of teachers. 98 F. Supp. 797. The case is here on direct appeal under 28 U. S. C. § 1253.

In the South Carolina case, *Briggs* v. *Elliott,* the plaintiffs are Negro children of both elementary and high school age residing in Clarendon County. They brought this action in the United States District Court for the Eastern District of South Carolina to enjoin enforcement of provisions in the state constitution and statutory code which require the segregation of Negroes and whites in public schools. S. C. Const., Art. Xi, § 7; S. C. Code § 5377 (1942). The three-judge District Court, convened under 28 U. S. C. §§ 2281 and 2284, denied the requested relief. The court found that the Negro schools were inferior to the white schools and ordered the defendants to begin immediately to equalize the facilities. But the court sustained the validity of the contested provisions and denied the plaintiffs admission to the white schools during the equalization program. 98 F. Supp. 529. This Court vacated the District Court's judgment and remanded the case for the purpose of obtaining the court's views on a report filed by the defendants concerning the progress made in the equalization program. 342 U. S. 350. On remand, the District Court found that substantial equality had been achieved except for buildings and that the defendants were proceeding to rectify this inequality as well. 103 F. Supp. 920. The case is again here on direct appeal under 28 U. S. C. § 1253.

In the Virginia case, *Davis* v. *County School Board,* the plaintiffs are Negro children of high school age residing in Prince Edward County.

was alleged to deprive the plaintiffs of the equal protection of
the laws under the Fourteenth Amendment. In each of the
cases other than the Delaware case, a three-judge federal district court denied relief to the plaintiffs on the so-called "separate but equal" doctrine announced by this Court in *Plessy*

They brought this action in the United States District Court for the
Eastern District of Virginia to enjoin enforcement of provisions in the
state constitution and statutory code which require the segregation of
Negroes and whites in public schools. Va. Const., § 140; Va. Code § 22-221
(1950). The three-judge District Court, convened under 28 U. S. C.
§§ 2281 and 2284, denied the requested relief. The court found the Negro
school inferior in physical plant, curricula, and transportation, and
ordered the defendants forthwith to provide substantially equal curricula
and transportation and to "proceed with all reasonable diligence and
dispatch to remove" the inequality in physical plant. But, as in the
South Carolina case, the court sustained the validity of the contested
provisions and denied the plaintiffs admission to the white schools during
the equalization program. 103 F. Supp. 337. The case is here on direct
appeal under 28 U. S. C. § 1253.

In the Delaware case, *Gebhart v. Belton,* the plaintiffs are Negro
children of both elementary and high school age residing in New Castle
County. They brought this action in the Delaware Court of Chancery to
enjoin enforcement of provisions in the state constitution and statutory
code which require the segregation of Negroes and whites in public
schools. Del. Const., Art. X, § 2; Del. Rev. Code § 2631 (1935). The
Chancellor gave judgment for the plaintiffs and ordered their immediate
admission to schools previously attended only by white children, on the
ground that the Negro schools were inferior with respect to teacher
training, pupil-teacher ratio, extracurricular activities, physical plant,
and time and distance involved in travel. 87 A. 2d 862. The Chancellor
also found that segregation itself results in an inferior education for
Negro children (see note 10, *infra*), but did not rest his decision on that
ground. *Id.,* at 865. The Chancellor's decree was affirmed by the Supreme
Court of Delaware, which intimated, however, that the defendants might
be able to obtain a modification of the decree after equalization of the
Negro and white schools had been accomplished. 91 A. 2d 137, 152. The
defendants, contending only that the Delaware courts had erred in ordering the immediate admission of the Negro plaintiffs to the white schools,
applied to this Court for certiorari. The writ was granted, 344 U. S. 891.
The plaintiffs, who were successful below, did not submit a cross-
petition.

v. *Ferguson,* 163 U. S. 537. Under that doctrine, equality of treatment is accorded when the races are provided substantially equal facilities, even though these facilities be separate. In the Delaware case, the Supreme Court of Delaware adhered to that doctrine, but ordered that the plaintiffs be admitted to the white schools because of their superiority to the Negro schools.

(3) The plaintiffs contend that segregated public schools are not "equal" and cannot be made "equal," and that hence they are deprived of the equal protection of the laws. Because of the obvious importance of the question presented, the Court took jurisdiction.[2] Argument was heard in the 1952 Term, and reargument was heard this Term on certain questions propounded by the Court.[3]

(4) Reargument was largely devoted to the circumstances surrounding the adoption of the Fourteenth Amendment in 1868. It covered exhaustively consideration of the Amendment in Congress, ratification by the states, then existing practices in racial segregation, and the views of proponents and opponents of the Amendment. This discussion and our own investigation convince us that, although these sources cast some light, it is not enough to resolve the problem with which we are faced. At best, they are inconclusive. The most avid proponents of the post-War Amendments undoubtedly intended them to remove all legal distinctions among "all persons born or naturalized in the United States." Their opponents, just as certainly, were antagonistic to both the letter and the spirit of the Amendments and wished them to have the most limited

[2] 344 U. S. 1, 141, 891.
[3] 345 U. S. 972. The Attorney General of the United States participated both Terms as *amicus curiae.*

effect. What others in Congress and the state legislatures had in mind cannot be determined with any degree of certainty.

(5) An additional reason for the inconclusive nature of the Amendment's history, with respect to segregated schools, is the status of public education at that time.[4] In the South, the movement toward free common schools, supported by general taxation, had not yet taken hold. Education of white children was largely in the hands of private groups. Education of Negroes was almost non-existent, and practically all of the race were illiterate. In fact, any education of Negroes was forbidden by law in some states. Today, in contrast, many Negroes have achieved outstanding success in the arts and sciences as well as in the business and professional world. It is true that public school education at the time of the Amendment had advanced further in the North, but the effect of the Amend-

---

[4] For a general study of the development of public education prior to the Amendment, see Butts and Cremin, A History of Education in American Culture (1953), Pts. I, II; Cubberley, Public Education in the United States (1934 ed.), cc. II–XII. School practices current at the time of the adoption of the Fourteenth Amendment are described in Butts and Cremin, *supra*, at 269–275; Cubberley, *supra*, at 288–339, 408–431; Knight, Public Education in the South (1922), cc. VIII, IX. See also H. Ex. Doc. No. 315, 41st Cong., 2d Sess. (1871). Although the demand for free public schools followed substantially the same pattern in both the North and the South, the development in the South did not begin to gain momentum until about 1850, some twenty years after that in the North. The reasons for the somewhat slower development in the South (*e.g.*, the rural character of the South and the different regional attitudes toward state assistance) are well explained in Cubberley, *supra*, at 408–423. In the country as a whole, but particularly in the South, the War virtually stopped all progress in public education. *Id.*, at 427–428. The low status of Negro education in all sections of the country, both before and immediately after the War, is described in Beale, A History of Freedom of Teaching in American Schools (1941), 112–132, 175–195. Compulsory school attendance laws were not generally adopted until after the ratification of the Fourteenth Amendment, and it was not until 1918 that such laws were in force in all the states. Cubberley, *supra*, at 563–565.

ment on Northern States was generally ignored in the congressional debates. Even in the North, the conditions of public education did not approximate those existing today. The curriculum was usually rudimentary; ungraded schools were common in rural areas; the school term was but three months a year in many states; and compulsory school attendance was virtually unknown. As a consequence, it is not surprising that there should be so little in the history of the Fourteenth Amendment relating to its intended effect on public education.

(6) In the first cases in this Court construing the Fourteenth Amendment, decided shortly after its adoption, the Court interpreted it as proscribing all state-imposed discriminations against the Negro race.[5] The doctrine of "separate but equal" did not make its appearance in this Court until 1896 in the case of *Plessy* v. *Ferguson, supra,* involving not education but

---

[5] *Slaughter-House Cases,* 16 Wall. 36, 67–72 (1873); *Strauder* v. *West Virginia,* 100 U. S. 303, 307–308 (1880):

"It ordains that no State shall deprive any person of life, liberty, or property, without due process of law, or deny to any person within its jurisdiction the equal protection of the laws. What is this but declaring that the law in the States shall be the same for the black as for the white; that all persons, whether colored or white, shall stand equal before the laws of the States, and, in regard to the colored race, for whose protection the amendment was primarily designed, that no discrimination shall be made against them by law because of their color? The words of the amendment, it is true, are prohibitory, but they contain a necessary implication of a positive immunity, or right, most valuable to the colored race,—the right to exemption from unfriendly legislation against them distinctively as colored,—exemption from legal discriminations, implying inferiority in civil society, lessening the security of their enjoyment of the rights which others enjoy, and discriminations which are steps towards reducing them to the condition of a subject race."

See also *Virginia* v. *Rives,* 100 U. S. 313, 318 (1880); *Ex parte Virginia,* 100 U. S. 339, 344–345 (1880).

transportation.[6] American courts have since labored with the doctrine for over half a century. In this Court, there have been six cases involving the "separate but equal" doctrine in the field of public education.[7] In *Cumming* v. *County Board of Education*, 175 U. S. 528, and *Gong Lum* v. *Rice*, 275 U. S. 78, the validity of the doctrine itself was not challenged.[8] In more recent cases, all on the graduate school level, inequality was found in that specific benefits enjoyed by white students were denied to Negro students of the same educational qualifications. *Missouri ex rel. Gaines* v. *Canada*, 305 U. S. 337; *Sipuel* v. *Oklahoma*, 332 U. S. 631; *Sweatt* v. *Painter*, 339 U. S. 629; *McLaurin* v. *Oklahoma State Regents*, 339 U. S. 637. In none of these cases was it necessary to re-examine the doctrine to grant relief to the Negro plaintiff. And in *Sweatt* v. *Painter, supra,* the Court expressly reserved decision on the question whether *Plessy* v. *Ferguson* should be held inapplicable to public education.

(7) In the instant cases, that question is directly presented.

[6] The doctrine apparently originated in *Roberts* v. *City of Boston,* 59 Mass. 198, 206 (1850), upholding school segregation against attack as being violative of a state constitutional guarantee of equality. Segregation in Boston public schools was eliminated in 1855. Mass. Acts 1855, c. 256. But elsewhere in the North segregation in public education has persisted in some communities until recent years. It is apparent that such segregation has long been a nationwide problem, not merely one of sectional concern.

[7] See also *Berea College* v. *Kentucky*, 211 U. S. 45 (1908).

[8] In the *Cumming* case, Negro taxpayers sought an injunction requiring the defendant school board to discontinue the operation of a high school for white children until the board resumed operation of a high school for Negro children. Similarly, in the *Gong Lum* case, the plaintiff, a child of Chinese descent, contended only that state authorities had misapplied the doctrine by classifying him with Negro children and requiring him to attend a Negro school.

Here, unlike *Sweatt* v. *Painter,* there are findings below that the Negro and white schools involved have been equalized, or are being equalized, with respect to buildings, curricula, qualifications and salaries of teachers, and other "tangible" factors.[9] Our decision, therefore, cannot turn on merely a comparison of these tangible factors in the Negro and white schools involved in each of the cases. We must look instead to the effect of segregation itself on public education.

(8) In approaching this problem, we cannot turn the clock back to 1868 when the Amendment was adopted, or even to 1896 when *Plessy* v. *Ferguson* was written. We must consider public education in the light of its full development and its present place in American life throughout the Nation. Only in this way can it be determined if segregation in public schools deprives these plaintiffs of the equal protection of the laws.

(9) Today, education is perhaps the most important function of state and local governments. Compulsory school attendance laws and the great expenditures for education both demonstrate our recognition of the importance of education to our democratic society. It is required in the performance of our most basic public responsibilities, even service in the armed forces. It is the very foundation of good citizenship. Today it is a principal instrument in awakening the child

---

[9] In the Kansas case, the court below found substantial equality as to all such factors. 98 F. Supp. 797, 798. In the South Carolina case, the court below found that the defendants were proceeding "promptly and in good faith to comply with the court's decree." 103 F. Supp. 920, 921. In the Virginia case, the court below noted that the equalization program was already "afoot and progressing" (103 F. Supp. 337, 341); since then, we have been advised, in the Virginia Attorney General's brief on reargument, that the program has now been completed. In the Delaware case, the court below similarly noted that the state's equalization program was well under way. 91 A. 2d 137, 149.

to cultural values, in preparing him for later professional training, and in helping him to adjust normally to his environment. In these days, it is doubtful that any child may reasonably be expected to succeed in life if he is denied the opportunity of an education. Such an opportunity, where the state has undertaken to provide it, is a right which must be made available to all on equal terms.

(10) We come then to the question presented: Does segregation of children in public schools solely on the basis of race, even though the physical facilities and other "tangible" factors may be equal, deprive the children of the minority group of equal educational opportunities? We believe that it does.

(11) In *Sweatt* v. *Painter, supra,* in finding that a segregated law school for Negroes could not provide them equal educational opportunities, this Court relied in large part on "those qualities which are incapable of objective measurement but which make for greatness in a law school." In *McLaurin* v. *Oklahoma State Regents, supra,* the Court, in requiring that a Negro admitted to a white graduate school be treated like all other students, again resorted to intangible considerations: ". . . his ability to study, to engage in discussions and exchange views with other students, and, in general, to learn his profession." Such considerations apply with added force to children in grade and high schools. To separate them from others of similar age and qualifications solely because of their race generates a feeling of inferiority as to their status in the community that may affect their hearts and minds in a way unlikely ever to be undone. The effect of this separation on their educational opportunities was well stated by a finding in the Kansas case by a court which nevertheless felt compelled to rule against the Negro plaintiffs:

Segregation of white and colored children in public schools has a detrimental effect upon the colored children. The impact is greater when it has the sanction of the law; for the policy of separating the races is usually interpreted as denoting the inferiority of the negro group. A sense of inferiority affects the motivation of a child to learn. Segregation with the sanction of law, therefore, has a tendency to [retard] the educational and mental development of negro children and to deprive them of some of the benefits they would receive in a racial[ly] integrated school system.[10]

Whatever may have been the extent of psychological knowledge at the time of *Plessy* v. *Ferguson,* this finding is amply supported by modern authority.[11] Any language in *Plessy* v. *Ferguson* contrary to this finding is rejected.

(12) We conclude that in the field of public education the doctrine of "separate but equal" has no place. Separate educational facilities are inherently unequal. Therefore, we hold that the plaintiffs and others similarly situated for whom the actions have been brought are, by reason of the segregation

---

[10] A similar finding was made in the Delaware case: "I conclude from the testimony that in our Delaware society, State-imposed segregation in education itself results in the Negro children, as a class, receiving educational opportunities which are substantially inferior to those available to white children otherwise similarly situated." 87 A. 2d 862, 865.

[11] K. B. Clark, Effect of Prejudice and Discrimination on Personality Development (Midcentury White House Conference on Children and Youth, 1950); Witmer and Kotinsky, Personality in the Making (1952), c. VI; Deutscher and Chein, The Psychological Effects of Enforced Segregation: A Survey of Social Science Opinion, 26 J. Psychol. 259 (1948); Chein, What Are the Psychological Effects of Segregation Under Conditions of Equal Facilities?, 3 Int. J. Opinion and Attitude Res. 229 (1949); Brameld, Educational Costs, in Discrimination and National Welfare (MacIver, ed., 1949), 44–48; Frazier, The Negro in the United States (1949), 674–681. And see generally Myrdal, An American Dilemma (1944).

complained of, deprived of the equal protection of the laws guaranteed by the Fourteenth Amendment. This disposition makes unnecessary any discussion whether such segregation also violates the Due Process Clause of the Fourteenth Amendment.[12]

(13) Because these are class actions, because of the wide applicability of this decision, and because of the great variety of local conditions, the formulation of decrees in these cases presents problems of considerable complexity. On reargument, the consideration of appropriate relief was necessarily subordinated to the primary question—the constitutionality of segregation in public education. We have now announced that such segregation is a denial of the equal protection of the laws. In order that we may have the full assistance of the parties in formulating decrees, the cases will be restored to the docket, and the parties are requested to present further argument on Questions 4 and 5 previously propounded by the Court for the reargument this Term.[13] The Attorney General of the

---

[12] See *Bolling* v. *Sharpe, post,* p. 497, concerning the Due Process Clause of the Fifth Amendment.

[13] "4. Assuming it is decided that segregation in public schools violates the Fourteenth Amendment.

"(*a*) would a decree necessarily follow providing that, within the limits set by normal geographic school districting, Negro children should forthwith be admitted to schools of their choice, or

"(*b*) may this Court, in the exercise of its equity powers, permit an effective gradual adjustment to be brought about from existing segregated systems to a system not based on color distinctions?

"5. On the assumption on which questions 4 (*a*) and (*b*) are based, and assuming further that this Court will exercise its equity powers to the end described in question 4 (*b*),

"(*a*) should this Court formulate detailed decrees in these cases;

"(*b*) if so, what specific issues should the decrees reach;

"(*c*) should this Court appoint a special master to hear evidence with a view to recommending specific terms for such decrees;

"(*d*) should this Court remand to the courts of first instance with

United States is again invited to participate. The Attorneys General of the states requiring or permitting segregation in public education will also be permitted to appear as *amici curiae* upon request to do so by September 15, 1954, and submission of briefs by October 1, 1954.[14]

It is so ordered.

---

directions to frame decrees in these cases, and if so what general directions should the decrees of this Court include and what procedures should the courts of first instance follow in arriving at the specific terms of more detailed decrees?"

[14] See Rule 42, Revised Rules of this Court (effective July 1, 1954).

"Restored to the Docket"

COMMENTARY

THE first thing one notices after crossing the Maryland border on a drive down U.S. 1 from Philadelphia to Washington is a large sign imploring us to IMPEACH EARL WARREN. The paint is beginning to peel, which gives it a pathetic quality, but in the summer of 1954, when it was doubtless put up, the command was a rebel yell. "Massive resistance" greeted the decision that segregated education violated the Fourteenth Amendment, not only in states of the old Confederacy, but in much of the rest of the country as well. The issue helped the New Conservative movement gain enough adherents to support both the *National Review*, as counter to the weeklies *New Republic* and *Nation*, and *Modern Age*, in opposition to the quarterly *Partisan Review*, when they were founded in the second half of the fifties. The more moderate of those opposed to Warren's decision charged that it violated legal precedent and was based upon sociological arguments instead of the intention of the Constitution. The more extreme felt that it was part of the Communist conspiracy. Richard Weaver, in an article in *National Review* during the summer of 1957 (an article that did not do his otherwise judicious mind justice), went so far as to assert that integration was Communism. Even some liberals felt, given the reaction, the decision inexpedient.

What were the bases of Warren's decision? Was the court merely "following the election returns" in *Brown*? How did the *Brown* decision reverse *Plessy* v. *Ferguson,* the 1896 Supreme Court decision that had made racial segregation a part of American legal structure? Does *Brown* indicate that the Supreme Court was beginning to place the wisdom of the judges above the competence of the legislators? Or does it follow the tradition of Supreme Court decisions? These are some of the questions the *Brown* decision has raised about our government of laws, not of men. They can be answered by looking closely at the development of Warren's argument.

This argument begins with the assertion that a "common legal question" justifies a single decision covering four cases. The particulars of the cases are given in the four-paragraph note to paragraph 1. This note allows for the economy with which Warren states the aspect of the cases pertinent for the Supreme Court's consideration: the decisions of the lower courts have been based upon the "separate but equal" ruling in *Plessy* v. *Ferguson*. By bringing these four cases together, Warren indicates, without explicit statement, in paragraphs 1 and 2, that his argument will be directed toward the validity of *Plessy*. He reinforces this indication in paragraph 3 through explicit statement of the plaintiffs' contention, while allowing the defendants' case to be inferred from the rulings of the lower courts. The history of the four cases is completed, with extreme economy, in the second and third sentences of paragraph 3, and Warren is ready to begin his examination of the *Plessy* doctrine with paragraph 4.

Paragraphs 4, 5, 6, and 7 build up to the last sentence of paragraph 7, which states the ground upon which a decision must be based: "We must look instead to the effect of segregation itself on public education." By taking this as a principle, Warren adopts a view of history and legal argument that exposed him and the *Brown* decision to hysterical criticism. The argument his ground implies is concerned with the future more than with the past. Traditionally, legal or forensic argument is directed toward the justice or injustice of past action, while argument concerned with the expediency, right, or harmfulness of a future course of action is considered deliberative or political. From this distinction stems the charge that the *Brown* decision was a political, not a legal action, on the part of the Supreme Court.

To see the changing view of history in *Brown*, we can compare Warren's skeptical statement in paragraph 4, concerning the possibility of recovering the full intention of the Fourteenth Amendment with statements made by Chief Justice Taney in his opinion in *Dred Scott* v. *Sandford* (1856) and Justice Brown in *Plessy*. Speaking before the Civil War, and before the Thirteenth and Fourteenth Amendments, Taney asserted that "the duty of the [Supreme] court is, to interpret the instrument [i.e., the Constitution] they have framed, with the best lights we can obtain on the subject, and to administer it as we find it, according to its true intent and meaning when it was adopted." He experienced no doubts in uncovering the "true intent," and he cited the legislation and histories of the times, and the language used in the Declaration of Independence, [to] show, that neither the class of persons who had been imported as slaves, nor their descendants, whether they had become free or not, were then acknowledged as a part of the people, nor intended to be included in the general words used in that memorable instrument.

The record of history spoke just as clearly to Justice Brown when he reasoned that

the object of the [Fourteenth] amendment was undoubtedly to enforce the absolute equality of the two races before the law, but in the nature of things it could not have been intended to abolish distinctions based upon color, or to enforce social, as distinguished from political equality, or a commingling of the two races upon terms unsatisfactory to either.

The Thirteenth and Fourteenth Amendments had clearly overturned the *Dred Scott* ruling that Negroes could never be citizens of the United States, but to Justice Brown's mind equal protection by the law did not prohibit segregation.

Beginning with a Massachusetts case of 1850, *Roberts* v. *City of Boston,* which had held segregated schools legal, Brown went on to assert a firm distinction between the equal treatment required for Negroes in political matters and the discretion allowed the states in social affairs under the Thirteenth and Fourteenth Amendments. The "underlying fallacy of the plaintiff's argument," asserted Brown, in a tortuous pursuit of error, was "the assumption that the enforced separation of the two races stamps the colored race with a badge of inferiority. If this be so, it is not by reason of anything found in the act, but solely because the colored race chooses to put that construction upon it." A reader of *Dred Scott* and *Plessy* today cannot help but feel that the clarity of the historical record and the ease with which "intention" was recovered must have been due to the case Justices Taney and Brown wanted to make.

American political mythology places a premium on the intention of the founders. Attempting to argue against this legal fundamentalism, Warren adopted a skeptical view of the limits of history that, however responsive he might find professional historians of the present generation and philosophers of history, was sure to challenge the commonplace attitudes. His skepticism concerning history, in paragraph 4, however, is mitigated by a use of the historical record in paragraph 5. Consistent with his attempt at economical writing, much of this record is cited professional histories of American education in footnote 4. The advancement in education, especially for Negroes, he argues, has changed the circumstances in which *Brown* must be decided. The changed circumstances account, in this argument, for part of the difficulty of uncovering the intention of the Fourteenth Amendment regarding education.

Paragraph 6 picks up the attempt to establish precedent on a different line from the discovery of intention in paragraph 4. The actual language of the first attempts to construe the Fourteenth Amendment are available in the record of the Supreme Court. By citing, in footnote 5, the opinion in *Strauder* v. *West Virginia* (1880) that the Fourteenth Amendment prohibits "discriminations which are steps towards reducing them to the condition of a subject race," Warren gives a precedent older than that of *Plessy.*

The "separate but equal" doctrine is presented as somewhat eccentric in American law in the rest of paragraph 6. Footnote 6, attributing its origin to the 1850 *Roberts* case in Massachusetts, implies its invalidity after the Fourteenth Amendment,

while attempting to placate the southern audience by identifying the problem as nationwide. *Plessy* itself had to do with
transportation. Two cases dealing with education, *Cumming*
v. *County Board of Education* (1899) and *Gong Lum* v. *Rice*
(1927), although settled by the *Plessy* precedent, were not, as
footnote 8 describes, a direct challenge to it. The four cases
dealing with graduate education, *Missouri* ex rel. *Gaines* v.
Canada (1938), *Sipuel* v. *Oklahoma* (1948), *Sweatt* v. *Painter*
(1950), and *McLaurin* v. *Oklahoma State Regents* (1950), were
settled using *Plessy* for the plaintiffs. The *Brown* case, then,
as Warren has developed the argument, is the first occasion
on which the Court has been forced to review the *Plessy* decision.

Having established the eccentric nature of the "separate
but equal" doctrine applied to education, Warren, in paragraph 7, acknowledged the equality or the tendency toward
equality in the separate facilities, insofar as the factors that
he carefully placed within inverted commas are concerned—
" 'tangible' factors." The statement that opinion cannot be
based upon these factors has been carefully prepared for
through the review of the *Plessy* doctrine. The last sentence
boldly states that the decision will be based upon equity because precedent is lacking. However, precedent for interpreting the Fourteenth Amendment was given in footnote 5 in the
quotation from *Strauder* v. *West Virginia*. Although the *Plessy*
had been based in part upon the "reasonableness" of the law
in question, Warren's willingness to move from judgment
based upon statute to equity decision shows a change from the
older decisions on race relations.

Paragraph 8 turns the argument from the ground for decision toward the movement that will lead to the conclusion at
the beginning of paragraph 12: "that in the field of public

education the doctrine of 'separate but equal' has no place."
The first step in this movement is to establish the principle
upon which an equity decision can be based. The first two
sentences of paragraph 8 express the attitude that history is
governed by the future rather than controlled by the past. The
trite phrase about not turning back the clock indicates that
Warren is more interested in past actions as a potential than
in the actual occurrences. The law, in this view, must concern itself with the present. It cannot be limited by past actions. The last sentence of the paragraph, however, indicates
that principles developed in the past do control the law. The
phrase ending the sentence comes from the last phrase of the
last clause of Section 1 of the Fourteenth Amendment: "nor
deny to any person within its jurisdiction the equal protection
of the laws." It is this principle that Warren will use to judge
the facts of the cases.

Paragraphs 9–11 present the facts for judgment. First, Warren points out (paragraph 9) that state and local governments
have assumed responsibility for education both through com-
pulsory-attendance laws and large expenditures. Then, he
asserts that an education is essential for success in American
society. From this he concludes that a state's own action in
providing educational facilities makes education an individual's right that must be given equal protection under the
state's laws.

An individual's right to equal educational opportunities
established, Warren straightforwardly questions and rejects
the contention that equal opportunity is afforded through
segregated facilities (paragraph 10). The evidence for this
rejection, presented in paragraph 11, is taken, with one exception, from the findings of the courts. Beginning with the
decisions that segregation in graduate education deprives Ne-

groes of equal opportunity, he applies these rulings to secondary and primary schooling. The longest quotation in the entire text of the *Brown* ruling is the one from the Kansas
court's findings against the plaintiffs, but nevertheless recognizing the inherent inferiority of segregated education.

The only evidence drawn from outside legal ruling is given
in footnote 11. These citations from psychological studies of
the effects of segregation led critics of the *Brown* decision to
charge that Warren had based his ruling upon psychology and
sociology instead of upon law. But the text of the decision
clearly does not substantiate this charge. Rather than relying
upon "modern authority," Warren solidly grounds his rejection of *Plessy* upon the Fourteenth Amendment and judicial
decision, using psychological studies only as corroborating
evidence.

Having established the principle of "the equal protection
of the laws" as the only basis for judgment in paragraph 8,
and having shown that segregated education does not afford
equal protection of Negroes' rights to education in paragraph
11, Warren must conclude for the plaintiffs in paragraph 12.
Segregation deprives Negroes of their rights and is thus contrary to the equal-protection clause of the Fourteenth Amendment. Having thus decided for the plaintiffs on the more general ground, Warren finds it unnecessary to consider the more
special allegation that segregation violates the clause of Section
1 of the Fourteenth Amendment that reads "nor shall any
State deprive any person of life, liberty, or property, without
due process of law." Footnote 12, however, points out that the
Court decided on the same day in *Bolling* v. *Sharpe* that segregation in the District of Columbia does deprive the Negroes
of "their liberty in violation of the Due Process Clause."

Warren's argument overturning *Plessy* combines a search

for precedent (paragraphs 4, 5, 6, 7, 11), an argument from cause to effect (paragraphs 7, 11), the assertion of a principle (paragraph 8) and its application (paragraph 12), with an argument from circumstances (paragraph 9). The predominating arguments through paragraph 12 involve the application of the equal-protection principle to the cause-effect analyses of segregation. If equal protection governs the laws, and if analysis shows that segregation is inherently unequal, then segregation is illegal. The argument, however, is based upon the notion that the ruling of the law must look to the present and future rather than to the past or precedent, as this circumstantial argument is presented in paragraph 9. It is this aspect that leads Warren into what may be considered the dubious ruling in paragraph 13.

If segregation is illegal, should it not be ordered stopped immediately? It would seem so, but in paragraph 13, Warren vitiates the decision through a concern for "complexity." His justification for postponing a decree for appropriate relief is based upon the limitation of the arguments presented to the Court. Because only the constitutionality of segregation has been considered, he holds that further argument is necessary before the Court can pronounce upon the questions given in footnote 13. Given the decision he has just rendered, however, it would seem that the answer to question 4 must be (*a*). Further, such an answer would preclude the necessity to consider question 5.

The second *Brown* decision (May 31, 1955), however, held that (*b*) was the proper answer to question 4 and that (*d*) was the correct answer to question 5. In his directions to the courts of first instance, Warren charged them to frame decrees on the principles of equity, which he characterized as "a practical flexibility in shaping . . . remedies . . . for adjusting and reconciling public and private needs." The private "interest of the plaintiffs in admission to public schools as soon as practicable on a nondiscriminatory basis," he asserted, may be balanced by "the public interest in the elimination of such obstacles in a systematic and effective manner." Although he charged that the "defendants make a prompt and reasonable start," this was mitigated by the opinion that "the courts may find that additional time is necessary to carry out the ruling in an effective manner." To gain additional time, "the burden rests upon the defendants. . . ." What the courts will require is that they move "with all deliberate speed" toward ending discrimination on the basis of race.

Remembering the summer of 1967, when adolescent Negro children seemed largely responsible for the mass burning and looting in cities throughout the country, it might be argued that the amorphous quality of such phrases as "practical flexibility," "as soon as practicable," "prompt and reasonable start," and "all deliberate speed" damn Warren's second *Brown* decision. The first *Brown* decision lacked this bureaucratic language. The illegality of segregated education was solidly established. The use to which those opposed to integrated education have put the quicksilver phrases of the second decision has been too obvious for belaboring. Such language is favored by those employing arguments from circumstances, for to them the complexity of the situation never allows firm statement. The first decision, although based upon the application of the equal-protection principle of the Fourteenth Amendment to the cause-effect analysis of segregated education, was prepared for through the circumstantial argument of paragraph 9. "Today," Warren asserted there, education "is a principal instrument in awakening the child to cultural values, in preparing him for later professional training, and in helping him adjust

normally to his environment." Many of the children seen looting on the evening television news were no older than the
Brown decisions. The bureaucratic language in which the
order ending educational segregation was couched served them
ill.

XV

The Decay of
American Political
Rhetoric

Principles, Rhetoric, and Action

For forty years, American intellectuals with an historical bent have found their perplexities shaped for them in the wry observations of *The Education of Henry Adams*. Disillusionment is nothing new in the history of American thought. All along the Atlantic seaboard, in the seventeenth and eighteenth centuries, men experienced the bitter disparity between the promise and the reality of American life, especially so in those colonies founded upon pretensions of reforming society. Before the Revolution was over, members of that generation were lamenting the decline from the spirit of '76. The Jeffersonians wished to return to it and the Jacksonians wanted to return to the spirit of the Jeffersonians.

And so it went until Henry Adams questioned the very attempt. The American style had been an appeal to the purity of past principles—right application of the Bible or of the Constitution would set all to rights. But Adams argued that the old principles had outlived their usefulness. He observed of the period immediately following the Civil War:

> the whole fabric [of government] required reconstruction as much as in 1789, for the Constitution had become as antiquated as the Confederation. Sooner or later a shock must come, the more dangerous the longer postponed. The Civil War had made a new system in fact; the country would have to reorganize the machinery in practice and theory.

Just as Ezra Pound was urging of literature early in this century, Adams was urging of government: "Make it new." But the question of how to make it new was one neither Pound nor Adams was able to solve. Both were reduced to quips like Adams's observation that "the progress of evolution from President Washington to President Grant, was alone evidence enough to upset Darwin," an observation like-minded men today extend to include Lyndon Johnson. Throughout his historical observations on the latter half of the nineteenth century, Adams analyzes situations as the expression of "an excess of power held in inadequate hands," a perplexity that seems to have become more and more common in the forty years since his death. In spite of realizing that past principles were incapable of solving future problems, Adams at once looked back nostalgically upon the eighteenth century as a time when principles applied to actions, looked forward quizzically to an age when that would once again be the case, and viewed his own time as one of disjunction between the two.

This stance Adams bequeathed to us. Although philosophical analysis shows that disjunction between principles and action is apparent, not real, the pose seems inescapable. It has led us into a corner where the very idea of principles seems suspect. We are all "pragmatists" in the popular sense of testing with trial balloons instead of questioning our contemplated actions to discover the principle that supports them. It is precisely this "pragmatism" that supports the professed contempt of "rhetoric" in an age whose best popular literature and art appears in the commercials that enliven the leaden banality of an evening's television, for it is rhetoric that forms a link between principles and actions. The decay of principles accounts for the decay of rhetoric, which the foregoing analyses witness. Although a thorough philosophical investigation of ethics would be necessary in order to demonstrate alternative principles for present action and a convincing contemporary rhetoric, a review of the techniques used in the examples drawn from the three-and-a-half centuries of American history may suggest lines of inquiry.

The most interesting way of proceeding seems a reversal of chronological order. By beginning with Warren's opinion in *Brown* and moving backward to Winthrop's sermon, the relationship between rhetoric, principles, and action may be indicated. Of each example we must ask, "does the rhetoric obscure or make clear the principles supporting the action?"

Analysis of Warren's opinion did not substantiate the charge that it was more sociological than legal. In overturning *Plessy,* Warren's argument combined a search for precedent with a causal analysis of school segregation, which showed its violation of the equal-protection clause of the Fourteenth Amendment. If the Constitution were the principle under which Warren was acting, then his argument clearly would have required an order barring further school segregation. Paragraph 13 shows, however, that his real principle was "complexity." The circumstances of American life, Warren believed, did not allow a court order until the case was reargued. Then, in the second *Brown* decision, Warren framed an order that added

to, rather than simplified, the complexities of school segregation. Although his action, the order, does not appear to be in
conjunction with the principle of equal protection, that was
not the principle under which he acted. There is no disjunction between Warren's order and his real principle. Unfor-
tunately, complexity, as his real principle, is undefined. He
acted, then, under a principle whose lack of clarity could only
add confusion to American life.

Truman, in his Inaugural Address, depended for persuasive
power upon his self-professed conviction in democracy. As a
principle, democracy is explicated in opposition to Communism. In this, he personifies the abstract concepts in such a
way as to convince an audience that there was virtue in belief,
as such. In comparing these abstract concepts, he opposes incomparable things to bring out an identification between
American interests and democratic principles. The four-point
program he proposes was subsumed under the protection of
democracy, but the identification of American interests with
democratic principles makes the actual principle for action
the protection of self-interest. This is masked with idealistic
appeals, but the mask barely conceals the pride that makes protection of self-interest the principle for action. It is difficult,
if not senseless, to argue that men ought to act against their
self-interest. Self-interest is one of those principles for action
that needs no justification. However, what constitutes self-
interest is not immediately clear. By justifying his Cold War
program under a mask of idealism, rather than straightforwardly setting forth his views of the nation's needs, Truman
expressed the confusion that led to the muddle the United
States has made of international relations in the past twenty
years.

The Agricultural Adjustment Act was based upon the myth

of agrarian virtue rather than upon rational analysis of an economic situation. Since agriculture is the floor of the economic pyramid in this myth, the depression must have been caused by an agricultural failure. Further, agricultural activity inculcates democratic principles into the whole society. Should the farmer fail, the whole nation would go with him. It is therefore the government's duty, in providing for the general welfare, to protect farmers even at the immediate expense of the rest of the population. The principle explicitly stated was the principle governing action. The effects, over the past thirty-five years, show, however, that action based upon a principle drawn from a myth can be as pernicious as actions whose principles are unarticulated or only partly understood.

Woodrow Wilson is often spoken of as a "man of principle," perhaps because the word occurs frequently in his writing. Analysis of his Fourteen Points speech shows that what we mean, or perhaps ought to mean, by that phrase is a man who insists upon others conforming to his statements. He pronounced without bothering to argue. Listeners are expected to believe simply upon the authority of the person pronouncing. The ambiguities in many of the points allowed the various audiences to believe Wilson was asserting what they already believed. His concern for his "image" as a peacemaker is the principle explaining the speech as an action. Perhaps the kindest thing one might say about the Fourteen Points speech is that even Wilson allowed himself to be fooled by this concern.

Unlike our two "major" parties, the Populist Party sought political power, not as an end in itself, but as a means for putting into effect its platform. Populists reasoned that the country's economic problems resulted from an international conspiracy of the moneyed to restrict the amount of currency.

This, according to the Populists' quantity theory of money, increased the value of monetary units, an obvious benefit for those already holding large quantities of money. The plutocrats had gained control over the federal government since the Civil War and were using it, according to Populist analysis, progressively to restrict the currency. In order to return the government to its constitutional role of providing common services, a change of political control was necessary. That Populists saw this change possible through constitutional means and not revolution is an expression of their belief in the uniqueness of America. Their theories of money, government, and the uniqueness of America, like Truman's pronouncements about democracy, are obvious expressions of self-interest. Although the platform has a self-righteous air, it lacks the sanctimoniousness of Truman's address partly because there is no attempt to mask self-interest. Today, the attempt to use abstract theories as principles for action gives the platform a certain quaintness.

In his Second Inaugural Address, Lincoln's initial concern is his image. Unlike Wilson, however, Lincoln's real concern is not for himself but for his audience. Beginning as a participant, Lincoln changes his stance to that of a commentator upon events before he concludes his remarks in the role of a high priest in a holy war. Behind this progression stands his conception of providence and man's inability to fully understand God's will. Victory, in the providential scheme, compels charity toward the vanquished. Speaking to an audience professing Christian principles, Lincoln manipulated his image in such a way as to force the audience to act emotionally according to their profession.

Like Agricultural Adjustment, the Morrill bill failed to produce the desired effect, and for similar reasons. The myth of agrarian superiority is assumed in both acts. Morrill, in defending his bill, argued that national welfare depended upon "natural" activities, like agriculture. Strangely, however, men have to be educated in the "natural." His view of education depended upon the notion that mental activity is separated into discrete faculties. The development of agriculture, in this argument, rested upon making it a science. Pure induction was Morrill's notion of science. Agricultural colleges collecting facts in every area of the country would place agriculture in America on a par with that in Europe. The device for securing endowment, land grants, was one that had failed since the beginning of the nation. Lack of imagination, together with an attempt to apply principles and plans that did not fit the facts, account for the bill's failure.

South Carolina's Ordinance of Nullification followed from the theory of state sovereignty. In this theory, the states had delegated specified functions to the federal government through their ratification of the Constitution. The federal government could act only as an agent for the states, who remained forever sovereign members of the federal association. Should the federal government exceed its delegated functions, a state's refusal to allow the action to affect its citizens could not be considered an act of revolution. Interposition is simply the protection from outside interference any government affords its citizens. In American history, this theory has developed into a myth that has operated rather like the myth of agrarian superiority. It is a principle for which there are no facts. As such, its application is an impossibility. Perhaps an uneasiness about this accounts for the progression from deliberation to indignation to defiance in the documents produced by the convention that passed the Ordinance.

Marshall's opinion in *Marbury* v. *Madison* is the only document in this collection that shows a sense of humor. He cleverly turned the Republicans' principles of strict construction of the Constitution and the priority of the legislature against their immediate political position. In his complicated argument from relationship concerning an act of will, Marshall reached a conclusion to which an application of his own principles concerning the priority of the executive and the government's duty to enforce agreements also would have led him. However, by reaching the conclusion through the application of Republican principles, he guarded the integrity of the Supreme Court. As action, his opinion was based upon a principle of the necessity of considering the circumstances rather than acting under abstract theories. The circumstances of the Court at the time dictated an opinion couched in Republican terms.

The image of the President Jefferson presented in his First Inaugural was that of a political midwife. The democratic executive puts into operation policies brought into the consciousness of the people through their political arguments. Jefferson assumes, in the speech, that his audience already agrees that the natural advantages of the United States allow republican government restricted to narrow functions. These functions, he argues through definitions and relationships, are largely negative. They preserve what already exists. As President, Jefferson took action fundamentally at variance with these principles. The purchase of the Louisiana Territory could not be defended on strict constructionist principles. The purchase, he felt, was a necessity of the time. America could not tolerate an expansionist France controlling her western border, with the power to cut off western commerce at New Orleans. Jefferson's theory could not deal with the facts and he had to resort to a principle like Marshall's.

The Northwest Ordinance was based upon neither principles of the rights of man nor principles of self-determination, but upon the hopes and fears of the newly independent states along the Atlantic Seaboard. The western territory, they hoped, would provide a capital resource, and so they tried to encourage buyers through provisions that would provide property with security equal to that in the states. A well-organized government, obviously, provides the greatest protection for property, and for a pattern of colonial government the states went to the British colonial system from which they had just freed themselves. They even strengthened the system by removing anomalies that the haphazard growth of the British system had allowed. Behind this stood their fear that untaught men were unlikely to form republican governments. In order for republican states to emerge from the Northwest, they reasoned, a period of tutelage under colonial government was necessary. Thus it was assured that additions to the United States would be forced to go through experiences analogous to that of the first thirteen states. The principle behind this action is that men learn only through the exigencies of experience.

Eleven years earlier, the Continental Congress had declared America's independence of the British colonial system through a formal argument based upon an implicit syllogism. This argument implied no fears about removing governmental restrictions since, as it was based upon a concept of eternal order, men fall back upon a benevolent order of nature when customary relations are destroyed. In this argument, government is a convenience, not a necessity. It is the opinions of mankind that matter, because these opinions are in some sense an expression of divine will. In the Declaration, there is a causal chain linking God, man, and government. The principle governing men's actions must be the attempt to discover God's will through the course of the natural progression of events. The appeal to heaven "for the rectitude of our intentions" indicated that Congress thought such a discovery had been made, at least insofar as the government of "one people" was concerned.

Almost a century and a half before, when the Puritans brought to America the principle that men must regulate their actions according to their attempt to discover the will of providence, there was no certainty that the discovery could be made. Although Winthrop argued with his audience as though men could be reasonable, this capacity was much more severely restricted than it was to be for the Continental Congress. Winthrop's techniques for argument were similar to the Declaration's, both relying primarily upon inferences drawn from definitions. However, the conditional tone and the use of arguments from testimony in Winthrop's sermon indicate the weaknesses of human reason and character that he felt in himself and saw around him. This weakness was primarily selfishness, the expression of original sin that made strict government necessary for community survival. Winthrop's attempts to understand Christian principles and to apply them in action were unrelenting. The failure of the Puritan community to continue these attempts is perhaps an indication that that was not the best way to apply principles to action.

In these examples, Marshall's opinion in *Marbury* v. *Madison* comes closest to uniting principle and action through rhetoric. Marshall, himself, had one of the most successful careers in one of the most honorable positions that American life holds. The principles of his opinions seemed to vary with the circumstances of the times, but they can be traced back to a fundamental position that to Marshall was like a categorical imperative, in Kant's terms. If an action is categorically good, then "it is conceived as good *in itself* and consequently as being necessarily the principle of a will which of itself conforms to reason. . . ." For Marshall, preservation of the integrity of the federal government as a body that could act to meet the exigencies of any situation was a principle from which all judicial decision stemmed. Behind the opinion on every case seems to stand the question, "How will a decision on this issue contribute to the effectiveness of the federal structure?" Adaptation of arguments to meet the particular circumstances, as we saw in *Marbury* v. *Madison,* were made in accord with this imperative. It is open to debate whether Marshall chose a legitimate imperative principle, but there can be no doubt that he succeeded in strengthening the federal structure.

Action not motivated by principle is impossible. Those who claim to do without principles actually are refusing to expend the mental energy necessary to discover what supports their action. Rather than thinking, they do the first thing that comes to hand, trusting in luck, or providence, or serendipity, or whatever the currently fashionable term for laziness happens to be. Laziness is a good deal more common as a principle for action than we like to admit. When men fail to take action because of complexities, as did Warren; when they pronounce instead of argue, as did Truman; when they act according to myth or theory regardless of facts, as did Congress in passing the Morrill and Agricultural Adjustment Acts and as did Jefferson in his argument restricting government to largely negative functions; or when they act from fears, as did Congress in passing the Northwest Ordinance and as did Wilson in his attempt to retain the name of the world's leading peacemaker; they act in such a way as to make their imperative principle laziness. A joke that makes the academic rounds concerns the grammar-school boy who turned in this review of Gibbon: "The decline and fall of the Roman Empire was caused by carelessness." Some equally perceptive historian of the decline and fall of the American Republic may one day sum up the causes under the heading: laziness.

Rhetoric studies the devices we use to mediate between principles and action. These devices may clarify as well as obscure the relationship, but more frequently they obscure it. To use a phrase of the late Richard M. Weaver's, "the ethics of rhetoric" compels it to make clear the principles for action. Rhetoric, then, is a part of practical ethics. In our day, ethics no longer follows from theological positions. This fact has produced a lack of recognizable principles for action, which, in turn, seems to have caused the perplexed stance Henry Adams bequeathed us. Any new guide for the perplexed, it would seem, must begin with a philosophical investigation of the theoretical bases for action. In moving from theoretical to practical ethics, such a guide would find the study of rhetoric useful, for rhetoric is, as Kant said of metaphysics, as inescapable as breathing.

Bibliographical
Essay

Bibliographical Essay

Preface and Chapter I

The questions, "What is history?" and "How can we know it?" are as old as the book of Samuel, the writings of Herodotus and Thucydides. The specific form in which these questions are debated today, however, stems from the early nineteenth century. Leopold von Ranke's doctrine that the historian must attempt to narrate the events of the past as they really were—*wie es eigentlich gewesen*—set off a debate concerning the status of historical knowledge which historians and philosophers have carried on to the present day. Can history be objective, or is the historian's account necessarily relative to his culturally determined preconceptions? What is the meaning of causation in history? How can the historian discover the connections between events? How can these connections be explained? Are events unique or are there general laws that can account for what happens? Such questions have implications both for the practice of historians and the speculation of philosophers. They closely parallel the debate concerning the status of our knowledge of the physical world that natural scientists and philosophers of science have carried on during the same century and a half.

The best introduction to the historical-practice aspects of these questions is Harry Elmer Barnes, *A History of Historical Writing* (2nd rev. ed.; New York: Dover Publications, 1962). For the philosophical-speculation aspects of the questions, the student would do well to begin with either William H. Dray's *Philosophy of History,* Foundations of Philosophy Series (Englewood Cliffs, N.J.: Prentice-Hall, 1964), or W. H. Walsh's *Philosophy of History: An Introduction* (New York: Harper & Row, 1960). Both books distinguish "critical" from "speculative" philosophy of history. The critical philosopher attempts to clarify the historian's actual practice—the assumptions that allow historians to get on with the business of writing accounts of past events—while speculative philosophers predicate theories of the historical process itself.

Several recent anthologies will provide students with an introduction to the debate. *Theories of History,* edited by Patrick Gardiner (New York: The Free Press, 1959), contains arguments by speculative philosophers of history, beginning with Giovanni Battista Vico and ending with Arnold Toynbee. In addition, the Gardiner anthology includes important statements on the status of historical knowledge as well as recent critical essays on such topics as relativism, causation, and explanation. Students should especially pay attention to the selections by R. G. Collingwood ("History as Re-enactment of Past Experience") and Carl G. Hempel ("The Function of General Laws in History"). The seeming opposition between the positions of Collingwood and Hempel has structured much of the debate over philosophy of history in recent years. The position upon which my work in this book has been based is that Collingwood presents the best discussion of the method of discovery and Hempel presents the best discussion of the means of explanation that we have to date. *The Philosophy of History in Our Time,* edited by Hans Meyerhoff (Garden City, N.Y.: Doubleday Anchor Books, 1959), covers about the same questions as the Gardiner anthology does, but with different selections. *The Varieties of History from Voltaire to the Present,* edited by Fritz Stern (New York: Meridian Books, 1956), deals more than the other two anthologies with statements by practicing historians.

By becoming familiar with the work being done in philosophy of history, students will recognize the context in which I have tried to use the model of rhetorical analysis as a device for understanding particular documents. Investigation through the use of models is familiar to natural scientists and is becoming familiar to social scientists. In my essay, "A Definition of the Humanities" (*Liberal Education* [May, 1965] 262–274), I argued that investigation through models was also applicable to the humanities. David Hawkins' *The Language of Nature: An Essay in the Philosophy of Science* (San Francisco: W. H. Freeman and Co., 1964) carries model-building as a device for understanding through the natural sciences and mathematics into psychology and ethics. Hawkins' is not an easy book, but the rewards are greater than the trouble. Those who find this subject interesting can continue it with Mary B. Hesse, *Models and Analogies in Science* (Notre Dame, Ind.: University of Notre Dame Press, 1966) and with R. B. Braithwaite, *Scientific Explanation* (New York: Harper Torchbooks, 1960).

Rhetorical analysis itself is best studied by beginning with Plato's *Phaedrus* (Indianapolis: Library of Liberal Arts, 1956) and Aristotle's *Rhetoric,* in Lane Cooper's translation (New York: Appleton-Century-Crofts, 1960). Some may wish to go on to Cicero, *De Inventione; De Optimo Genere Oratorum; Topica* (Cambridge, Mass.: Loeb Classical Library, 1949). The best modern book on rhetoric is Richard M. Weaver, *The Ethics of Rhetoric* (Chicago: Henry Regnery, 1953). George Kennedy's *The Art of Persuasion in Greece* (Princeton, N.J.: Princeton University Press, 1963) is the only adequate history of Greek rhetoric in English. In *History as Argument: Three Patriot Historians of the American Revolution* (The Hague: Mouton & Co., 1966), I applied certain aspects of rhetorical analysis to a problem in historiography. Students who would like to see how rhetorical analysis can be adapted to fiction will find Wayne C. Booth's *The Rhetoric of Fiction* (Chicago: University of Chicago Press, 1961) interesting. For a minimum background in the logic necessary for rhetorical analysis, students will be wise to study a text such as Wesley Salmon, *Logic,* Foundations of Philosophy Series (Englewood Cliffs, N.J.: Prentice-Hall, 1963), or W. Fearnside and W. Holther, *Fallacy: The Counterfeit of Argument* (Englewood Cliffs, N.J.: Prentice-Hall, 1959).

A good example of an extended debate for students to analyze rhetorically is Edmund Burke's attack on the French Revolution, *Reflections on the Revolution in France,* together with Thomas Paine's reply, *The Rights of Man.* Both books were issued under one cover by Dolphin Books, Garden City, New York (Doubleday & Company, 1961). Ray B. Browne has combined an abridgement of the two with a selection of both eighteenth- and twentieth-century criticism. See *The Burke-Paine Controversy: Texts and Criticism* (New York: Harcourt,

Brace & World, 1963). Burke's speech "On Conciliation with
the Colonies" can be found in Edmund Burke, *Speeches and
Letters on American Affairs* (New York: Everyman's Library,
E. P. Dutton & Co., 1956). The best, most conveniently arranged edition of *Federalist Papers* is the one edited by Jacob
E. Cooke (Cleveland: Meridian Books, World Publishing Co.,
1961). A handy collection is *Churchill in His Own Words* (2
vols.; New York: Capricorn Books, G. P. Putnam's Sons, 1966).

Chapter II

Serious students of the American past need to own a few
reference works and keep them at hand. The single most important is *Historical Statistics of the United States, Colonial
Times to 1957* (Washington, D.C.: Government Printing Office, 1960). This Bureau of the Census publication ought to be
consulted before generalizations are made by either amateur
or professional students of the American past. Close reading
of the documents in Henry Steele Commager's *Documents of
American History* (7th ed.; New York: Appleton-Century-
Crofts, 1963) is an additional corrective to hasty judgments.
Richard B. Morris' *Encyclopedia of American History* (New
York: Harper & Row, 1961) and Thomas H. Johnson's *The
Oxford Companion to American History* (New York: Oxford
University Press, 1966) are useful for checking one's memory.
The Harvard Guide to American History, edited by Oscar
Handlin *et al.* (Cambridge, Mass.: Harvard University Press,
1955), and *A Guide to the Study of the United States of Amer-
ica,* prepared under the direction of Roy P. Basler by Donald
H. Mugridge and Blanche P. McCrum (Washington, D.C.:
Library of Congress, 1960), only partially overlap each other.

The American Historical Association's Guide to Historical Literature, edited by George Frederick Howe *et al.* (New York: The Macmillan Company, 1961), contains a large section on the Americas as well as covering other areas of world history.

For background on John Winthrop, students will do well to begin with Edmund S. Morgan's *The Puritan Dilemma: The Story of John Winthrop* (Boston: Little, Brown and Company, 1958). The text of "A Modell of Christian Charity" is from *The Winthrop Papers,* edited by A. B. Forbes (5 vols.; Boston: Massachusetts Historical Society, 1929–1947). Those interested in Puritanism as a topic might do well to begin with Alan Simpson's *Puritanism in Old and New England* (Chicago: University of Chicago Press, 1955) and the first chapter, "A City Upon a Hill: The Puritans of Massachusetts Bay," in Daniel J. Boorstin's *The Americans: The Colonial Experience* (New York: Random House, 1958) before going on to Perry Miller's *The New England Mind: The Seventeenth Century* (New York: The Macmillan Company, 1939). A good example of a study on a more specialized, but nevertheless important, topic for understanding Puritanism in New England is Bernard Bailyn's *The New England Merchants in the Seventeenth Century* (Cambridge, Mass.: Harvard University Press, 1955).

Chapter III

Carl Becker's *The Declaration of Independence: A Study in the History of Political Ideas* (New York: Vintage Books, 1958) and Julian P. Boyd's *The Declaration of Independence: The Evolution of the Text as Shown in Facsimiles of Various*

Drafts by Its Author (Princeton, N.J.: Princeton University Press, 1945) seem to exhaust the possibilities of textual analysis of the document. Becker's book argues for one hypothesis of the document's intellectual context as well. Those interested in the Revolutionary movement should begin with what I consider the best single-volume study: Edmund S. Morgan's *The Birth of the Republic: 1763–1789* (Chicago: University of Chicago Press, 1956). The intellectual development leading up to the Declaration, as this was expressed in the pamphlets of the time, is being made available in *Pamphlets of the American Revolution,* edited by Bernard Bailyn, of which Volume I of the projected three-volume series has appeared (Cambridge, Mass.: Harvard University Press, 1965). This volume contains a long introduction, which has been issued as *The Ideological Origins of the American Revolution* (Cambridge, Mass.: Harvard University Press, 1967), and is a masterpiece of intellectual history. Serious students of the thought of the Revolutionary generation will want to consult the generation's historians: Mercy Otis Warren, *History of the Rise, Progress and Termination of the American Revolution* (3 vols.; Boston, 1805); John Marshall, *Life of George Washington* (5 vols.; Philadelphia, 1804–1807); and David Ramsay, *History of the United States* (3 vols.; Philadelphia, 1816–1817). Ramsay's earlier *History of the American Revolution* has been reprinted recently by Russell & Russell. The Marshall and Warren volumes have been reprinted recently by AMS Press. They are analyzed in my *History as Argument. The American Revolution: Two Centuries of Interpretation,* edited by Edmund S. Morgan (Englewood Cliffs, N.J.: Prentice-Hall, 1965), provides a beginning for those interested in the changing views on the Revolution. The text of the Declaration is from a photostatic copy of the parchment.

Chapter IV

An excellent synthesis of the period that culminated in both the Northwest Ordinance and the Constitution is Merrill Jensen's *The New Nation: A History of the United States during the Confederation, 1781–1789* (New York: Alfred A. Knopf, 1950); it is an especially good book with which to begin one's study of the period because it challenges naive assumptions and commonplaces about the necessity of the Constitutional Convention and the everlasting value of its production. The importance of new lands to the Revolutionary generation is narrated by Thomas Perkins Abernethy in *Western Lands and the American Revolution* (New York: Appleton-Century-Crofts, 1937). John Franklin Jameson's *The American Revolution Considered as a Social Movement* (Princeton, N.J.: Princeton University Press, 1926) is still a good beginning for those who wish to study that topic. Serious students will need to consult such sources as: *Journals of the Continental Congress,* edited by W. C. Ford *et al.* (34 vols.; Washington, D.C.: Government Printing Office, 1904–1937); *Letters of Richard Henry Lee,* edited by J. C. Ballagh (2 vols.; New York: The Macmillan Company, 1911–1914); *The Papers of Thomas Jefferson,* edited by Julian P. Boyd *et al.* (Princeton, N.J.: Princeton University Press, 1950–). The Harper Torchbooks edition (1964) of Jefferson's *Notes on the State of Virginia* is valuable as a record of his thinking about issues touching on land. The text of the Ordinance is from the *Journals of the Continental Congress.*

Chapter V

The best introduction to the period is Henry Adams, *History of The United States during the Administrations of Jefferson and Madison* (9 vols.; New York: Charles Scribner's Sons, 1801–1896). Adams' history is a masterpiece of historical writing. Those who want to investigate the intellectual context of the inaugural address should begin by becoming familiar with the arguments in the *Federalist Papers* (issued in a number of recent editions) and *The Antifederalists,* edited by Cecelia M. Kenyon (Indianapolis: The Bobbs-Merrill Company, 1966). Studies such as those of Leland D. Baldwin, *Whiskey Rebels: The Story of a Frontier Uprising* (Pittsburgh: University of Pittsburgh Press, 1939); Joseph Charles, *The Origins of the American Party System* (Williamsburg, Va.: Institute of Early American History and Culture, 1956); Noble E. Cunningham, Jr., *The Jeffersonian Republicans: The Formation of Party Organization, 1789–1801* (Chapel Hill, N.C.: University of North Carolina Press, 1957); Alexander De Conde, *Entangling Alliance: Politics and Diplomacy under George Washington* (Durham, N.C.: Duke University Press, 1958); Stephen G. Kurtz, *The Presidency of John Adams: The Collapse of Federalism, 1795–1800* (Philadelphia: University of Pennsylvania Press, 1957); Robert Allen Rutland, *The Birth of the Bill of Rights, 1776–1791* (Chapel Hill, N.C.: University of North Carolina Press, 1955); James Morton Smith, *Freedom's Fetters: The Alien and Sedition Laws and American Civil Liberties* (Ithaca, N.Y.: Cornell University Press, 1956); and Leonard D. White, *The Federalists: A Study in Administrative History, 1789–1801* (New York: Free Press Paperback Edition, 1965) will take interested students into the political background of the period. The text of Jefferson's address is from

Inaugural Addresses of the Presidents of the United States from George Washington 1789 to Harry S. Truman 1949 (Eighty-second Congress, Second Session, House Document No. 540).

Chapter VI

Students of American constitutional history ought to own *The Constitution of the United States: Analysis and Interpretation,* edited by Edward S. Corwin (Washington, D.C.: Government Printing Office, 1953). The Supreme Court reports are contained in a series beginning with A. J. Dallas, *Reports of Cases in the Courts of the United States, and Pennsylvania, 1790–1800* (numerous editions) and continued by William Cranch, *Reports of Cases Argued and Adjudged in the Supreme Court of the United States, 1801–1815* (9 vols.; Washington, D.C., 1804–1817); Henry Wheaton, *Reports of Cases Argued and Adjudged in the Supreme Court of the United States, 1816–1827* (12 vols.; Philadelphia, 1816–1827); Richard Peters, Jr., *Reports of Cases Argued and Adjudged in the Supreme Court, 1828–1842* (17 vols.; Philadelphia, 1828–1843); B. C. Howard, *Reports of Cases Argued in the Supreme Court, 1843–1861* (24 vols.; Philadelphia, 1843–1861); J. S. Black, *Reports of Cases Argued and Determined in the Supreme Court, 1861–1862* (2 vols.; Washington, D.C., 1862–1863); J. W. Wallace, *Cases Argued and Adjudged in the Supreme Court, 1863–1874* (23 vols.; Washington, D.C., 1864–1876); and *U.S. Reports, Supreme Court, 1875–* (Washington, D.C., 1876–). Andrew C. McLaughlin's *A Constitutional History of the United States* (New York: Appleton-Century-Crofts, 1936) is still a good place to begin this study. Students interested in John Marshall should read Albert J. Beveridge, *The Life of*

John Marshall (4 vols.; Boston: Houghton Mifflin Company, 1919) as well as Edward S. Corwin, *John Marshall and the Constitution* (New Haven, Conn.: Yale University Press, 1921). Henry Adams' *History,* as well as Leonard D. White's *The Jeffersonians: A Study in Administrative History, 1801–1829* (New York: Free Press Paperback Edition, 1965), provides valuable information on the period. The text of Marshall's decision is from I Cranch 153.

Chapter VII

William H. Freeling's *Prelude to Civil War: The Nullification Controversy in South Carolina, 1816–1836* (New York: Harper & Row, 1966) is the most recent book on the subject. The intellectual context of the Nullification Ordinance should be studied in connection with John C. Calhoun's treatises, *A Disquisition on Government* and *A Discourse on the Constitution and Government of the United States,* which first appeared in his posthumous *Works* (6 vols.; New York: Appleton-Century-Crofts, 1851–1855). Marvin Meyers' *The Jacksonian Persuasion* (New York: Vintage Books, 1960), Arthur M. Schlesinger's *The Age of Jackson* (Boston: Houghton Mifflin Company, 1945), and Leonard D. White's *The Jacksonians: A Study in Administrative History, 1829–1861* (New York: Free Press Paperback Edition, 1965) will lead students into a broader study of the age. The text of the Ordinance is from *Statutes at Large of South Carolina,* Vol. I.

Chapter VIII

The proceedings of Congress have been issued beginning with *Debates and Proceedings in the Congress of the United States, 1789–1824* (42 vols.; Washington, D.C., 1834–1856) and continued by *Register of Debates in Congress, 1825–1837* (29 vols.; Washington, D.C., 1825–1837), *Congressional Globe, 1833–1873* (Washington, D.C., 1834–1873), *Congressional Record, 1873–* (Washington, D.C., 1873–). These proceedings are not to be completely relied upon and must be checked against other sources such as newspapers, letters, etc. Federal laws are contained in *Statutes at Large* (issued after each session of Congress or for each calendar year). Recent evaluation of the effects of the Morrill Act are given by Allan Nevins, *The State University and Democracy* (Urbana, Ill.: University of Illinois Press, 1962), and James Lewis Morrill, *The Ongoing State University* (Minneapolis: University of Minnesota Press, 1960). Paul W. Gates, "The Homestead Law in an Incongruous Land System," *American Historical Review* (July, 1936), pp. 652–681, and Thomas LeDuc, "State Disposal of Agricultural College Land Scrip," *Agricultural History* (July, 1954), pp. 99–107, investigate the more immediate effects of the bill. Histories of education seem, almost always, to be special pleading for some theory of education. Laurence R. Veysey's *The Emergence of the American University* (Chicago: University of Chicago Press, 1965) is a useful corrective and should be read by anyone interested in the subject. The text of the Act is from *United States Statutes at Large*, Thirty-seventh Congress, Second Session, Chapter 130.

Chapter IX

Lincoln's papers have been issued as *The Collected Works of Abraham Lincoln*, edited by Roy P. Basler (8 vols.; New Brunswick, N.J.: Rutgers University Press, 1953). Anyone interested in Lincoln ought to read Herndon's *Life of Lincoln: The History and Personal Recollections of Abraham Lincoln as Originally Written by William H. Herndon and Jesse W. Weik* (Greenwich, Conn.: Fawcett Publications, 1961). Otherwise, books on Lincoln and the Civil War are as common as newspapers, and in some parts of the country, more common. The text of Lincoln's Address is from *Inaugural Addresses of the Presidents of the United States from George Washington 1789 to Harry S. Truman 1949.*

Chapter X

Although opinion on the Populists was mixed until John D. Hicks wrote *The Populist Revolt* (Minneapolis: University of Minnesota Press, 1931), his glorification went largely unchallenged until Richard Hofstadter's *The Age of Reform* (New York: Alfred A. Knopf, 1955) appeared. Since then, it has been popular to malign Populists in a fashion that seems as little critical as William Allen White's famous editorial, "What's the Matter with Kansas," which set the tone for dismissing the Populists in their own day. Paul M. O'Leary's "The Scene of the Crime of 1873 Revisited: A Note," *Journal of Political Economy* (August, 1960), pp. 338–392, shows that their charges were not as farfetched as it is popular to think. Some knowledge of economic theories is important for anyone wanting to investigate Populism. Both Karl Marx's *Capital* and Adam

Smith's *The Wealth of Nations* are available in Modern Library editions (Random House). The third work of economic theory important for nineteenth-century studies is David Ricardo, *The Principles of Political Economy and Taxation* (New York: E. P. Dutton & Co., 1960). Students will again find Leonard D. White's *The Republican Era: A Study in Administrative History, 1869–1901* (New York: Free Press Paperback Edition, 1965) interesting on the subject. The text of the platform is from *Documents of American History,* edited by Henry Steele Commager.

Chapter XI

Documents relating to American diplomacy appear under the title *Papers Relating to the Foreign Relations of the United States, 1861–* (Washington, D.C.: Government Printing Office, 1861–). Woodrow Wilson's *Public Papers* appear in an edition by Ray Stannard Baker and William E. Dodd (6 vols. in 3; New York: Harper and Bros., 1925–1927). Baker's work on Wilson resulted in a documentary biography, *Woodrow Wilson: Life and Letters* (7 vols.; New York: Charles Scribner's Sons, 1946). Earlier, he had written on *Woodrow Wilson and World Settlement, Written from his Unpublished and Personal Material* (3 vols.; Garden City, N.Y.: Doubleday, Page, 1922). More recently, Arthur S. Link has been turning out a more critical multivolume life and times in *Wilson* (Princeton, N.J.: Princeton University Press, 1947–), of which five volumes have appeared. Students of Wilson will find Edward M. House's *Intimate Papers,* edited by Charles Seymour (4 vols.; Boston: Houghton Mifflin Company, 1926–1928), interesting. A shorter introduction to Wilson is Link's

Woodrow Wilson: A Brief Biography (Cleveland: The World Publishing Company, 1963). H. G. Wells' newspaper pieces appeared in *The War That Will End War* (New York: Duffield and Co., 1914). The text of Wilson's Address is from *Messages and Papers of the Presidents* (20 vols. ending with Dec. 7, 1920 [Wilson]; Washington, D.C., 1907–).

Chapter XII

There is no shortage of material on the "age of Roosevelt." Most of it, however, is partisan. One of the more objective studies is William Edward Leuchtenburg, *Franklin D. Roosevelt and the New Deal, 1932–1940* (New York: Harper & Row, 1963). Students of the period will find Dexter Perkins' *The New Age of Franklin Roosevelt, 1932–1945* (Chicago: University of Chicago Press, 1957) and Arthur M. Schlesinger's *The Age of Roosevelt* (3 vols.; Boston: Houghton Mifflin Company, 1957–1960) interesting. The agricultural statistics of G. F. Warren and Frank A. Pearson were issued as *Wholesale Prices for 213 years, 1720–1932* by Cornell University Agricultural Experimental Station, Memoir 142 (Ithaca, N.Y., 1932). Histories of agriculture are much like histories of education, in that theory overcomes facts. Rational attempts to deal with the facts must begin with the statistical evidence available. The text of the Act is from *United States Statutes at Large,* Seventy-third Congress, First Session, Chapter 25.

Chapter XIII

Those interested in the origins of the cold war ought to be familiar with Harry S. Truman, *Memoirs* (2 vols.; Garden City,

N.Y.: Doubleday & Company, 1955–1956). Two very recent books attempt to put the last twenty years in perspective: Louis J. Halle's *The Cold War as History* (New York: Harper & Row, 1967) and Ronald Steele's *Pax Americana* (New York: The Viking Press, 1967). It is really quite early to judge the mass of material coming out, except as rhetoric. The text of Truman's Address is from *Inaugural Addresses of the Presidents from George Washington 1789 to Harry S. Truman 1949.*

Chapter XIV

The article cited in the text by Richard M. Weaver appeared as "Integration Is Communization," *National Review* (July 13, 1957), pp. 67–68. The mass of material in print on race lacks permanent value, except as an indication of the confusions of the times. The text of Warren's decision is from 347 U.S. 483.

Chapter XV

The Education of Henry Adams is readily available in a number of inexpensive editions. One of the more recent is Houghton Mifflin's Sentry Edition (1961). There is no lack of books commenting on the American character. Those interested might well begin by contrasting nineteenth-century views of two Europeans, Alexis de Tocqueville in *Democracy in America* (New York: Vintage Books, 1959) and Harriet Martineau in *Society in America* (New York: Doubleday Anchor Books, 1962) with James Fenimore Cooper's *The American Democrat* (New York: Alfred A. Knopf, 1931), and continue by contrasting the twentieth-century views of the French priest, R. L. Bruckberger, in *Image of America* (New York: The Viking Press, 1959); the South African novelist, Dan Jacobson, in *No Further West* (London: Weidenfeld & Nicolson, 1959); and the American, Elinor Castle Nef, in *In Search of the American Tradition* (New York: University Publishers, 1959). From there, the field is wide open for further reading.

Anyone interested in pursuing the ethical implications of rhetoric should start his study of ethics with Aristotle's *Ethics* (most of which is readily available in Philip Wheelwright's *Aristotle* [New York: Odyssey Press, 1951]) and Kant's *Fundamental Principles of the Metaphysic of Morals* (Indianapolis: The Bobbs-Merrill Company, 1949). Richard M. Weaver's *The Ethics of Rhetoric* is the best book on the connections between ethics and rhetoric, but a more thorough philosophical investigation of the subject is needed.

Index*

* This index does not cover material in the Bibliographical Essay.